Secret Pa...

Secret Passages provides a theoretical and clinical exploration of the field of psychoanalysis. It looks at the pivotal relationship between analyst and client and its importance to the psychoanalytic process. Offering a uniquely global perspective, Bolognini considers the different trends in contemporary psychoanalysis, charting a course between the innovative and traditional.

Divided into three parts, the areas of discussion include:

- plurality and complexity in the internal world
- the complex nature of psychoanalytic empathy
- from the transpsychic to the interpsychic.

Drawing on vivid clinical examples throughout, *Secret Passages* will be of great interest to all psychoanalysts, in particular those with an interest in gaining a more global theoretical perspective.

Stefano Bolognini is a Psychiatrist and a Training and Supervising Analyst and is President of the Italian Psychoanalytic Society. He works and lives in Bologna, and is consultant and supervisor of the Italian National Mental Health Service. He is a member of the European Board of the *International Journal of Psychoanalysis*.

THE NEW LIBRARY OF PSYCHOANALYSIS
General Editor: Alessandra Lemma

The New Library of Psychoanalysis was launched in 1987 in association with the Institute of Psycho-Analysis, London. It took over from the International Psychoanalytical Library which published many of the early translations of the works of Freud and the writings of most of the leading British and Continental psychoanalysts.

The purpose of the New Library of Psychoanalysis is to facilitate a greater and more widespread appreciation of psychoanalysis and to provide a forum for increasing mutual understanding between psychoanalysts and those working in other disciplines such as the social sciences, medicine, philosophy, history, linguistics, literature and the arts. It aims to represent different trends both in British psychoanalysis and in psychoanalysis generally. The New Library of Psychoanalysis is well placed to make available to the English-speaking world psychoanalytic writings from other European countries and to increase the interchange of ideas between British and American psychoanalysts. Through the *Teaching Series*, the New Library of Psychoanalysis now also publishes books that provide comprehensive, yet accessible, overviews of selected subject areas aimed at those studying psychoanalysis and related fields such as the social sciences, philosophy, literature and the arts.

The Institute, together with the British Psychoanalytical Society, runs a low-fee psychoanalytic clinic, organizes lectures and scientific events concerned with psychoanalysis and publishes the *International Journal of Psychoanalysis*. It also runs the only UK training course in psychoanalysis which leads to membership of the International Psychoanalytical Association – the body which preserves internationally agreed standards of training, of professional entry, and of professional ethics and practice for psychoanalysis as initiated and developed by Sigmund Freud. Distinguished members of the Institute have included Michael Balint, Wilfred Bion, Ronald Fairbairn, Anna Freud, Ernest Jones, Melanie Klein, John Rickman and Donald Winnicott.

Previous General Editors include Dana Birksted-Breen, David Tuckett, Elizabeth Spillius and Susan Budd.

Current Members of the Advisory Board include Liz Allison, Giovanna di Ceglie, Rosemary Davies and Richard Rusbridger.

Previous Members of the Advisory Board include Christopher Bollas, Ronald Britton, Catalina Bronstein, Donald Campbell, Sara Flanders, Stephen Grosz, John Keene, Eglé Laufer, Alessandra Lemma, Juliet Mitchell, Michael Parsons, Rosine Jozef Perelberg, Mary Target and David Taylor.

The current General Editor of the New Library of Psychoanalysis is Alessandra Lemma, but this book was initiated and edited by Dana Birksted-Breen, former General Editor.

ALSO IN THIS SERIES

TITLES IN THE NEW LIBRARY OF PSYCHOANALYSIS TEACHING SERIES

THE NEW LIBRARY OF PSYCHOANALYSIS

General Editor: Dana Birksted–Breen

Secret Passages

The Theory and Technique of Interpsychic Relations

Stefano Bolognini

Translated by Gina Atkinson

Foreword by
Glen O. Gabbard

Routledge
Taylor & Francis Group

LONDON AND NEW YORK

First published 2008 in Italian as *Passaggi segreti: Teoria e tecnica della relazione interpsichica* by Bollati Boringhieri Editore Vittorio Emmanuele II, 86–10121 Turino, Italy

English language edition first published 2011
by Routledge
27 Church Road, Hove, East Sussex BN3 2FA

Simultaneously published in the USA and Canada
by Routledge
270 Madison Avenue, New York NY 10016

Routledge is an imprint of the Taylor & Francis Group, an Informa business

© 2008 Bollati Boringhieri Editore, Torino

English language translation © 2011 Gina Atkinson

Typeset in Bembo by RefineCatch Limited, Bungay, Suffolk
Printed and bound in Great Britain by TJ International Ltd, Padstow, Cornwall
Cover design by Sandra Heath

This publication has been produced with paper manufactured to strict environmental standards and with pulp derived from sustainable forests.

British Library Cataloguing in Publication Data
A catalogue record for this book is available from the British Library

Library of Congress Cataloging-in-Publication Data
Bolognini, Stefano.
Secret passages : the theory and technique of interpsychic relations / Stefano Bolognini ; translated by Gina Atkinson.
    p. cm.
"First published 2008 by Bollati Boringhieri, Italy."
"Title of the original Italian edition: Passaggi segreti: Teoria e tecnica della relazione interpsichica."
Includes bibliographical references.
ISBN 978–0–415–55511–1 (hardback)
ISBN 978–0–415–55512–8 (pbk.)
1. Psychoanalysis.   I. Title.
BF173.B635 2008
150.19′5—dc22

2010016550

ISBN: 978–0–415–55511–1 (hbk)
ISBN: 978–0–415–55512–8 (pbk)

Contents

Contents

Acknowledgments

I wish to thank *Rivista di Psicoanalisi*, the *International Journal of Psychoanalysis*, *Revue Française de Psychanalyse*, *Psicanàlise*, *Revista de Psicanàlise da Sociedade Psicanalitica de Porto Alegre*, *Setting*, *Cahiers de Psychanalyse*, *Gli Argonauti*, and *fort da*, for allowing me to publish papers (partially revised here) that had previously been published in their annals.

I am deeply grateful to Paola Golinelli for her careful and patient reading-through of the drafts and for her invaluable and insightful comments on both theory and clinical matters over the years.

Special thanks are also due to all those colleagues who have so generously contributed to the evolution of the thoughts set out in this book, through lively debate on my papers at various congresses.

Foreword

Glen O. Gabbard

There can be little doubt that the era of pluralism has descended on the field of psychoanalysis. Globalization has arrived and has impacted psychoanalysis just as it has many other disciplines. With Internet access to the world literature, international conferences, and the availability of Web discussions involving analysts from every corner of the globe, we now regard psychoanalysis as a chorus of diverse voices, usually singing independently of one another, occasionally creating harmony, but for the most part producing a cacophony of dissonance. Today's analyst has to cope not only with the theories of one's own psychoanalytic community, but also with those psychoanalytic ideas that emanate from other languages and other cultures that may be quite unfamiliar. One solution to this extraordinary challenge is to retreat into orthodoxy and shore up the boundaries of one's preferred approach to psychoanalytic work in the service of sharply distinguishing it from those of others (Gabbard, 2007). This strategy lends itself to casual disregard of those who think differently from oneself.

A more challenging response to the globalization and pluralization of psychoanalysis is to set out on a journey of discovery in an attempt to learn how others think. The task is formidable, to be sure, and analysts today must learn something about the culture, the language, and the philosophy of different analysts in different regions of the world if they are to become full citizens of the pluralistic psychoanalytic world. Such psychoanalytic clinicians and scholars are few in number because much is asked of them in their pursuit of breadth and depth in the psychoanalytic enterprise.

One such person who has risen to this challenge and managed to integrate many different perspectives in a remarkably clear and useful discourse is Stefano Bolognini. Rather than shrinking from the rigorous challenge now facing analysts in Europe, Bolognini sees pluralism as an opportunity to expand his psychoanalytic knowledge and expertise. More than any other European analyst working today, he has systematically studied perspectives from North America and South America as well as those of French and British authors to provide a state-of-the-art commentary on contemporary psychoanalysis in this well-written and comprehensive new volume. He turns our 'problem of abundance' into a feast of many flavors, all of which are to be savored. Bolognini is like a cultural anthropologist studying the various psychoanalytic civilizations around the world with assiduous scholarship and contagious enthusiasm. He discovers that a process of transformation is occurring in contemporary analytic discourse where incompatibilities and discontinuities of different theories are giving way to meaningful parallel observations and constructive dialogue among those with diverse points of view.

Bolognini provides the reader with a veritable *tour de force* of international psychoanalysis today. He has the facility to describe similarities and differences between the approaches that are used in various regions of the world and examine the similarities and differences. He uses my own work on rethinking therapeutic action (Gabbard & Westen, 2003) as a stepping-off point to look at the multiple theories of how analysts work today. This exploration into therapeutic action allows him to contemplate the differences between the intrapsychic and the interpsychic. The technical strategies that are currently advocated by analysts of different theoretical persuasions are also considered. Bolognini is thoughtful, measured, and fair in his appraisal of the different trends that are prevalent in contemporary psychoanalysis. He values innovation while always being careful to preserve what is best about traditional psychoanalysis and the writings of Freud.

Bolognini is blessed with what Eugene O'Neill called 'a touch of the poet.' He knows how to write in metaphor in a way that vivifies his topic rather than obfuscating it. Indeed, his emphasis on language and words is refreshing at a time when others would minimize the importance of language in psychoanalysis. He sees the value of both a one-person psychology and a two-person psychology, while always being careful to parse the differences.

Bolognini's exploration takes the reader to unexpected places. To my great delight, he shares my love for dogs as valuable companions on the journey through life. He plumbs the depths of the relationship between dogs and their human counterparts, beginning with Freud and his near-inseparable tie to his faithful companion, Jo-fi. We learn that Jo-fi's uncanny knack of stretching and yawning at the end of an analytic hour replaced Freud's need to look at a clock to see when the session was over. Humorous and compelling anecdotes about dogs are recounted with a penetrating analysis of what dogs represent for us and how they have fulfilled human needs for millennia.

Other areas addressed in this magnificent work include one of Bolognini's favorite topics, psychoanalytic empathy; his approach to dreamwork, which is particularly novel; and his work with severely disturbed patients. Throughout his book, Bolognini provides vivid clinical examples so that a psychoanalytic reader can gain an unusual clarity in understanding how exactly Bolognini melds theory and technique. The clinical data is provided in sufficient detail so the reader will feel as though he or she is in the room with the analyst following the step-by-step developments of the project.

Throughout this survey of contemporary psychoanalytic work, Bolognini serves as a respectful guide with encyclopedic knowledge. One cannot fail to be educated and enlightened by his observations. The reader also begins to appreciate the integrity of the author and his wish to understand rather than to disparage the views of those who come to psychoanalysis with an entirely different set of assumptions from his own. We are fortunate to have this book available to us at a time when the cacophony of voices may be overwhelming and may tempt us to withdraw from meaningful dialogue. We should all be grateful to Stefano Bolognini for leading the way for the rest of us to follow. He has blazed a trail, and now it is incumbent upon the rest of us to make our way along that trail and join him in the new country of global psychoanalysis.

References

Gabbard, G. O. (2007). 'Bound in a nutshell': Thoughts on complexity, reductionism, and 'infinite space'. *International Journal of Psychoanalysis*, 88: 559–574.

Gabbard, G. O., & Westen, D. (2003). Rethinking therapeutic action. *International Journal of Psychoanalysis*, 84: 823–841.

Introduction

This book is divided into three parts.

The first part contains a description of the general premises of the theoretical–clinical elaboration contained in these pages: my relevant cultural and emotional background with respect to this object, psychoanalysis, that has occupied the greater part of my life; my vision of the putting together of the principal therapeutic factors, utilizing as a foundational departure point the exemplary work of Gabbard and Westen published in the *International Journal of Psychoanalysis* in 2003; and a reflection on the relationships between words and things, which I believe are crucial to our working activity and which, as a result, are as important in the technique as in the theory of our discipline.

In this first part, only 'tastes' of the specific theme of this text are presented, but I found it appropriate in this section to provide some basic elements about the terrain from which this text is born. In a certain sense, these elements constitute a natural 'antechamber' with respect to the chapters that follow.

The second part of the book is more specifically dedicated to the theme of the interpsychic. Here I explore various spheres in which the interpsychic is manifest and is developed, from a theoretical and a clinical point of view, including the technical aspect of 'interpret-action.' And it may not be surprising if in this context a chapter pertaining to dogs as an important part of our lives finds a place as well, because – beyond the collection of anecdotes that I have allowed myself to include with undeniable pleasure, and that can constitute a rejuvenating break during a reading that may otherwise be rather demanding – our relationship with dogs has much to teach us concerning some of the basic functions of human relations, including therapeutic ones.

To give an idea of the variety of themes entailed in the concept of the interpsychic, I have freely revisited the psychosomatic area (something that others have been doing for decades with a specialized competence; I think especially of our French colleagues in De M'Uzan's group, as discussed extensively in Birksted-Breen, Flanders, & Gibeault, 2010), with the purpose of examining in particular the natural functions of interconnection and interchange carried out by the mucosal areas of the body, tracing as well some functional analogous equivalents that fall within the territory of the interpsychic.

I then return to a topic that is dear to me – empathy – with the intention of demonstrating once more its two fundamental characteristics: complexity (functional and structural) and innate undecidability. My goal is not at all to deny the existence of empathy, but to remove any delusions regarding the simplistic intentions of a certain 'methodical' utilization, as well as those regarding a sweetened, simplified, and unconflicted image of this concept, which instead deserves a much more comprehensive and potentially problematic consideration. I am also a supporter of the specificity of psychoanalytic empathy, which I consider profoundly different from common empathy among human beings.

An excursion into the territory of dreams could not be left out, and even if the focus has been shifted to elaborating the actual meaning of some of the phases of oneiric activity, I have taken care to put forward interpsychic passages that flourish in the analysis of dreams in the session. Analyst and patient work together on dreams, sometimes succeeding in sharing the exploration of secret passages that suddenly open up for both, like the ravines of the ancient city of Petra, unexpectedly leading to broad panoramas and previously unimagined discoveries.

The third part of the book ventures into some less habitable zones, in several cases for a long time less cohabitable during the analytic experience, at the border between the transpsychic and the interpsychic.

I have tried to describe the primary function of the containment of those aspects that are most essential – and, in a certain sense, preelaborative – in the analytic experience. I take very much to heart the connection with psychiatric work, which I firmly believe must not be lost and which represents a territory to be reconquered (both as a conceptualization and in practice) for many psychoanalysts who have preferred to radically withdraw from it.

I then take up the topics of fear and panic: two very strong emotional conditions that test the analyst's fortitude and capacity for elaboration no less than they do the patient's, given that the need for the latter is often not only that of an external diagnosis, but also that of a co-experience to be undertaken together, in order to experience containability and transformability.

'Trusting one's self' becomes, then, the goal of a journey that risks going on without end unless one meets someone who accepts getting to know together – and confronting together – the conditions that are potentially most destructive of mental life (and of life in general).

One more thought before getting to the heart of the individual chapters – or rather, a wish and a goal: that here and there, during the reading, 'something of the interpsychic' can be accomplished between the reader and the author. That is, that – with however much natural discontinuity obtains, given that the two are not the same person and have different ideas – a dialogue may be established, a dialogue facilitated by good intentions, by the sensation of having understood that which the other is saying or writing.

I consider the ambition of imposing my vision of things to be unrealistic (I take for granted that every analyst, as a result of his or her own journey, will have such a vision, more or less consolidated, and thus rightly all his or her own); but I would like it very much indeed if my psychoanalytic thoughts have been rendered in a way that is sufficiently comprehensible and expressed with clarity – perhaps communicating some feelings, too, as many of the colleagues whom I admire know how to do, and whose works I read gladly, and who end up becoming meaningful conversationalists in my internal laboratory.

We'll see whether I succeed.

PART ONE

Three Prefaces to the Discussion

1

FREUD'S 'OBJECTS'

Plurality and complexity in the internal world and in the analyst's working self

---

In a touching and well-researched book written in 1989, Lynn Gamwell, Director of Binghamton University Art Museum in New York State, examined Freud's notable collection of antique art. She observed that Freud began to surround himself with antique objects of great value (primarily little sculptures) after his father's death, in the 1890s, which were also the years of his greatest scientific and professional isolation.

Freud created for himself, in that period, 'an attentive audience of objects, which included an Egyptian scribe, a Greek goddess of wisdom, and a Chinese sage' (Gamwell, 1989, p. 21). 'These hundreds of human and animal figures all faced him like a huge audience. . . . He wrote thousands of manuscript pages facing Imhotep, the Egyptian architect who, in late antiquity, was revered as a healer. . . . Several accounts reveal that Freud treated these figures as his companions' (p. 27).

But these figures were not only the surrogate colleagues that at that time he did not yet have. Even after the success of psychoanalysis, continuing theoretical and group conflicts deeply grieved him; oppressed by these diatribes, 'the beleaguered founder of psychoanalysis always returned to his desk and to his dependable, silent audience, which represented for him the wisdom of the ages' (p. 28).

This was a world made up of external and internal objects, then, a source of comfort and of inspiration at the same time, in an illusional, intermediate area of potential creativity. At the end of his life, after a long illness, Freud decided to die in his studio, among his little objects, 'his ancestors of choice, his most faithful colleagues, and the embodiments of his excavated truths of psychoanalysis' (p. 29).

Today we are less alone.

In my colleagues' offices in other cities and countries, which I like to visit in order to be able to imagine them at work in my personal evocative thoughts during sessions, I have often seen at least a photo of Freud, sometimes of Klein, a few of Winnicott, and in some cases personal portraits of the analyst and his supervisors. Almost never — and appropriately so — have I seen images of family members, the patient's obvious rivals behind the scenes, out of respect for the patient's temporary centrality, and with full liberty for him to fantasize.

I must say that only very rarely have I discovered in offices the characteristics of the indecipherable and Spartan neutrality that were recommended until a few decades ago as a guarantee of the 'blank screen.' Today's analysts — in their exterior settings as well — seem to have in part renounced the pretext of an ideal undetectability of the analyst's self in the professional relationship. If anything, judging by the distinctive language of their office furnishings, they appear inclined to officially admit to their existence as individuals, in addition to their identities as those who merely fulfill a function. Nevertheless, they certainly retain their good sense and good taste in limiting themselves to a perceptible but usually sober personalization of the environment, avoiding a narcissistic invasion of the working field with the exhibition of their private iconography.

The true presences in that room, then, are those that count and that make a difference; the patients do not see them, even though for years they live with them without knowing it, because they are in the mind and heart of the analyst.

An 'ex-officio' presence is *a priori* taken for granted, and that is precisely that of Sigmund Freud, whom everyone knows and of whom patients cultivate an absolutely subjective image.

And he is 'their' Freud, almost never the analyst's.

They ignore, then, those who may be the analyst's other relevant teachers, the more loved authors, the colleagues with whom external and internal dialogues are developed, and the cultural community in which the analyst actively co-participates.

Today we are less alone, as I mentioned, and our collegial exchanges are so alive and frequent that, like Freud, we are not in need of interlocutors *in effigie concreta* in such a quantity (on the contrary, I think of the various pointed comments that we would hear today about a psychoanalytic office furnished like that of Berggasse 19).

A century of psychoanalysis confronts us, instead, with the difficult complexity of theoretical models and poses a problem of hosting in our scientific–professional imagination scientific presences in addition to that coveted uniqueness and unity that narcissism tends to strongly defend as the preferred dimension.

What still impedes us from recognizing and appreciating at least a little of that complexity and plurality is, at times, a transference problem (Klauber, 1981; Rangell, 1982; Eisold, 1994; Smith, 2003; Reeder, 2002; Spurling, 2003; Ambrosiano, 2005; Bolognini, 2005a, 2005b; Foresti & Rossi Monti, 2006), or one of *multi-object cohabitation* in confronting inspirational figures that are at times experienced not so much as parental or familial equivalents in an evolved sense (and thus with their characteristics and limitations not overly idealized), but as the archaic 'total parent,' unique and preoedipal – a parent who must not be 'betrayed,' putting him in a broader familial context, and then growing and differentiating oneself from him, but to whom or with whom one completely identifies, rather than only partially so.

In his very original work, 'On Psychoanalytic Figures as Transference Objects,' Laurence Spurling (2003) supports the utility, for every analyst, of an examination of his own internal relationship with the author to whom he refers. He notes: 'The value of an investigation of one's relationship to a psychoanalytic figure is that it is an excellent medium for revealing one's transference, as the figure in question is not a real person but only exists through his/her writings' (p. 31).

Spurling quite honestly analyzes his transference in relating to Winnicott, annotating the theoretical and affective changes that, with time, have developed in him in regard to this figure and his thought.

Freud, Ferenczi, or Klein, or Winnicott, Bion, Kohut, or Lacan – it isn't important who: the *transferential* copy that at times can come on the scene, at a level not so evolved, in the unconscious area of the analysts' internal world or that of psychoanalytic societies, is basically always the same. It risks leading to a restricted hypersimplification of the internal field and, correspondingly, of the professional–institutional one.

Two preliminary specifications: the first is that many subsequent observations will be read in free reference as much to the analyst's internal world as to the offshoots and reciprocal repercussions between the internal world and the institutional world, which do not coincide but are not independent of each other either.

The second: the discussion that I will develop is not in favor of a generic theoretical–clinical eclecticism, but – I repeat – it is in favor of the recognition of plurality and complexity of our contemporary horizons, which are in continual, compelling evolution, and of their utilizability in interchanges among colleagues and in the privacy of daily theoretical–clinical reflection.

Continuing my panoramic shot of the 'language of objects' in the workplaces and offices of my colleagues – that is, in the institutions and society headquarters of the three psychoanalytic continents – I am struck by how the official iconography hung on the walls suggests, for the most part, two series of portraits: that of international Grand Masters, who make official the historical developments and diffusion of psychoanalytic research; and that of the more homespun and reassuring local predecessors (usually a portrait gallery of presidents), who serve as a link between the ideal and the family history, as well as a shock absorber of the tension between the dilemma of plurality and the guarantee of identity and of institutional continuity.

The fact that such portraits may be exhibited with the greatest frequency in the centers of psychoanalytic societies with the longest traditions does not surprise us, of course – that is, in those centers where time and the progressive institutional *working through* have permitted a calming and sufficiently serene recomposition of that specific family history, consensually accepted by subsequent generations – even though there is likely to have been a considerable degree of conflict in the first generation after the founding fathers.

Transferential oneness

It is completely natural for every analyst that there may be a theoretical choice adopted, and that one author more than others may satisfy the demands of a complex scientific vision of an individual or of a group, characterizing its scientific identity. It is also realistic that, beyond choices of final allegiance, the analyst undergoing a formative evolution may choose an author as a single beacon who signals the way to navigators, necessitating a temporary, natural simplification of the theoretical field in order to construct the foundations of his own nascent theoretical–technical subjectivity.

But I am concerned here with a gray area, a 'shadow zone' that can be hidden behind certain excessive simplifications of the theoretical field, which is due to an excess of the analyst's transference to the parental or narcissistic equivalent represented by the inspirational object and which can constitute an obstacle to a collegial intersubjective exchange.

The symptom of this shadow zone is precisely the incapacity for an interchange with the 'non-self,' which is unconsciously feared as dangerous and too disturbing.

This shadow zone does not at all coincide with the strong and authentic core identification that in many cases can be well constructed, using a theoretical setup based on a single inspirational figure, with a simple internal identity and, in fact, an authentic one (i.e., well individuated and separate from the relevant internal object); but it is distinguished by its *symptomatology of narrow-mindedness toward an externality that may not be immediately corroborating.*

It is the task of the sufficiently mature analyst to keep himself vigilant, reflective, and self-analytic in the face of a possible tendency toward an idealizing archaic transference to a specific hyperpossessive object (of the kind: *'You will not have any other god apart from me!'*), a transference that functions as a protective element with respect to the disturbing experience of plurality among the family figures.

Plurality, in fact, sounds offensive to our originary narcissism – which, deep down, intimately, would demand an exclusive and privileged union, both internal and external, with a unique parental or narcissistically confirming equivalent.

My first analytic patient comes to mind: a young engineer, the second son of four brothers, who could not tolerate that, on his favorite soccer team – the 'Inter' soccer team of Milan – someone other than his favorite player, Karl Heinz Rummenigge, might actually have scored a goal. This player was the symbol of an idealized and perfect narcissism and of an invincible 'German' technology that obviously represented the projection of his ideal self.

This patient had no peace due to the fact that, in his field of work (building engineering), there was no single, masterful person to whom he could refer, someone who was good with every technical problem. True, there was a certain Mr. Leonhardt, whom the patient

11

continually quoted to me, and who seemed to combine within himself the height of the profession (in addition to which, through the assonance of his name, he evoked the absolute and universal genius of Leonardo da Vinci).

But, tragically, this protective figure – though dominant – was not enough in the face of more complex and diverse eventualities. For example, having been charged with designing his town's sidewalks, my patient noted with dismay that on this task, the immense Leonhardt had written nothing; so he would have to go to the extreme length of asking for advice from another engineer, Mr. Semenzato, an unknown colleague for the past few years. Semenzato was a few years older than my patient and had previously arranged the same sort of project in a nearby town, so he was someone who might be able to tell him something useful about it.

This prospect of consulting him seemed quite offensive and narcissistically unacceptable to my patient: to move from Leonhardt to . . . this Semenzato?!? Unthinkable! 'Why?' my patient cried out in his session, 'Why in the field of building engineering isn't there someone unique and absolute who corresponds to a Dante Alighieri, unquestionably considered by everyone "the supreme poet"?'

It is unnecessary to point out that, at the time, I was older than he by a few years, and that I came dangerously close to being the equal of this provincial Semenzato, the professional 'older brother' who interfered in an annoying manner with the unique and symmetrical relationship with the patient's narcissistic ideal.

It must also be pointed out in my patient's defense, as a mitigating factor, that true complexity and plurality do not constitute agreeable reality; they require work and a much greater interior space with respect to the elementary functions of an 'either/or' type.

In a paper dedicated to this formative background ('La Famiglia Interna dell'Analista' [The analyst's internal family]; Bolognini, 2005a), I pointed out the opportunity to enlarge the familial field of the professional self to a broadened structure including the equivalents of grandparents, uncles and aunts, cousins, and analytic siblings, because the totality of these figures, of these potential interlocutors, can constitute a considerable richness in furthering the aim of *internal consultation* during the clinical work.

We know very well that many authors, in the past more than 100 years, have accurately described a specific aspect or portion of the mental functioning of human beings. We also know that many of these may, for narcissistic reasons, oedipal or intergenerational, have emphasized their own discoveries and acquisitions as though they had to supplant those of their predecessors, invalidating them. Others, with greater moderation, have realized they were proposing extensions, variations of perspective and additional integrations, not substitutive ones. They (I think of Klein and Kohut) officially stated that they offered an ideological continuity of the works of those who had preceded them, but they then dedicated almost all their work to the carefully honed presentation of only the new aspects of their 'copyright.'

In this way, they actually provoked in their readers and followers the implicit conviction of a complete substitution of the new for the old, with the predictable opposing effects of rejection in some and proselytism in others.

Today as yesterday, some psychoanalysts express themselves in their writing as though Freud (speaking theoretically) did not still constitute one of their fundamental sources of reference – which, conversely, he always ends up being, if nothing else because of their implicit assumptions of where to begin. They seem to negate the fact that Freud, first of all, certainly asked himself many questions and threw out exploratory thoughts in reasonable anticipation of subsequent verifying developments.

Others, on the contrary, maintain that Freud actually said everything himself, and that successive developments are not 'derivatives' (perhaps inevitably and appropriately integrative ones), but new 'spins' on his work. These analysts put forward stern warnings not to go beyond what they maintain to be the proper realm of orthodoxy, as though every novelty were invariably the expression of a resistance (an assumption that – if not discriminately modulated – risks being transformed into a paralyzing, viselike grip).

Conversely, what takes no notice of *a priori* rejections or total proselytisms is our preconscious, which – in very specific stages of treatment, or in the present moment of an individual session, in bypassing the barriers of our preferences with impudence, precisely when (and if) we do not expect it – brings to our mind this or that author, perhaps a disagreeable one, or one of whom we have taken little account. This author, with regard to certain configurations or certain developments, has written pages on that moment right there, and – damn! – they fit perfectly and, if we are honest, permit us to see or to understand something new: a little as though a not very well-liked relative has provided us with useful tools in an unexpected and a bit disconcerting way.

It is not that the preconscious is always taken literally as a revealed truth; the ego still has the absolute right to carry out its own reflections and to draw from them some choices considered at the secondary level.

However, the preconscious is a respected interlocutor, because – if placed in a condition to express itself – it has its own unforeseen and irrepressible originality, and it is worth listening to; free association, at times, seems to gain access to theory as well, through a creative and reflective intersection with clinical work.

It falls to us to integrate or, more modestly, to allow certain unexpected and logically inconsistent connections to cohabit an intermediate, interlocutory area – connections that surprise us in sessions. Sometimes, if one has the patience, they can reveal themselves less incompatible and contradictory than imagined, more or less as sometimes happens in a family or group setting, when contributions that seem to undermine the coherence of a certain way of seeing things then demonstrate an unforeseen generativity.

And it must also be said that a presumed theoretical rigor on the *logical* level, in certain cases, can be a sign of some rigidity and intolerance on the *psycho*logical level, impeding contact and consultation with more of the internal interlocutors endowed with various skills (like the original mother and father, with their respective languages and mental perspectives, in the child's formative experience and the adult's internal consultation).

The problem that I am describing, in fact, is that of the contactability and consultability of a broad internal group that can (and I emphasize 'can,' not 'must') become part of the authentic interior world of the contemporary analyst.

I want to add that I carefully maintain a certain distinction between the 'working ego' and the 'working self.' Internal interlocutors play a part in the latter, while the working ego consults them, and in the end, if it is sufficiently autonomous and mature, it takes a position, chooses, and decides.

The complex articulation of our internal organization in the session does not constitute in and of itself an insurmountable difficulty for analysts. We are sufficiently trained, for example, in the exercise of suspending judgment, in the consideration of well-balanced points of view, in the alternating and interwoven identification with various characters on the scene, in the continual referral of the present to the past and vice versa – from the inside to the outside of their co-presence, to the perception of desire behind the defense, etc. In general we are in a sufficiently proven condition to stage a complex mental scenario.

Certainly, others surpass us in this sense – for example, philosophers, because they have at bottom a dynamic advantage: they more often deal with abstract concepts rather than emotional experiences. I would say that, usually, differently from us and with due exceptions, philosophers 'travel without baggage in hand' – the baggage of memories, of the emotions and sensations that we always carry with us because of their inevitable associations, since every theoretical reference reconnects them to us in sessions, in our clinical and personal stories, in more or less painful and difficult situations of therapeutic cohabitation.

Philosophers, our fellow travelers in thought, specialize in conceptual explorations that for the most part evoke other conceptual explorations. Because of this – being, at least apparently, less weighed down by dense emotional charges – they seem to better tolerate complexity.

It is also in discussing our theories that I think we analysts must frequently tolerate a not yet rational complexity, but an evocative one, much greater than that demanded of those who, in their rationality, are legitimately released from continual and intense experiential evocation.

The other highly specific point at which psychoanalysis proves to be a 'science with a special mandate' resides, in my opinion, in its acceptance of the *alternation of primary process with secondary process as a functional realm specific to the mind of the analyst.*

The problem I pose is whether that is valid only for clinical activity, or is it also valid for theoretical reflection on the psychoanalytic mission?

I understand that, for a 'normal' epistemology, an answer that may allow for a certain *modality of theoretical reflection* – the alternating primary/secondary functioning – may seem unacceptable. In that alternating functioning, the principle of contradiction can come to be suspended, and in weighing the validity of two theories that are not in agreement, Occam's razor can also fail to function, since it does not take into account the *cohabitability* or its lack in two theories that are consistent in their interior, but not between themselves, and sometimes with fruitful results, in the analyst's *real* mind (not the ideal one).[1]

Antithetical theories and models, then, can coexist with a certain degree of 'truth' (or, more modestly, of utility), even though they might rationally exclude each other. It is possible that in other cases, one perspective might seem more fertile or more livable than another, and in certain cases vice versa, so it happens that, at the present time, they may coexist (and not inappropriately) from a clinical point of view.

There is a diversity of opinions on what can be defined as 'research' in psychoanalysis today: there are those who restrict the term to empirical research; those who extend it to conceptual research; those who rely on clinical material as creative investigation; those who require objective, statistical, or psychometrical measurability of observable variables; and so on. Such diversity is emblematic in our field, and it seems to me to suggest a certain caution in the face of a possible categorization of methodological judgment.

One can observe, for example, the exchange of opinions between Otto Kernberg (2006) and Roger Perron (2006) in the *International Journal of Psychoanalysis* in regard to this topic. I am aware of stepping into a hornet's nest there, and I will limit myself to outlining the problem.

But let us return to complexity and plurality, and to their ramifications for theory and technique. For example, a critical point for us analysts is that of the theoretical–clinical choice to 'condense' representations of the object to the point of arriving at the uniqueness of the underlying transferential relationship. Or, at the other end of the spectrum, of articulating, tolerating, and sharing a certain plurality of presences in the analytic scene, succeeding in playing with them in the session in a creative way, on an oneiric level as well, with the 'one,' 'two,' 'three,' and the 'more than three,' according to various situations.

The multiple figures of a discussion or of a dream can be understood as split products or fragments of a narcissistic representation (= only

---

1 Occam suggested that, among the different explanations of a natural phenomenon, one would have to prefer the one that does not multiply useless entities (*entia non sunt multiplicanda*). Usually, 'Occam's razor' comes to be applied as a practical rule for choosing among hypotheses that might have the same capacity for explaining one or more observed natural phenomena.

images of parts of the self) or of a dyadic situation (= images of the self and the object). Alternatively, they can be considered pertinent to more evolved spheres of organization of the internal world, such as oedipal triangulation, the family scheme, an important and meaningful group reality for the subject in a given moment, etc.

In each case, then, we work primarily to reintegrate that which is split in the self. In other cases, the dispersion of the object's representations into multiple figures present on the scene suggests the opportunity to interpret transferentially this multiplication of representations, re-unifying the apparent plurality of figures into the representation of the object-analyst.

Yet at times we find ourselves facing the possibility of granting, or not, a certain degree of objective dignity of its own to a figure that can begin to exist in the external world and in the patient's internal one, in continuity with the transference − of which, certainly, it is an extension. On the basis of its characteristics of continuing existence and substance, it gradually gains a different status, an autonomous right of citizenship in the patient's life and in the treatment scenario.

A classic case, in this sense, is evident in the way of treating the patient's development of loving feelings in analysis. According to the clinical context, the analyst will be able to appreciate the preeminence of aspects of defensive displacement from himself to an external object. Alternatively, those aspects can be seen as more mature ones − as an evolved transfer to a new, realistic, and possible object (with the analyst becoming, in that case, a post-oedipal parent who can be renounced). Or, at a much more regressive level, the analyst will be able, through a *new entry*, to catch on the fly an opportunity to 're-dredge up' some element of the patient that − after a split, and after having been launched like a projectile far into the distance, remaining in exile and entirely remote from the confines of the self − was awaiting, for who knows how much time, the opportunity of representation and introjective reintegration into a self that can still be represented only through the image of a couple. And so on, with other possibilities.

The important thing is for the analyst to be keenly perceptive (today one works with a 'perceptivity with complex stripes'), and to make use of a sufficiently broad array of configurations and models in his 'working self,' and also to characterize himself as having a certain internal mobility in his 'working ego.'

In regard to the idea of having a sufficient endowment of models and con-figurations, I am reminded of a curious episode of forty years ago.

At the end of the 1960s – in tandem with the economic boom – new habits, new cultural perspectives, and specialists in new careers began to make themselves known in Italy. Among the latter (in addition to psycho-analysts) were sommeliers, refined advisors for a new sensibility in wine drinking.

I was quite impressed and admiring when, in an elegant restaurant in Rome, one of these specialists came to our table, displaying a silver *tastevin* around his neck, and after having taken note of the dishes we had chosen (with lamb as the entrée), he recommended, with thoughtful and focused precision, a 1965 Blauburgunder Sudtiroler, which in his words was perfect for the occasion. These were the years in which James Bond ordered an exclusive champagne vintage with a self-confident air, and I thought that this expert must have been, within his chosen field, a font of science.

I was perplexed, however, when he moved two tables away from us and I heard him recommend the same Blauburgunder, with the same concen-trated haughtiness, to a couple who had ordered prosciutto and melon. I then dedicated my interest to eavesdropping on his subsequent conversa-tions at various tables here and there in the room, only to discover that he managed to offload an entire case of Blauburgunder, regardless of whether the hapless diners had ordered the Adriatic sole or game from the mountains of Veneto.

Nevertheless, from the way in which he assumed a particular attitude and expressed himself, that guy had seemed to me to be a great professor.

Now, I suspect that it may be rather difficult to work with this internal mobility if one is not inclined to collaborate at least a little with some of the inspirational objects that are *different among themselves*, that may have entered to become a part of, with introjective authenticity, our interior psychoanalytic family.

These objects can function as a 'third' with respect to the analyst–patient dyad, or with respect to that mixture of the analyst and another internal object who is more universal: with respect to a dyad, that is, more than with respect to a couple.

I think that, at times, the analyst risks forming *an excluding, narcis-sistic dyad, instead of a differentiated, generative couple* – also in the case of a relationship with a *teacher or an author of reference*.

Furthermore, just as happens almost regularly in the first stages of clinical work, the internal realm of identification can work things out such that the analyst *'becomes'* his own analyst or his own supervisor, *'behaving as he'* and losing contact with the self, rather than remembering them and consulting them while remaining one's own self.

> [In short], . . . the force of transference is destined to considerably condition the theoretical–conceptual openings and closings toward this or that colleague or teacher, favoring them or inhibiting them, at times, to set aside the actual value or scientific interest of various proposed contributions.
>
> Transferences are created that apparently point toward an object-theory (Leo Rangell's 'transference to theory,' 1982) – that is, transferences behind which there is always a more or less complex involvement with a figure that inspires areas of great transferential significance.
>
> According to Falzeder (1998), who cites in this sense the American 'filiations' of Ferenczi and Rank, the underlying inspirational figure is usually a unique one.
>
> (Bolognini, 2005a)[2]

Certainly, the analyst's theoretical–technical harmony and integration depend on his basic nature, on his development as a person, and on his formative course during his training years. These fundamental factors come to make up a sort of 'complex personal equation' of the analyst, which will render him unique and specific with respect to every categorical standard.

What I am trying to indicate here is that this harmony may also be the fruit of a relative (and thus temporary) acceptance of the plurality and conflictuality of a sufficiently loving internal environment, possibly making use of an underlying, good narcissistic physiological endowment.

This latter element comes to be provided primarily by the mother and father and by their subsequent equivalents; then by the analysis; and later on – I would add – by an adequate and not unrealistic, complex valorization of the family/institution in which one has grown up, which forms a foundational internal object for the analyst.

The much-reviled larger psychoanalytic institutions, which certainly have many well-documented defects, fulfill, however, a

---

2 Translation by Gina Atkinson.

foundational function as an antidote to the theoretical–clinical endogamy (which is, on the other hand, a risk in small groups). This, in my view, is not sufficiently recognized.

Daniel Widlöcher (2004) asks himself about the deep meaning of the enormous quantity of seminars, conventions, and conferences developed by psychoanalysts in every geographical region. While recognizing a variety of possible motives for this rather surprising fact (if ophthalmologists or surgeons had as many conventions, this would indicate enormous scientific progress, which in reality in our field is not the case), Widlöcher hypothesizes that the basic function of all these meetings may be the function of the 'third' – that is, the need to give notice of and to verify elaborative internal results to the individual, or to the local group, experienced as an entity that is not sufficiently 'other.'

Plurality in psychoanalysis today

Although André Green (2005) has recently decidedly contested Wallerstein's idea of *common ground* and of 'many psychoanalyses' (Wallerstein, 2005), the IPA Congress in Rio (in 2005) and the one in Berlin (in 2007) have to my mind confirmed the fact of gradual, substantial, community acceptance of a fertile variety of currents of analytic thought. The novelty here is not in the '*variety*' (already noted), but in the '*fertile*' aspect, since it can now be seen with clarity that analysts are rather tired of religious wars, and they find it more and more the norm to exchange ideas and organize panels with colleagues of different origins and varying formulations.

Fertility is evidenced by the fact that analysts of different origins no longer limit themselves to stating their own opinions, each on his own, functioning – so to speak – 'in parallel.' Instead they begin to exchange ideas in a spirit of curiosity, without the pretext of 'converting' the other, in a perspective of interchange that does not threaten respective identities. This is what verifies, in fact, the international clinical discussion groups.

The 'monochrome' panel, in contrast, is less attractive at meetings than it once was, and it has a taste of the provincial, sometimes risking the repeat of a self-confirming atmosphere of parochialism. Conversely, a panel regains its particular attraction when it deals with the reexamination of a strongly characterized cultural biotope that can be utilized in the internal references that every analyst adopts to orient himself and to form conceptualizations.

These considerations are valid yet again, without too much discontinuity, for external reality just as for the analyst's internal reality. Overall, they refer not so much to having few or many teachers in one's own formation, as to having few or many interlocutors – and, if possible, ones who are sufficiently different among themselves, belonging to both the parental series and the fraternal one – with whom to engage in a creative dialogue on the external and the internal.

Incidentally, the 'mono-Leonhardt' engineer consulted Semenzato, in the end, and for better or for worse, those famous sidewalks sprang forth – the result of a collegial genesis, rather than a self-sufficient or a divine one.

For some years, moreover, as happens with many of my colleagues, I have had the opportunity of entering into exchanges with psychoanalysts of different histories, schools, residences, and traditions. I can say – with a feeling I have discovered to be shared – that the first meetings resemble those with third- or fourth-generation family branches of immigrants: there is reciprocal curiosity, some trepidation, the certainty of a common 'old-style'/family history, and, however, at the same time – powerful and undeniable – the experience of being an outsider.

In the beginning, certain phantasms (which are at least in part protective ones) generated an initial ill-concealed tension. Even the promising diversification along genealogical lines, which in meetings with foreign colleagues could have allowed a real possibility of cross-fertilization, carried the risk – without the predictable marching in place of the usual reassuring and confirming discussions (already noted to be a sort of 'closed farm') – of giving rise to the construction of a preliminary defensive bastion.

Attendance at international discussion groups, with colleagues of different nationalities but especially of *different schools*, have permitted me to dissolve some of these phantasms, a little at a time, without having to lose my original familial identity. I have met people who are desirous of working on clinical material with real curiosity about the contributions of others, united perhaps by an implicit, spontaneous pre-selection. In those groups, people come together who are already inclined to set aside their often very particular histories and to grasp the occasion for contact and exchange in a climate of what is effectively a cultural otherness.

Much more complex is the experience of the CAPSA forum (the Committee on Analytic Practice and Scientific Activity), the initiative instituted in 2005 by the IPA president, Claudio Eizirik, to promote theoretical–clinical, intercontinental exchanges through an official network of specific invitations issued by the Association to colleagues who bring direct testimony of the diverse ways of working in the three major geographical areas of the IPA.

In summary, I can say that the few initial resistances to these inter-woven exchanges came, really, from those nations strongly character-ized by local theory, perhaps more accustomed to self-confirming situations and, all in all, more inclined to export their psychoanalysis than to import something of others'. The overall good start of these meetings seems to open a new era in the history of our Association.

Regarding the various 'psychoanalytic families,' in the following pages, I will not propose an update about 'which Freud' or 'which Klein,' which Winnicott, Lacan, Kohut, Bion, etc., one meets in visit-ing the psychoanalytic societies of various continents, according to local stock-exchange quotations or perhaps making recourse to the *impact factors* provided by the frequency of citation of these various authors. Instead, I want to report an underlying impression that has formed in me with time and with ongoing contacts and that contrib-utes today to my overall analytic view.

To me it seems that, in many countries, a process of transformation of many 'incompatibilities' may in fact be taking place, not in the sense of a destructive denial of discontinuities or of different theories, but in the sense of a *recognition of the existence, of the consultability and dignity, of the various psychoanalyses* (in a meaningful parallel with the very recent official acceptance of the existence of different models of training in the IPA). Meanwhile, there is a laborious but progressive attenuation of conflicts surrounding the historical, scientific, insti-tutional, familial, and theoretical–clinical figure of Sigmund Freud.

Do I run the risk of putting forth a version of the facts that is too simple if I say that Freud, in our collective fantasy, 150 years after his birth, is slowly, arduously 'becoming a grandfather'?[3]

---

3 I intend here to refer not to the fact that Freud may have been 'surpassed' – a problem that the press periodically suggests to analysts in a perfunctory and provocative way – but to the fact that others who came after him may have continued the intergenerational chain with the characteristics and the prerogatives of equally worthy and original forms of generativity and parentage that are their own. I think that this point – of the possible

Can we think that truly by virtue of his extraordinary (but not divine) fertility, he has many grandchildren today, and that none of them is, intergenerationally, 'the only' son with the right of primo-geniture and of exclusive heredity to his title and goods?

Generally speaking, the recognition of one's own Freudian line of descent is, for the analyst, the natural result of an authentically rooted gratitude and admiration.

Not only that: beyond recognition of common genealogical and historical roots, the majority of analysts do not at all repudiate the importance and substance of Freudian discoveries, but one feels encouraged – more than authorized – to extend research work into new areas also, utilizing new theoretical and technical tools – *also*, I intend to emphasize.

If, on the one hand, one must not lose sight of the unforsakeable pole of a discriminating, necessary rigor for a scientific psychoanalysis, I would like to contribute, in the pages to come, toward giving a dialectic representation to the other pole, within which the range of our discipline can come alive and enrich itself – a range that includes a cautious, attentive, and not indiscriminate faith in its possible developments.

I feel myself to be a son of classical psychoanalysis, which I hold dear and of which 'I don't throw anything away' – but I feel a familial relationship with it, not a sacral or idealizing one, and even less a fetishistic one. This permits me, I think, to look at what is new with interest, without feeling myself to be too much at fault or too intimidated under the gaze of my ancestors.

I think that, if anything, our teachers of the past may have had the courage to explore the unknown without contenting themselves with 'sacred scriptures' and that we must learn from them, first of all, precisely this, while also not abandoning an appropriately critical spirit.

At the same time, I do not harbor any compulsive fervor to have to rid myself by force of the family notebooks and library; I do not

---

'grandfathering,' so to speak, of Freud into analysts' internal world – must be well clarified. To know how to become grandparents means accepting that others, too, after us, may be generative and that, indeed, precisely the generative capacity of our successors may confirm the goodness of our original roots. We would not render Freud a good service – and not our internal Freud either – if we imagine his children and grandchildren as uniform automatons who follow canonical codes.

feel any intolerance toward the roots from which we have come, as long as I do not feel constrained to religiously repeat them without being able to reach my personal creativity or our shared, fraternal, generational creativity. I understand our 'post-modernism,' in short, as the following: a substantial familial appreciation, humanizing and not idealizing, of our original psychoanalytic objects, in full recognition of our received heritage.

From here, in addition to our transference – but possibly utilizing the energy of our transference – we can proceed, moving between two poles: that of appreciation for a precious heritage that is not to be wasted, and that of courage with which to face the new that is yet to be conquered, just as Freud and his students did, the pioneers, sometimes alone and sometimes in groups.

Today we are truly no longer alone, if we choose not to be, and if we know how to utilize the presences and the resources of our field.

Precisely from my clinical encounters in recent years, I draw the most comforting thoughts. It may seem banal, but with the effort of working together, among colleagues, the push of the drives and the vicissitudes of the subject's narcissistic equilibrium, the intersubjective implications of the encounter and the overdetermination of transference journeys, the reintroduction of split elements, the activity of reverie, and the recovery of memory – all are concepts that become less and less alien and are always less incompatible in the analyst's actual mind (not the ideal one). Most often, analysts retain a clear ideal of the origin and distinctive relevance of concepts with respect to diverse models.

I am describing, perhaps, a complex movement or groundswell that pertains to the evolution of the international psychoanalytic community in its scientific and institutional aspects (CAPSA is, at bottom, an 'emerging idea' of this multifaceted project) – that is, *the movement toward meeting and interchange with respect to differences and plurality.*

And I would like to conclude this chapter by commenting on this subject (which – given today's geographical diffusion of psychoanalysis – risks assuming a planetary dimension) at a more individual and possibly more homespun level: in emptying the suitcase (our already-cited 'baggage in hand') after a clinical meeting with faraway colleagues, we often return to our offices with an abundance of paper material.

Photocopied articles, books, recovered notes from discussions – all lie for some time on our desks, to be later thrown away or, alternatively, placed in a bookcase or in categorized files for future usage, becoming part of that plankton that Cesare Musatti[4] (personal communication) spoke of and through which the analyst nourishes himself, following his rambling needs and inspirations.

But another, less tangible treasure will sneak out of the just-opened suitcase, and it will follow us, invisible, all the way to our workplace: an efficacious expression, an unusual concept, a meaningful back-and-forth between two colleagues, a surprising interpretation, even a special way – for us, a little bit 'foreign' – to create a pause or to keep hold of an uncertainty, which will return to our minds when we least expect it and which will probably contribute to a not insignificant moment in a session.

Maybe it will be useful to us as well, provided that we are not offended, provided that we are not frightened off by it.

4 Cesare Musatti was one of the early founders of the Italian Psychoanalytic Society.

2

PROPOSAL FOR AN ALTERNATIVE REVIEW OF THERAPEUTIC FACTORS

In the margins of Gabbard and Westen's 'Rethinking Therapeutic Action'

When Gabbard and Westen's article dedicated to the developments of the therapeutic perspective in contemporary psychoanalysis appeared in the *International Journal of Psychoanalysis* in 2003, I, like many of my colleagues, greatly appreciated the broad, balanced nature – in some ways an intentionally 'ecumenical' one – of this review of therapeutic factors put forward by the two authors.

The vastness of their vision of the whole picture, the expository clarity and accuracy of their assessments, make this definitely a work worthy of praise. It must be said, preliminarily, that although this is a valuable article, it is basically a regional one, absolutely North American, as can be seen from the bibliographic references, almost all of which represent authors of that continent, even though the article begins with a decisive recognition of the current pluralism in the field.

Authors of other theoretical–cultural constellations (French, English, Italian, Latin American) probably would have put forward, with equal naturalness, different viewpoints and different evolutionary journeys, examining other developments in contemporary psychoanalysis. And while it is certain that Gabbard and Westen trace a necessarily partial picture, it is also a rich, stimulating one, and is rather a 'layman's' view (from the standpoint of not belonging to a particular school), which invites reflection and comment in a pleasantly free atmosphere. There is no intolerance, and there are no implicit preclusions (such as implications between the lines that 'only *this* is psychoanalysis'), nor any explicit, overly restrictive and absolutist comments (such as the anathema that 'this is *not* psychoanalysis!'). And in this sense, my choice of their text as a starting point definitely facilitates further elaborations of my thinking.

Theoretical pluralism, the complexity of therapeutic factors, articulation of operative strategies and treatment techniques, recognition of the diversity of needs of different patients and of the same patient at different times and in different circumstances, the importance of the person of the analyst and of his capacities to relate to the patient's internal objects (now differentiating himself from them, now knowing how to be consonant with them), the intrapsychic and interpsychic interplay, negotiation of the therapeutic climate, attention to the defensive overinvestment of internal reality or of external reality, an appreciation of possible connections and interdisciplinary confirmations with the neurosciences, development theories, ethology, nonpsychoanalytic psychotherapeutic techniques from which we can also learn something – all these elements seem to me to have been taken into account in this contribution from two colleagues who, in effect, have carried out an encyclopedic undertaking in providing a summarized view of the state of the art, from their North American orientation.

I will not examine all the concepts they have put forth, but will instead limit myself to integrating them, drawing out in particular the therapeutic factors that have perhaps been a little undervalued by them or synthesized into general formulations.

To state that my choice will be totally personal is to put it mildly. On the other hand, every barrel yields the wine that it contains, and every colleague will sing a different song from that of others, because his story and his journey are different, and he is different; nor will I be able to thoroughly analyze the arguments I quote because that would require writing another book, or focusing all my attention on only one of these.

Thus, what I express will be a broad spectrum of my personal opinions.

What would I add to Gabbard and Westen's article?

Quite arbitrarily, I find it both appropriate and realistic to highlight the following therapeutic passages as particularly important in analytic treatment:

1 Establishing the setting.
2 Permitting the experience of regression.
3 Constructing a certain therapeutic alliance and sharing the recognition of psychic reality.
4 Gradually getting to know the patient and learning to synthesize oneself with him.
5 Learning to work together.
6 Promoting cohesion of the self if it is lacking.
7 Creating internal space if it is not there.
8 Gaining familiarity with the preconscious and the transitional area.
9 Experiencing the existence of the unconscious.
10 Recognizing and rehabilitating relationships with objects: integrating splits, tolerating ambivalences and separation.
11 Showing how an evolving personal perspective is possible.
12 Gradually accepting separation and loss while becoming and remaining one's own self.

I would like to highlight that some of these 'passages' may be, in and of themselves, therapeutic 'provisions,' 'actions,' 'tools,' and 'factors,' in the sense that, correspondingly:

a They describe phases of the treatment.
b They are part of methodical, planned care.
c They require a series of concrete facilitating interventions by the analyst.
d They constitute a technical system.
e They function as transformative efforts.

Regarding the setting: it is a situation in which the patient comes to find himself a part of (= the passage), but it is also an operative context that we maintain as useful and appropriate (= provision), which we decide to give notice of and apply concretely with deliberate communication (= action), and which we use with technical cognition (= a tool), and which in itself is already operating in various ways

(= a transformative factor; for example, as the first containing and regulating factor, even before it becomes a standard capable of making evident the intemperate exigencies of the unconscious).

Moreover, 'the maternal function of the setting, the basic, silent support of the associative/interpretive work, and the even more silent repository of the psychoses and the bastions of the analytic couple, has been well observed by all of us for fifty years' (Berti Ceroni, 2002).[1]

To Winnicott (1954) we owe a detailed description of the setting (he summarized twelve fundamental elements of it) as the *facilitating environment*.

Naturally, I will not embark on a detailed *réportage* of the subsequent literature on the subject, rich with highly elaborated contributions, such as the very carefully written and accurate one by Meissner (2004) on the use of the couch.

What I would like to keep in mind here is that the setting is also – in and of itself – a structuring therapeutic factor, a carrier of new developments and often of benefits from the very beginning of treatment, surprisingly capable of inducing long-term structural transformations for those patients who have not known a primary regulating experience; conversely, it is also a source of crisis when it becomes significantly altered in the context of persistent regression.

Intrinsically correlated with the setting and promoted by it, *regression*, in turn, does not only come about as a phenomenon that forms a part of the process, but results in also becoming, in its benign and useful version, a therapeutic factor in itself. As many authors have demonstrated (Winnicott, 1954; Balint & Balint, 1959; Kohut, 1971, 1984; Searles, 1986), the very fact of coming into contact with one's own primitive states or childhood repressions in the unconscious and detached from the self by early dissociations – while making use, however, of analytic assistance and the elaborating support of an ego now more appropriately equipped – already leads to a transformation and to a broadening of the sense of self.

The enormous therapeutic potential of regression is especially evident in those cases in which dissociative defenses that have long been detached from the self's central ego are overturned by a sudden upward thrust in the tide of experience, requiring the subject to reexperience this as his own. In such circumstances, an astonished

1 Translation by Gina Atkinson.

and at times alarmed ego must recognize that it 'holds in suspense' an experience of the self (e.g., a grief reaction, a vital potentiality eliminated as provoking guilt, an old jealous furor, etc.), which, paradoxically, becomes asymptomatic once it is no longer repressed but split (Bolognini, 2003a). Only the regimen of intra-analytic regression can effectively permit renewed contact with this split-off experience of the self.

Technically speaking, it is not at all taken for granted that the analyst will succeed in promoting and allowing the patient's regression, given that at times analysts (especially the younger ones) are afraid of this apparently negative turn of events. It may be seen as an infantilizing and distressing picture of the patient's internal movements, and some analysts, more or less unaware of it, discourage regression through a perceptible coldness.

And the patient is no less afraid – such that, very often, we could help him by pointing out to him that he is succeeding in reestablishing contact with certain experiences, traveling a path that he has avoided until now. It is a path that requires being re-traveled, perhaps with the help of someone capable of sharing the experience and the investigation of its deep personal meaning.

Now the construction of the *therapeutic alliance* enters the picture.

Certainly, the therapeutic alliance is a passage in the analytic process, an intentional provision actualized by the analyst with a series of directed interventions that are also utilized as tools. But it is also an absolutely efficacious factor at various levels; one could say that it is not only 'an alliance to accomplish a therapy' but is also 'an alliance *that is therapeutic in itself.*'

Now that the field of well-described neurotic and psychotic 'pseudo-alliances' has been appropriately cleared by Greenson and Wexler (1969) and by Rabih (1981), with all their collected samples of false collaboration, hypocrisy, compliance, and artificial reasoning, we see that the gradual construction of the working alliance permits the recovery of lost and unsaturated valences of the model of the newborn baby's suction-interaction with the breast (Etchegoyen, 1991) and of the cooperative desire between the baby and the adult (Sandler, Kennedy, & Tyson, 1980). This recovery, made possible by the therapeutic alliance, leads on to the exploration of advanced levels of analytic cooperation that can make the experience of a dialogue between the adult parts of the analytic couple feel natural (Meltzer, 1967) and to a frank and even harsh intersubjective and interpersonal comparison, provided that it is founded on faith in a common task (Renik, 1995, 1999) and can promote an evolved genital-level collaboration between two persons (Lopez, 2004).

Many authors agree that the working alliance may be more a product of an underlying framework than of an intentional, conscious plan and that cooperative unconscious levels (Segal, 1994), activated by the analysis, may be simultaneously both the cause and the effect of therapeutic progress.

The symmetrical experience of a collaboration contained in the asymmetry of the analytic relationship permits, furthermore, a natural and gradual distribution of the gradients of cohabitation with the objects of the self or with the area of 'non-self' (Kohut, 1971), according to individual tolerances that vary considerably from patient to patient.

All authors agree that the therapeutic nature of the cooperative experience in analysis depends heavily on the patient's capacity to introject that experience in an authentic and deep way, structurally acquiring it as his own so that he can reproduce it in extra-analytic situations as well.

Gabbard and Westen (2003) dedicate a few paragraphs (p. 833) to the process of internalization of the analyst's functions and modality that, with time, can become the patient's procedural memories of the therapeutic help received. I think that this may be true, generally speaking, but I would add that *the specific levels of internalization* (Grinberg, 1967) of the object-analyst and its way of functioning[2] *are crucial,* and the knowledge of them is not a doctrinaire fixation, but one of the key points of monitoring the work in progress.

I have dedicated various earlier contributions specifically to the theme of empathy and its vague and elusive nature (Bolognini, 1997a, 2001, 2002a, 2004a, 2004b, 2004e), in order to discredit a sort of sugary, romanticized, and voluntaristic version of this concept that in reality, by contrast, has its own complex, articulated, and conflictual psychoanalytic dimension.

In a perspective that is tied to the real, daily work of analysis, the task of *gradually knowing the patient, learning to synthesize oneself with*

---

2 The levels of internalization to which I refer are: *incorporation*, which produces control and imitation; *interiorization*, which brings an object into the internal world, but does not adequately connect it with the self and does not metabolize its useful components; and *deep introjection*, which, by contrast, permits these latter transformative and constructive passages.

him – beyond every intentional empathistic pretext and the clear sense of obviousness that could arise at first glance – is reinserted, with full rights, into the series of therapeutic 'passages,' 'provisions,' 'actions,' 'tools,' and 'factors' that I am examining.

This gradual knowledge is the product of a prolonged psychic cohabitation, and it requires that the analyst know how to go beyond the universality of the analytic process, and of theory, in order to recognize the patient's personal individuality.

Gabbard and Westen appropriately cite Mitchell's (1997) concise formulation: 'There is no general solution or technique, because each resolution, by its very nature, must be custom designed. If the patient feels that the analyst is applying a technique or displaying a generic attitude or stance, the analysis cannot possibly work' (Mitchell quoted in Gabbard & Westen, 2003, p. 826). In a certain sense, then, it is 'no' to the Procrustean bed, and 'yes' to the personalization based on specific, case-by-case knowledge.

It is a fact of life that is equally true outside of analysis: every parent, every instructor, every trainer, even every animal breeder (I hope that no one will be shocked by this last category – those who love dogs and other animals will understand) must oscillate between general concepts of evolutionary and formative developments, on the one hand, and the directed recognition, the concern *ad personam*, and the gradual, relational process of coming to terms with the uniqueness of the individual (Racamier, 1992), on the other. And if things go well enough, that ends up in the achievement of a certain pleasure and a physiological dose of libidinal investment and narcissism that enriches the object and the relationship.

The therapeutic action of progressive knowledge of the patient on the analyst's part develops, in fact, in my opinion, more or less along two lines:

1   By producing a growing appropriateness in the analytic inter-action.
2   By producing an effect of enrichment on the patient and on the relationship.

One could object that this is basically a dimension of the 'one-person analysis' type and that I am perhaps neglecting the reciprocal side – that is, the effects of a gradual knowledge of the analyst on the patient's part. But on this last point, I am not opposed to particular resistance; I, too, believe – like many – that often enough the patient ends up knowing the analyst regardless of what the latter does or does not do, says or does not say, even though I am reluctant to generalize too much because, in some cases, I have also had surprising evidence to the contrary.

I think that the power of deep needs, of residual projections, at times even of a relative unacceptability or inauthenticity of the real object, may determine – in certain cases, to a disconcerting degree – the amount of the patient's knowledge of the analyst. But this matter (a discussion of which would take us far afield) must not be seen as absolute, and I think that the final sentence of Ferdinando Camon's novel *The Sickness Called Man* (1981), 'This man, I do not know him' – which is the thought of the protagonist who has gone to see his analyst some time after the conclusion of treatment – is not in reality representative of the experience of many patients or ex-patients.

Excluding biographical information, the two people in analysis usually know each other reciprocally well enough: 'The analysand "knows" many things about us (or rather all that which we express in the relationship), but makes use only of the things that restore something of himself to him' (Thanopulos, 2003).[3] And this – if there are really no characterological exhibitionisms or perversions on the analyst's part – forms part of a natural process, in my view, that is totally compatible with the analyst's respectful air of reserve, dedicated especially to allowing space for the individuality of the patient and his needs (Bonaminio, 2003), more than for the narcissistic defense and self-idealizing of a mythological, impersonal inscrutability of the analyst himself.

Even self-disclosure, the chosen battleground for many analysts who have had different training and come from different theoretical perspectives, is an event that comes to be refigured, to a substantial degree, if considered with enough critical serenity.

By chance, I happened to be the discussant for a paper of Owen Renik's (1995) on three separate occasions (see also Sechaud, 2000) at professional meetings where the subject of self-disclosure was discussed, and I must say that, although there were divergences at the beginning regarding basic technical orientation, after a long and involved discussion, we ended up converging on many significant points. An initial area of consideration was the fact that such an

3 Translation by Gina Atkinson.

operation must be attentively and honestly centered around the patient's needs, and not on those of the analyst, who tempers a substantial portion of his overly frequent choices to self-disclose, which probably occur more as a result of the analyst's own tendencies than of therapeutic opportunities.

A second area of discussion focused on revelation of the counter-transference experience: certainly an uncommon activity, but not exclusively one of the intersubjectivists, if we think of Winnicott's views as expressed in 'Hate in the Countertransference' (1949), or of the utility of knowingly bringing back to the field an emotionally split element, one that the analyst finds himself having to undergo internally without being able to speak of it (in situations of a 'The emperor has no clothes!' type), utilized by many authoritative analysts of other eras and other schools. I think, for example, of Meltzer's 'routine and inspired interpretations' (1978), in which he describes his communication to the patient of his own stupor and perplexity at the patient's apparently incongruous association by recounting his own dream of a Velásquez painting, or of Winnicott's *Psychoanalytic Explorations* (1989), in which he says to the male patient: '*I see a girl!*'

It is only that they did not call their actions 'self-disclosure.'

The real problem pertains to how much, when, and how one can make use of this technical provision, in relation to its possible therapeutic or anti-therapeutic effects. And this, in my opinion, brings us back to the starting point of gradually getting to know the patient, of how we function together, and what is useful or damaging in that particular analysis, given the specificities of the field, taking into account also – in an integrative but not 'integralistic' way – the general theoretical principles that inspire us in our work.

Renik (1999), in a face-to-face, intersubjective meeting that is hard for us Europeans to conceive of, rather harshly confronts the young and reticent patient Robert in order to demolish, to good effect, a characterological defense that paralyzes his life and that holds the analyst, too, in check. Strangely, in his *réportage*, Renik does not describe an aspect of his clinical stance – one that I could discover only in our discussion – as operating effectively in him, and I will mention it in the next paragraph. Renik took this aspect of his stance to be implicit, at least during his work with Robert, whereas I feel, in considering it a crucial aspect not to be taken for granted, that it would have to be specified as a necessary condition in order to be able to eventually proceed to such an incisive interpersonal exchange.

I refer to the analyst's *attention to the patient's self-cohesion*. To my way of thinking, this is a further fundamental therapeutic factor that harmonically regulates the conduct of the analysis in that it permits the analyst not to require of the patient's ego what that ego cannot give or tolerate in the analytic work, if it is not supported by basic conditions of the self that permit the patient to function adequately.

The concept of the self has been explored and developed by authors who have highlighted principally its self–representative aspect (Jacobson), the internal object (Klein), narcissism (Kohut and subsequent followers of self psychology), relational–libidinal aspects (Winnicott, Khan, Bollas), and the bodily aspect (Gaddini). To my mind, the moment for a possible integration of these different perspectives is not far off, as we recognize that each of them identifies and highlights something of deep truth.

This can appear to be a rudimentary epistemological standard for those who love more refined philosophemes, but the fact that, during certain sessions, certain authors and their concepts – which in that moment and that situation fit perfectly with what is emerging – come to my mind, in a natural way, has over the years assumed for me an orienting function that is extremely valuable.

Specifically, as far as attention to the level of overall self-cohesion in order to further the analytic work is concerned, it is certain that today we owe much to Kohut's observations. Even though we may not fully agree with him – as is true in my case – in regard to some nonconflictual aspects of his comprehensive vision of the human being, I nevertheless find extremely valuable his constantly keeping in mind the basic conditions of the patient's self in regulating the exploratory analytic phase in process.

The functional relationships that intervene between the ego and the self of the patient and the analyst have been the object of study (Bolognini, 1991; Jacobs, 1991) directed toward establishing the opportunity for technical choices (we would ask ourselves, for example, with Micati, 1993, 'how much reality can be tolerated?') that are useful in identifying 'points of coincidence' and experiential contact between the ego and the self of the interlocutors (Fonda, 2000). These points of coincidence and contact are indispensable in order to produce a deep change, and not only an informative and cognitive acculturation at the level of the ego. And in effect, one must take the pulse of the situation and understand what the patient is capable of accepting and elaborating in that particular moment. In this regard,

I dedicate my next point of discussion to an operative factor in an initial condition of elaborative impossibility.

To create an internal space if it isn't there is an indispensable necessity in those cases in which internal persecutory pressure (which can be occasional and reactive) – or, more unfortunately, a basic, structural, characterologically narcissistic–evacuative disposition – impedes any and all introjections. I am referring to all those situations, that is, in which the patient simply cannot take in anything that originates from the analyst. And the analyst's specific attention to this functional parameter (which corresponds, then, to an internal structural organization of the patient, temporary or chronic) results in a very particular therapeutic factor of which one often does not have adequate awareness.

There is a spatial component in the analytic work connected to the 'placement' (the 'positioning,' the 'positive') – that is, the speaking/giving of something to the patient in order for him to take it in internally and be able to make use of it. One 'places' or 'positions' if there is space in which to place something, if there is (etymologically) a 'place,' a 'position' (*positum, positio,* etc.) for it.

In this sense, the 'negative' in analysis is not so much what comes to be negated, erased in perceptions and representations; rather, it has another meaning: the breaking-down component, the toxic, lethal aspect of internal contents, of the relational connotations and the experience of self and of the world – something that takes up internal space and that impedes mental nutrition and transformation.

Colleagues at loggerheads with patients who do not listen, who do not 'take in' anything, usually give space to the negative, if they see that no interpretation relative to the roots of oppositionality obtains the hoped-for effect. That is, they proceed, as a consequence, like a mother who has understood that her child cannot take in any food if his visceral turmoil is not first evacuated.

The analyst cannot and must not 'negate the negative,' expecting to force the positive (either in the sense of 'placing' something, in general, or in the sense of proposing vital and 'positive' things, such as interpretations, representational associations, etc.) inside the patient's mind if there is no space in it.

More precisely, I maintain that one may be able to speak of an 'internal pressure' of the negative, which must be recognized and which one must not oppose; *the acceptance of its 'ex-pressure' (ex-pression)* is part of the treatment process, *before the interpretation.*

The analytic space/laboratory, intra- and interpsychic, that is necessary for representational elaboration, for integration and for subsequent interpretations is not a pre-guaranteed component of the analytic couple at work and much more often requires, in our clinical work, a long process for its formation, in part based in a specific way precisely on the sharing of experience, when this function has been primarily carried out to a sufficient degree by the person who has reared and functionally trained the child.

Once this space is set up, entry into the field of the factor I am about to describe becomes possible.

Familiarization with the preconscious is a fundamental goal of analysis, and I will not dwell on this aspect, which many authors (and among the most convinced and convincing, Davide Lopez, in all of his work – e.g., 1983, 2004) have taught us to privilege. Here I would like to emphasize the vital therapeutic action exerted in analysis by the work that the analyst carries out with the preconscious, in more direct aspects of the relationship with the patient.

I mean to say that the analyst's mental style – when he is capable of utilizing, with a certain freshness and respect for the other, his own initially superior associative fluidity and the broader functionality of preconscious channels in the analytic dialogue – ends up experientially communicating to the patient a way of functioning, in a certain sense a way of being, that over time will 'infect' him with success.

I consider this an important therapeutic factor, one based more on the shared interpsychic experience (Bolognini, 2004a) than on the ego–ego, conscious dialogue between the two who speak in sessions.

Certainly, the analyst must avoid excessively exhibiting himself and must avoid crushing the other with his own probable evocative freedom, intuitive and representational, in order not to demoralize the other by comparison and not to induce in him an excess of envy that would kill the desire to emulate.

As he does in demonstrating a good relationship with his own self (Bollas, 1987), the analyst must provide a taste of a functional internal climate, not an essay on virtuosity; otherwise, he can easily end up humiliating the patient or inducing imitation.

In continuity with what I have just set out, I consider shared experiences of, respectively, the transitional area and the dimension of reverie to be psychoanalytic therapeutic factors as well. I join these concepts together here with full awareness of being overly concise, and of an inappropriate matching, from a theoretical point of view, given the diversity of functional levels involved. But I connect these concepts to a familiarization with the preconscious based on the fact that I believe in the primacy of the shared experiential dimension, with the aim of a gradual access to all these fundamental dimensions of functioning, both intra- and interpsychic.

What I feel pressed to emphasize is that these functional capacities do not develop in the subject only by spontaneous reproduction, through a natural, *ab interno* process – perhaps reactivated by an appropriate analysis of blocking and distorting elements that had until then created impediments and that utilize an intrinsic and innate potential for intrapsychic liberation. Rather, they also develop in part – and in my opinion, especially – through a shared formative experience, which gradually makes new ways of cohabiting with the self and the other experienceable and which renders *cohabitation* possible, session after session, over the years of the analysis.

Beyond the officially expressed theoretical positions, I find rich examples of this functional, protracted cohabitation in the clinical descriptions of Lore Schacht (2001), regarding the transitional area, and of Antonino Ferro (2002), regarding the activity of reverie.

An aquatic interlude

In my imagination, many patients arrive for treatment in conditions similar to those of an individual who, standing on the beach, has never put a foot into the water.

The first analytic session is, for the patient, 'going into the water.'

The problem is to learn and to allow oneself to let go, initiating a process of acclimatization (this is what swimming instructors call the first phase of contact with the new environment) and learning to be confident in the fact that one can float.

The first great obstacle for neophytes is to have faith in playing dead: having one's pelvis above and one's ears under the water clearly goes against the defensive ego's agonizing need to keep the situation under control, and the tendency is to keep oneself vertical from the neck up, using one's head as a periscope.

In this phase, the instructor's basic assistance is decisive. With empathic perception, he synchronizes himself with the pupil's level of alarm, and – partly by example, partly by appropriate instruction – he permits the pupil to reach, a little at a time, a certain level of confidence with the practicability of the aquatic medium.

If the course is successful, after a period of time, the pupil is capable of submerging himself, of swimming, and of exploring the subaquatic environment to some degree of depth, descending and ascending with a certain pleasure. Some will also be able to go down a little farther, while the great abyss will remain prohibited from direct exploration and will, instead, be known from the inside of a submarine or a bathyscaph, from behind glass.

I like to turn to this allegory in order to represent what I think of our different relationships with, respectively, the preconscious and the unconscious. I believe that the human being, having *experience with the existence of the unconscious* through dreams, slips of the tongue, symptoms, and the retrospective examination entailed in reconstruction, may acquire a mature sense of the depth and complexity of the internal world. This will make him thoughtful, open to interrogation and to listening, and interested in the knowledge possible in the light of the ego, from behind glass.

In the deep unconscious, no swimmer will ever move experientially or in real time, his strokes encompassing the ego and the self together; it is too dark, too cold, and there is too much weight to bear for his limited physical and mental structure.

But to see the marine floor some meters down from the surface is already in itself a great event, which completely changes one's perspective and opens up new worlds. We appreciate this possibility, and we enjoy it as much as we can.

In my chapter on *the recognition and decontamination of internal object relations* (chapter 5), the analyst's availability/willingness to find himself again involved in split experiences relative to the relationship with the patient's internal objects is selected as a specific therapeutic factor in contemporary psychoanalysis.

I refer to the new and more complex role of interpreter that falls to the analyst, who is inevitably called upon to impersonate figures of the internal world, not only as the symbolic support of projection, but also as the active co-interpreter – often unknowingly, but subjectively involved – of an internal scene that comes to be experienced interpersonally with full pathos and is often put forward in an enactment (Jacobs, 1986).

The great disadvantage of this function resides in the increased probability that the optimal psychoanalytic structure of the analyst's working ego may come to be temporarily unsettled by immersion in the patient's experience, a split experience that requires being re-experienced, this time together with a competent object. Our 'swimming instructor' (the analyst) finds himself turning involuntary somersaults under water, dragged down by the pupil and by an experiential vortex that overwhelms him, at least a little. We are no longer in the situation of a comfortable and pristine swimming pool, lucidly attributing to the patient the 'projections' that touch the analyst only on the surface, the obvious dysfunctional productions of an ego to be warned of its own oversights.

The contemporary analyst is always more disposed to provide (and fortunately, in my opinion, more competent to do so) a shared revisiting of scenes in nonmetabolized internal areas, where we are not only dealing with reconstructively indicating the existence of the depths, but also of actualizing the experiential recovery, utilizing the powerful effect of regression.

Attention, however – I am indicating as a therapeutic factor a capacity for immersion and reimmersion that does not, most of the time, correspond to being able to elegantly maintain oneself in perfect form, in whatever phase of these processes, which in reality are necessarily chaotic given the rather murky waters.

In scientific meetings, the infrequency of being able to listen to clinical summaries that are somewhat true to the material of the session – frequently lamented by colleagues from every part of the world – very often stems from the fact, in my opinion, that an embarrassing disparity exists between the ideal of aesthetic analytic technique and the reality of things as they are. In my view, contemporary analysts often dive into the depths and are, on the average, rather good at returning to the shore with the patient, in some manner, but a full *réportage* of the sequence would indicate (referring again to the metaphor of an aquatic rescue) an array of fumbling, collisions, mistakes in direction, jerks, and swallowing of water such that the public, desirous of absolute, elegant, and stylized configurations, is sadly disillusioned.

Today we give aid to and rescue – at least every now and then – borderline and psychotic shipwreck victims who at one time would have been left to their destiny.

It is understood that I am not defending a courageous but slapdash spontaneity; to venture into the waters that I describe, one must be the best of swimmers and have a basic technique that is absolutely rigorous and proven.

However, one must also have the courage to take risks, knowing that, most probably, one will not go on to stage textbook forms of synchronized swimming with the patient, and that one may return to the shore somewhat agitated and in need of a rest, or at least of being able to recount one's adventure to a colleague, usefully reflecting on what has happened.

Well, today this situation happens rather often, in my view.

Analysts are understanding the advantages of being able to belong to a collegial 're-elaborative cooperative.' Also, with the difficulties and constraints mentioned above, we are becoming accustomed to utilizing the help of other colleagues-lifeguards, taking advantage of clinical discussions, which are almost always very useful.

With regard to *making it possible to perceive an evolving personal perspective*, I would like to propose a minimalist therapeutic factor, one that is admittedly partial: the analyst's capacity to perceive, appreciate, and point out the patient's progress in an acceptable and credible way – not so much in his life external to the analysis (which more often than not it is not for us to judge) as in the session, but outside, too, when the patient is alone with himself.

We have the competence to evaluate such progress, and our judicious but careful checking that the patient 'has succeeded at' or 'is succeeding at' (e.g., associating, remembering, communicating effectively, establishing a connection, recognizing a possible connection, giving notice of something painful or unpleasant, allowing the self a satisfaction, admitting a fear, etc.) has a powerful effect of encouragement and faith in the possibility of proceeding in an evolving personal way.

Gabbard and Westen (2003) mention something similar, in a rather generic way, referring to secondary facilitative strategies (p. 836), but in my opinion, the therapeutic factor that I am describing must be taken into account to an even greater degree.

In Herrigel and Suzuki's famous book *Zen in the Art of Archery* (1953), the Master observed somewhat absent-mindedly the pupil who busied himself, in a forced and unrealistic way, at bending his archery bow to his conscious intentions. When the pupil's defensive ego, exhausted and exasperated, loosened its control and an arrow was finally released from his grip – passing from his heart to his hands without passing through his brain – the Master experienced a jolt of interest, got up, and bowed in recognition of the event, saying, 'Today one has shot [an arrow].'

The Master's use of the impersonal tense, while celebrating, in fact, an event that went beyond the individual person, did not diminish the merit of the pupil, who thus received a strong push toward believing in the possibility of further growth.

I have been able to verify that knowing how to provide the patient with recognition of the steps he has achieved (usually with a thousand conflicts and considerable toil) – at the right moment, with frugality but also with sincerity – produces substantial benefit for the analytic work.

Precisely the 'analytic third' (in the North American sense, that of Ogden, 1994a, of the co-creation of a new analyst–patient subjectivity, shared and combined) is 'celebrated' and confirmed by a similar verification.

In a more European sense, the 'third' (as a paternal equivalent with separate functions pushing toward the recognition of reality) enters into the session, in my view, primarily when the patient perceives the presence of an authentic, internal, almost parental brotherhood between the analyst and the psychoanalysis – a brotherhood that pre-exists him, but one that is oriented in favor of his growth. This also occurs when the patient feels he has been reached in a respectful way, not paternalistically and not seductively, by a confirmation that is directed not at his narcissism but at his work.

Finally, in regard to *gradually accepting separation and loss, becoming and remaining oneself*, I believe that the most important therapeutic factor may be the fact that the analyst keeps a good memory of what he himself has experienced, in the analysis as in life, during certain passages of his own. This memory, among other things, keeps him from posing as a 'great sage' in the face of one who is doing his best, in some way, or who is defending himself with ignorance. The analyst will thus avoid adding to the patient's charge the burden of an indefinitely idealized object who shows that he believes in this idealization through and through, and that he enjoys it, satisfied, projecting onto the patient his own past and troubled self instead of giving him a hand.

Nor can one save the patient, in a pitying way, from the healthy suffering that he has tried to avoid. I do not believe that the analyst can substitute himself for the forces of life in facilitating the natural process of ascertainment and painful acceptance of separations and losses, but I think that he can do a lot to identify the specific defenses that come to be adopted along the way and that very often involve another serious loss, frequently not noticed or undervalued by the patient: that of elements of his own identity and of the contact with himself and his internal world.

The analyst's experience will register the maniacal 'gyrations,' the identifications in which the object substitutes for the self, the massive denials, the falls into melancholic holes in which one desires to reach the dead object in order not to detach from it, and, little by little, all the unhealthy versions of the suffering involved in living connected to separation. The analyst will bring these forward, gauging the times and ways to do so according to the patient's possibilities for working through.

The analyst capable of good recollection will re-travel with the patient some of the paths of his own evolving and formative route, including the one leading to acceptance of his own natural identity, refinding and making his traveling companion refind the meaning and flavor of existence.

Like a great many colleagues – and so without any pretext of being original in this thought – I think that *the constant call to self-analysis* may be the fundamental therapeutic factor. From this internal structure comes all the creative movement that primes the analytic couple's work, opening perspectives that were previously unthinkable and that can produce transformation and change.

3

SPEAKING OF THINGS, SPEAKING OF WORDS

Analysts are traditionally very attentive – and with good reason – to the always-impending risk of an actual anti-analytic drive discharge in the session, in the direction of 'acting out,' rather than producing thought and causing it to be produced, and transposing unelaborated elements into words and causing them to be thus transposed ('*Vorstellungen*' [representations], 'beta-elements,' '*cosomi*' [clusters of beta-elements], etc.).

At times analysts seem somewhat less concerned about facing the prospect of 'speaking of words' – that is, of making a sterile, empty, impoverished, and disconnected use of the experience, of using words that have no function other than to repeat themselves and that mean little more than their simple sounds and have no symbolic significance, rendered to the self and the other, in the interchange, like watered-down markers that evoke little or nothing and that 'do not carry things with them.'

Words can be *empty*, when the memory trace that connects them to things is prohibited or weakened.

A word that 'doesn't tell us anything' is a phoneme or a grapheme that is disconnected from other representations, from affects and drives; it is an isolated element, a cold fragment without life or meaning. Sassanelli (2007) writes:

> Oral is our origin; but the word
> that is – a sign – does not know how to make flesh of itself,
> loses itself in vain sounds and absurd flaws.[1]

1 Translation by Gina Atkinson.

In a session, if we mention 'the mother' to a patient as an absolute concept, without *we ourselves* having in mind, at least a little, *his* mother (and him with his mother) and how he has represented her – and perhaps also something of ourselves with our own mother, in order to really step into the fray – 'the mother' will become a sidereal, derealizing concept instead of an object of subjective life.

When the abstraction under discussion supersedes certain limits, word-presentations risk losing their 'weight' and 'sense,' and the subject who listens soon makes known his need to integrate them with thing-presentations – that is, if he does not, for whatever reason, collude with the intentions of the other, who is speaking with the intent to communicate almost nothing.

Not by chance did the ancients sometimes suggest following the opposite path, in regard to thoughts on their way to formulation: '*Rem tene, verba sequentur*' (meaning 'keep solidly [in mind] the thing, the words will follow'), as the Roman statesman Cato wrote.

In certain extreme forms of schizophrenic pathology, words and things are tragically disjointed. Like a cyclist who pedals uselessly while his bike chain is disengaged, the schizophrenic cuts off all links, and his words can burst out in a barrage, tumbling over themselves, without a connection among them. His words are also without intrinsic weight, and in the end they are without meaning, as in the celebrated 'salad of words.'

At the opposite end of the spectrum, in the language of some poets, certain words can be hyperdense, with a level of evocability or allusion that is rich, intriguing, and impossible to ignore.

In the language of philosophy, one tends toward strong abstractions; in technological language, the reverse is true, and a descriptive, precise reference to what is being represented and intended is more common. So there is a delicate and complex, *quantitative* balance in internal life, as there is in interpsychic communication between individuals, in regard to the investments of word-presentations and thing-presentations.

And humanity has always provided for this equilibrium through a balanced recourse to metaphors and examples, which enriches the representational legacy that is available and exchangeable among people, to a great degree.

The metaphor – that is, *metà-foréi*, 'to pass through' – permits otherwise unexpressed and difficult-to-communicate contents to go beyond barriers and to set in motion elaborations and new integrations. *Metaphors create passages* where earlier it seemed there could be none.

The symbol, in turn – that is, *syn-bàllei*, 'launches, throws' – can be said to 'launch' (to the other) the sensation, the representation, and the meaning implied by the represented thing, and it *unites the two subjects with a sort of communicative bridge*.

These exchanges, too, imply passages, sometimes public ones – clear, legitimate, evident to all and to all parts of the selves of individuals, exposed 'to the light of the sun' of the conscious ego. At other times, in contrast, the passages are private, secret, prohibited, subterranean – directed toward certain parts of the recipient's self and not to its totality. With the latter, the ego is temporarily excluded from the game, or, more often, it watches from another area, or functions as though it is rather drowsy.

The example (*exemplum*, from *eximere*, 'to take out') is a way to decipher and unpack a combined concept (expressed by a single word) through a more articulated and visualizable representation that brings facts into the picture, as well as things that are endowed with a comprehensible meaning when taken together. This meaning can be transferred by analogy: *the example is a way to 'explain'* (*ex-plicare*, 'to take out of the folds'*) something that is 'hidden in the folds.' But it is also a way to quantitatively balance the relationship between words and things, *to give*, precisely, *a body and an image to the words*. Otherwise, words only appear to be carriers of meaning.

The 'sense' of words is, etymologically, tied to *sentito*, '[what is] felt' – from *sensoriality* to *sentiment*. These terms refer to orbits that are functionally rather distant from each other, covering as well the external perception of affect, but it is not by chance that they have a common etymological root linked to the body.[2]

2 Zucchini (personal communication) reminds us of the common etymology that connects the Italian words *pensare* [to think] and *pesare* [to weigh], confirmed by the verb *ponderare* [to ponder], meaning *to attribute weight*. Chianese (2006) noted: 'In Freud's discourse, and even more so in Lacan, Leclaire, and Laplanche, there seems to be, substantially, a prevalence of Logos [that is, reason, thought of as the controlling principle of the universe and as manifested by speech]. . . . In this regard, Merleau-Ponty, in opposition to the logocentrism of Leclaire, Laplanche, and Lacan, will courageously state that the advent of the being is not linguistic; the birthplace of the word is in perception. . . . In the wake of Merleau-Ponty, that dialogue has been taken up again by Pontalis. Along other avenues, Aulagnier will formulate the concept of the "pictogram," a pre-linguistic and pre-symbolic area, and will come to define three layers of the psyche: the originary, the primary, and the secondary' (translation by Gina Atkinson).

In short, words without contact with things are inconsistent, gratuitous, volatile, and *sine materia*.

Agostino Racalbuto (1994) was convinced of this as well. An author who greatly loved words and knew how to use them extremely well, he wrote: 'If it is true, then, that the analyst must "treat" the link between "things" and "words" (for example, by refinding words that may give "soul" to things), it is also true that, in some cases, his treatments will have to be directed at things, because they are libidinally dense things that render words "alive." '[3]

But it is especially in the contributions of the English school of psychoanalysis that we find guidelines for a theoretical comprehension of this argument. Hanna Segal, in 1957, conceptualized the distinction between healthy symbolism and the 'symbolic equation' characterized by concrete thought.

Segal was able to connect these functions or dysfunctions to the degree of intensity of projective identification and to the modulation of the internal structure between the paranoid-schizoid and depressive positions. She then returned to a discussion of the process of symbolization in 1991, considering it in the light of not only its communicative aspects, but also its intrapsychic ones.

In the meantime, W. R. Bion (1962) conceptualized the distinction between alpha- and beta-elements, taking as his starting point the analysis of the difficulties of schizophrenic patients in giving meaning to their experiences, organizing their thoughts, and communicating them to others.

I think that these fundamental conceptualizations may be extended to physiology. One could say that someone who is capable of communicating knows how to balance the mobile distribution of cathexis between self and other, that he knows how to use introjective identification, as well as projection of the communicative type, in appropriate and fluid ways. He knows how to 'track' well enough between the depressive position and the paranoid-schizoid one, with a flexible versatility in processes of identification (Bolognini, 2002a, 2004e) and contact.

On the other hand, all those situations in which a certain capacity is disturbed require work on comprehension and reparation of the symbolic and communicative functions, which is not always within our reach.

3 Translation by Gina Atkinson.

An example of 'thinking/weighing words'

Paolo, an intelligent but neurotic bank executive, at the beginning of his fifth year of analysis, began a session appearing unusually emotional. In contrast, he was typically rather cold and reluctant, basically withdrawn and mistrustful.

> 'Doctor, I really want to talk to you about something that astonishes me and moves me very much emotionally. Today, after four years of work with you, I think I've finally understood something fundamental for me, something extraordinary.'

Naturally, I set about listening closely to him, with interest.

> 'Look, Doctor – only now I understand it . . .' (Here Paolo became even more thoughtful, and concentrated carefully.) '. . . that I . . .' (He articulated his words with great attention and intensity, to communicate to me the importance of his discovery; at this point I became extremely curious) '. . . that I . . . I would like only the *pleasant side* of things, and . . . I do not want . . . *the unpleasant side*!!!'

And after having pronounced this with an apparently enormous elaborative effort, he dropped down on the couch, exhausted, as though he had just given birth.

I must admit that at the time I was a little disappointed; I had hoped for something better, and frankly it seemed to me that the patient was getting carried away by an obvious banality. It is obvious that all of us would like the pleasant sides of things and not the unpleasant ones.

Taken as I was by the logical content of his communication, I had not given adequate weight to his sudden and powerful subjective experience. In truth, I had fully perceived his state of mind, but since I was looking at things from the vertex of logical content, it was really his vivacious state of mind, at that point, that seemed to me the anomaly; after all, why should one become so emotional about having 'discovered the wheel'?

For the patient, that seemed to attain the status of a memorable analytic event, capable of changing him – if not his life – and his self-image. And in fact, he reconfirmed this to me, not only by insisting on speaking of it for the entire session, but also by returning to it again in the next one.

He felt the need, he told me, to 'fix it into place,' this conquest, and he gave the example (being an expert amateur photographer) of the importance of printing a photograph, and another of 'fixing' a biological specimen of some type – one that would otherwise be perishable – onto a laboratory slide.

With the distance of years, I now think that Paolo had reason to attach such importance to 'fixing' that moment, that psychological condition that was so unusual for him. His ego was easily distracted in situations of conflict and was capable of repressions and splits that were rather disconcerting; in short, his idea of the importance of having to 'fix into place,' black on white, what he had seen with clarity during that moment of insight was a realistic one.

In this phase of the analysis, for this specific patient, our principal interlocutor (his and mine) was his central ego. Due to his resistances and some of his still-intense defensive activities, it placed major obstacles in the way of the fluid unfolding of a stable internal analytic function.

In this case, the ego appeared to be primarily in need of integratively aligning this new knowledge of a real element, which up to then had been denied, with the rest of the self. Paolo, who as I mentioned was an intelligent person, was aware of that, and our working alliance took account of the necessity of not undervaluing this apparently elementary work at the level of the ego.

Today, however, I also reflect on my relative deafness with respect to the authenticity of the patient's emotion. Literally, I had not given weight to his words, instead considering them too objectively. It was as though I, too, with him, had become accustomed to functioning in the session with a relative detachment, to considering things more rationally than emotionally, to giving words a value that was more logical than experiential.

All things considered, since I did not function in the same way with other patients who were different from him, I must admit that probably I had somewhat identified with his way of interacting – such that, when he noticed that he 'would like the pleasant sides of things and not the unpleasant ones,' I had looked from the top down, with detachment, as he usually did with others. In that truly important moment for him, his statement was not obvious because he was experimenting with the self – and not abstractly reasoning with the ego, the internal reality that was so repetitive and conditioning.

In order to give 'adequate weight' to the word, one must refind the connection with things (in this case, with emotions), and, more than an 'ego working-through,' a process of 'self working-through' is necessary, one that permits recuperation of the meaning of the experience. Otherwise, 'one speaks of words.'

In the seventh chapter of his 'Papers on Metapsychology' (1915a), Freud explicitly addresses this 'speaking of words': 'When we think in abstractions there is a danger that we may neglect the relations of words to unconscious thing-presentations, and it must be confessed that the expression and content of our philosophizing then begins to acquire an unwelcome resemblance to the mode of operation of schizophrenics' (p. 204).

In general, the *composition of a harmonious mixture* between *word-presentations and thing-presentations* is a hoped-for result, but it is not at all to be taken for granted, and it is not easy to obtain. Furthermore, the knowing, intentional – and, at the same time, creative – use of 'word bridges' (Freud, 1915a) requires a natural talent that may also be exercised and educated, in playing as in cultural formation.

In analysis, we are concerned every step of the way with the symbolic livability of the relationship. There must be something of truth, even if it is not real, in the analytic relationship, and something of experience, even if not of action. Affects, sexuality, aggression, pain, tenderness, joy must be felt, experienced, communicated – not 'realized' and acted on, but felt and experienced symbolically, yes.

Some time ago, a patient who was rather fun, good with quick retorts, gave me a sample in the session of her notable capacity to play between the two registers of the concrete and the symbolic, speaking precisely of this – that is, of the concrete and the symbolic. She did not call them by these names, but the substance of her remarks was this: 'You know, Doctor, I talked plainly to my fiancé: I want a ring, and I want it with a sparkling jewel. I need to symbolize . . . in a concrete way!'

The spontaneous, shared laughter that followed was testimony that the dialogue had unfolded along a common register of internal and interpsychic contact at the border between the symbolic and the concrete, in a dimension that was partially playful but not completely so.

When analysts speak among themselves

In order to avoid falling into an excessive defense of idealization of our professional group, I have no difficulty adding that we analysts, too, often risk 'speaking of words,' and that happens especially when, in our communications with colleagues, we too frequently turn to theoretical formulism, in a protracted and automatic way, without more humbly giving space and breath to an evocative representation of the clinical material to integrate the theory.

It is true that today we are all sufficiently savvy and disenchanted on the epistemological level to be aware that much of the clinical material presented can easily be bent and reoriented in the service of the theoretical presuppositions (or, worse yet, the 'scholastic' ones) that we start out with. As a consequence, we do not cultivate an ingenuous pretext of providing, through clinical presentations, a demonstration that absolutely confirms in truth what we have argued theoretically.

Instead, we try to give an appreciable and shareable representation to abstract conceptual formulations through a summary of clinical experience. In the transformative exchange among colleagues, too, an appropriate balance of investment between 'words' and 'things' creates richer mental objects, more integrated and complete ones, which are, all in all, more transmissible or more capable of being further elaborated as well.

But the difficulty remains, and we notice it even more when we must communicate something of our work and our theories to people outside our field. In such situations, the difficulty analysts have of expressing themselves in a comprehensible way – and, if possible, in a creative way as well – has been frequently noted.

Analysts often have a tendency to utilize ultra-specialized jargon that circulates, like a kind of regional currency, only in the interior of their entourage. Have you ever tried to surmount the difficulty of converting it, this currency, into something of 'international' value – that is, accessible to more people?

It is not really an easy task to speak of psychoanalysis to a public that is not part of the 'authorized staff.' How can one describe 'transference,' for example, with a word, an expression, or a sentence that takes account of the complexity and psychological reality of this abstract concept?

Unfortunately, very often, in speaking our jargon with others, we too are 'speaking of words.'

In truth, at least two giants of our discipline have given proof of the capacity to make themselves understood by everyone in a harmonious way: Freud (in some ways the theorist *par excellence*), thanks to his extraordinary creativity as an inventor of metaphors; and Winnicott, perhaps for his proximity to caretaking experiences, which permitted him to make effective radio broadcasts aimed at a vast public, for which he adopted a simple language, dense with experientiality.

In reality, in our scientific exchanges as well, a good and well-integrated mix of substantiality and abstraction seems important and advantageous.[4]

Reeder (2002) noted that analysts' reflections on their work necessitate three levels of elaboration, in order to be sufficiently harmonious and complete: if the second level (clinical theory) and the third (metapsychology) are regularly attended to and reported in descriptions of their work, the first level is much less so.

The *first level* is the *experiential* one, connected as much to conducting analysis as to having been an analysand in the past. And the adequate clinical language to express it is that described by the author as '*common-sense psychology*.' This is intended in neither a reductive nor a pejorative sense; it is that natural knowing (*savoir*, different from *knowledge* and *connaissance*) of which all of us are in possession for our reflections regarding ourselves and others.

My idea is that, on this first level, thing-presentations, then, must be *quantitatively commensurate* with word-presentations. It is understood that 'to give words to things' is a fundamental part of our work, and on this topic much has been written, to the point of exhaustion. But 'to give things to words' is also a part of our work (in the sense of making words evocative, endowed with substance, with sensation and possible feeling) – without degenerating into intentional suggestion, of course. It is an aspect of the analyst's art and craft.

Every analyst–patient couple sooner or later finds, with patience and often with suffering, its *madeleines* – words connected to things, to facts and images, to scents, colors, memories of faces, sounds,

---

4 Incidentally, this is one of the topics that the 'Theoretical Working Party' of the European Psychoanalytical Federation of (EFP) has addressed. For those who would like to go deeper into the argument, I recommend the excellent work of Parsons (1992) on the internal relationship that analysts have with their theories.

to atmospheres and experiences – from living or at least revisiting together.

These are shared metaphors that are not only rarefied signs, but that also integrate and transmit the experiential richness of human life; and I know I am here describing something felicitously natural, or – *post morbum* – something deeply reparative and rebalancing: the most refined and craftsmanlike part, perhaps, of a careful analytic treatment.

PART TWO

Interpsychic Passages

4

THE INTRAPSYCHIC AND THE
INTERPSYCHIC

It is the ambition of all psychoanalysts to be able to change, to some extent, certain aspects of the patient's intrapsychic life, in a long-lasting and structural way.

Every school has its specific goals for the change process, depending on its theoretical assumptions, but all agree that the patient should terminate analysis (though not self-analysis, a 'never-ending' contact with the introjected analytic function) once crucial and lasting changes within him have come about.

There are, in fact, no real differences of opinion on the next step either – that is, on the general principle that the patient's intrapsychic changes are *also* the result of work *on* the patient's intrapsychic *with* that same patient's intrapsychic (development of transference, stream of associations, reemergence of memories, insight, and so on) and *with* the analyst's intrapsychic (analysis of his own transference and countertransference, the use of his associations, memories, and so on to formulate interpretations).

All analysts agree with these propositions in what I might call an 'unsaturated' way, in that they by no means exclude these passages from their analytic work. Speaking in general terms, everyone likewise maintains that there is inevitably interaction between analyst and patient (without being 'interactivists' by this admission), just as there is between mother and child, and that the intra- and intersubjective dimensions cannot be separated during treatment, though there may be oscillation, with one occasionally predominating over the other (Green, 2000).

Differences arise when it comes to discussing how and how much

57

this interaction comes about, in what direction and with what effects, with what advantages or what risks, and what its technical use is, given the complexity of the conscious, unconscious, and preconscious levels involved. To sum up, the question is: what importance should we give to the work of the intrapsychic through the interpsychic in bringing about changes?

It is at this point that we have a branching out of innumerable personalized viewpoints. Following my detailed examination of recent literature on the subject, I suspect there may be as many different viewpoints as there are psychoanalysts. Along the axis that links the two extremes, 'intrapsychic' and 'interpsychic,' each thinker places himself in his own way, producing so many possible positions as to recall the Greek philosopher Zeno's famous paradox: Achilles can never catch the tortoise because between the two there is an ideal straight line consisting of an infinite number of points – *Tot capita, tot sententiae*. To make matters worse for the reporter, we show endless creativity in constantly renaming and redefining the concepts and configurations we observe: a cross to bear and a delight, a source of progress and perennial labor for a 'science with special rules' like ours.

It must also be pointed out that the different theoretical–clinical positions, correlating with the different training and the subjective nature of each analyst, nevertheless correspond (more or less consciously) to different concepts of the mind. The idea of a psychic apparatus predominantly overdetermined by internal drives and fantasies – as in classical Freudian and Kleinian thinking, or, conversely, much more capable of being modulated in its functioning in connection to relational developments, as in subsequent thinking of the followers of Winnicott, Bion, Kohut, or the intersubjectivists (though so very different among themselves) – then generated a remarkable variety of technical systems, and consequently different investments on the intra- and interpsychic sides.

So, I would ask you to accompany me in this challenge against complexity and to tolerate, or contain with patience, the manifold sides to the question. I ask you to exercise your usual aptitude for suspension and retain a potential appreciation of the various points, in anticipation of the personal synthesis that each of us will produce at his own pace.

Along the axis that links but also separates the two positions, we find the supporters of the intra- and interpsychic. I want to make it clear right from the start that I am not going to deal with the caricatures proposed by each of the opposite extremes to describe the other; I feel they are unrealistic and biased. For too long we have been swamped with improbable depictions of the 'mirror-like analyst,' dehumanized and impersonal, an awesome cleric or functionary of a superhuman entity called psychoanalysis, with a splitting between 'supposed knowledge' and supposed existence, 'passed through by the discourse of the unconscious,' inflexibly 'other' with respect to the patient but also – going by these descriptions – with respect to himself and human society, 'pure analyzing function,' and so forth; the analyst 'non-persona' who *non per-sonat* (i.e., is unable to perceive and use his own internal resonance in his patient's communications [Lopez, 1983]), and cannot partially or temporarily feel for the characters (*personae*) in the internal world of others without necessarily identifying himself with them; he who takes the ideal – to be hoped for, in certain cases – of knowing how to be *personne* ('no one,' like Ulysses [Sechaud, 2003]) to extremes when the analytic work requires or allows it.

This legendary type of analyst, faithful to the 'myth of the isolated mind' (Stolorow & Atwood, 1992) is a myth in itself, perhaps required to configure 'strong' differentiation and counterpositions; but it is really an improbable construction, the stuff of films.

At the other extreme, I find no less disquieting the descriptions of 'horizontal' analysts, a-generational, heedless of the past, of the unconscious, of transference, of their patients' individuality and sexuality, projected into the 'here and now' of the actual situation, corrective, transgressive, and hypersymmetrical.

Perhaps I might have caught a glimpse of someone who came across as embodying this stereotyped image, but, even in this case, I have to say that the formidable literary character never really corresponded to the real person: even the 'undifferentiated analyst' in jeans (and I apologize to those who thought up this caricature) is more of an oversimplified myth than a precise reality and, on closer observation, is more complex, three-dimensional, and thoughtful than he appears at first.

Having rid ourselves of these caricatures, I will attempt to describe what one really finds along the axis that links the two poles. I hope to be respectfully perceptive toward the two orientations I will present, although theoretical developments are currently moving toward a growing appreciation of the interpsychic. We should bear in mind

Aron's (1996) observation that, in many cases, both options function in the service of resistance.[1]

Above all, we should note a trend toward integration (leading to a broadening and greater extension of the theoretical view). Thus, while recognizing the richness of analytic exchange, many analysts believe it absolutely necessary to refer to both the intrapsychic model and the bipersonal one, two dimensions that are in dialectic equilibrium during an analysis, and even within a session itself (Ponsi & Filippini, 1996; Rocchi, 1997; Grispini, 2000).

In what follows, the adverb 'predominantly' appears frequently to indicate partial and relative tendencies occurring to various extents and in highly personal ways among various analysts – even more so, in actual fact, than among various schools of thought.

The 'intrapsychic' side

Those who stress the importance of the intrapsychic generally agree on certain basic points:

1 The patient's transference and that of the analyst, as well as their respective countertransference, develop in a highly overdetermined way, in close relation to the internal situation and, at least partially, regardless of external reality (including the analyst), which, especially at the start of treatment, functions essentially as a support for projections coming from within. This account is shared – though with quite different theoretical premises and technical perspectives – by many classical Freudians who, while not holding with the ideal of the mirror-like analyst, do not think it unrealistic to have 'relative objectivity' (Gabbard, 1997; Smith, 1999) as the patient's unconscious unfolds; something quite distinct from an 'idealized version of objectivity.'[2]

1 On the subject of current predominating trends, Bonaminio, an author with a keen interest and an open mind for new developments, makes the following interesting observation: 'the hypertrophy of the relational model may – for the sake of co-participation – lead to the risk of the analyst's usurping or eroding the patient's own space, his incommunicable and uncommunicated privacy' (1996, p. 109; translation by Malcolm Garfield).
2 Moccia, in his balanced review on the analyst's subjectivity and objectivity, notes that, curiously, American analysts are now reconsidering this theme: 'Even though the ideal of

Gabbard, in particular, states that 'no sensible observer would dispute the idea that the analysand has preexisting character-istics based on a lifetime of unique experiences that can be observed by others with some degree of consensus' (1997, p. 23). This view — and even beyond, in the sense of a certain radicalism in favor of the intrapsychic — is also held by a number of Kleinians (particularly in Latin America), who trad-itionally regard almost all analyst–patient interactions as forms of transference and countertransference based on unconscious fantasy.

2   This emphasis on the intrapsychic by no means goes hand in hand with a denial of interaction in analysis, whose existence is clear to all if only in the important moments of listening and interpretation. However, working together does not seem to be regarded as something that particularly influences the quality of what emerges, which is preexistent and must be brought to light. From this viewpoint, fundamental importance is placed on reconstruction rather than on the construction of something new.

3   The work is predominantly *on* the patient's intrapsychic *with* the intrapsychic of the patient himself (e.g., gradually canalizing the stream of associations by pointing out and clarifying; fac-ilitating connections; the re-emergence of memories) and *with* the analyst's intrapsychic (associations, memories, correlations, explanatory hypotheses, analysis of his own transference and countertransference, and so on), in a regime of intentional and careful separateness.

The analyst's familiarity with the preconscious enables him to fish down in the depths, like an Eskimo through a hole in the polar ice floe. The configuration and interpretive models he has at his disposal help the analyst find what is most suited to the material the patient offers. The fruit of the working through (which takes place predominantly in the analyst's mind) allows him to provide 'analytic gold' in the form of interpretation of the material itself. The patient's intrapsychic and that of the

analyst as anonymous interpreter of the patient's psyche is an impossible one, it is import-ant that he should MAKE AN EFFORT to achieve it. L. Friedman (1996), for example, wonders how the analyst can work without assuming that something exists there in the patient's mind ready to be discovered' (2002, p. 681; translation by Malcolm Garfield).

analyst 'flow together' from separate places as interpretations are formulated. They combine, above all, within the analyst's analyzing apparatus. Their experiential superimposition in countertransference is very often a drawback that the analyst's self-analysis must resolve each time.

4   The predominant concept of countertransference is, therefore, the classical one. Topically unconscious, activating the analyst's resistance and produced to a great extent by the preponderant projective efficacy of the patient, countertransference impairs our understanding of transference and 'if it is successful . . . we will not realize it, or at least, not immediately' (Semi, 1998).[3]

Clinical material predominantly in support of the intrapsychic

Luciana is a 35-year-old university researcher in her fifth year of treatment, tackling a problem of separation, which presents itself practically in analysis as a period of study and research abroad in order to gain the qualifications for promotion to the post of associate professor.

We reached a contractual agreement that allowed her six months' absence and then to take up sessions again (she was to pay for one session in four symbolically, and in exchange I would keep those times for her when she got back; both parties found this solution satisfactory). But, within herself, Luciana was far from finding internal agreement on her decision. The guilt and fear bound up with her painful personal initiative was in clear conflict with her desire to grow.

A crucial emotional problem was then added to this, that of 'leaving the field free' in her internal fantasy to her eternal rivals, a brother and sister, two and five years, respectively, younger than herself. Luciana is extremely jealous of her parents' attention toward them; right from the beginning, this analysis was transferentially characterized by anger and pain in regard to the analyst's possible interest in other patients.

In a dream one weekend, *Luciana was not sure whether she should get up from the sofa – where she was sitting during a party, chatting to her much loved and respected professor – to go to the buffet, for fear that rival colleagues might take her place in the meantime.* The dream had been clear to her in its institutional importance; she had not, though, associated it to her analysis.

3 Translation by Malcolm Garfield.

At the end of one mid-week session, she brought up an image that caused her great suffering in a dream: *there were eight small leaves on a tree, arranged in a regular pattern; one of these detached itself and Luciana felt much grief.* I interpreted this as her making contact, in the dream, with her grief for her imminent departure, since the other seven leaves/ patients (she has more than once conjectured out loud during sessions that 'every analyst must have on average eight patients, more or less') stayed attached to the tree/analyst, whereas she did not.

The following session began in an atmosphere of aggressiveness and persecution, with an explicit reference to my interpretation:

Patient (*angry, she twists and turns on the couch as she speaks*): You say that the leaf went off on its own initiative, but a leaf is inert! No – the tree sent it away! Or it might have been the wind.

Her tone is angry and accusing; I feel it through countertransference – I realize afterward – but do not grasp that 'the wind' may already figure, in the sequence, as a less persecutory agent than the analyst/ tree, actively and intentionally sending the leaf away. 'The wind' might represent her unstoppable process of development and growth, which leads to separation, or her professional career, and so on. In actual fact, it surprised me; I was satisfied with the solution we had agreed upon and was not expecting that turbulent outburst. Pervaded by the patient's massive negative projection, I urgently feel the need to free myself of it. My next response is, in effect, a micro-acting out in countertransference.

Analyst (*tense*): Actually, *you* said it was the leaf that detached itself from the other seven leaves, arranged in a regular pattern.

We might observe that the analyst's countertransference is caused both by the extreme aggressiveness of the patient, who, by projecting the guilt for separation, induces defense and counterattack, and by the analyst's own feelings, since he is narcissistically disillusioned in regard to his adroit and 'magnanimous' capacity for drafting a good agreement for the coming suspension. In fact, the analyst also suffers at being abandoned for six months by the patient, despite consciously understanding the adult, emancipating reasons for it. Certainly, although these last aspects are involved, the first outweighs them: we are within the sphere of 'classical' transference–countertransference interaction in which the countertransference is, for the moment, predominantly an obstacle.

> Patient (*still very agitated*): Last night I had two dreams. In the first, *I felt disgust and hate for my drug-addicted boyfriend and his druggie friends. I went away, slamming the door, decisively and without suffering.* In the second dream, on the other hand, *I suffered a lot: there was a puppy with a nasty cut on its back; I felt really sorry for it, I couldn't leave it to its fate like that.*
>
> [*Pause.*]
>
> Analyst (*much more relaxed and in control*): You have represented two internal moments of yours — two opposite ways of reacting to your future detachment from analysis. In the first dream, you 'discharge' your dependency [characterized as 'drug dependency,' i.e., an unhealthy dependency] on the other [the boyfriend /analyst] and your friends/other patients, so that you can leave cheerfully, with a sense of liberation, as if to say, 'I lose nothing by going away, in fact I even gain by it; I rid myself of someone or something that's sick, that's not me and not part of me.' In the second, you make contact again with a more human and suffering 'self' [the puppy, a creature that feels emotional bonds deeply].

The analyst's countertransference reaction was solved *partially* by the analyst's self-analytic introspection in asking himself why he had had to point out that it was the patient who had said that the leaf in the first dream 'wanted to detach itself'; but it was solved *mainly* by a perceptible movement by the patient toward depression, as testified by the dream sequence from 'I lose nothing by leaving you' (a narcissistic–autonomy defense) to 'I recognize my grief at leaving you' (the expression of a libidinal–affective–dependent side). The puppy's injured back corresponds to the part of the patient turned toward the analyst, a part the patient herself is unable to see, but only — with a great deal of resistance — to 'feel.'

Luciana, who has calmed down, now associates to a memory of family life: her sweaters, folded and protected with mothballs, in the drawers of her mother and 'dada.' I tell her she wants to refind her analysis carefully preserved by me in six months' time.

We will come back to Luciana in another clinical fragment at the end of this chapter. For the present, I would like to point out that this somewhat unexceptional clinical material can, I believe, represent work carried out *predominantly* on the patient's intrapsychic level, through the patient's dreams and associations and interaction with the analyst. In this interaction the analyst's functioning was significantly and to a great extent influenced by the patient's internal movements, rather than by his own subjectivity.

Transmission between the two psychic apparatuses developed *predominantly* at the 'classical' transference–countertransference level, in that the initial aggressive–persecutory emotional contagion provoked a counterreaction by the analyst, who was certainly not empathic at the time. On the other hand, the patient's depressive movement – which developed after the initial anger, perceptible thanks to a reduction in projections and a lowering of the persecutory pressure – made it possible for the analyst to recover extensive contact with the patient's internal complexity (what I consider *psychoanalytic empathy*).

It must also be pointed out that a substantial part of the analyst's contribution to the interpretation of the dreams, related to introducing the element of 'other patients' into it, was the result of the repeated presentation of this element in the patient's associations right from the beginning of the analysis.

For the sake of accuracy, in the first part of this material I will not, therefore, speak of the 'interpsychic'; instead, I will use the concepts of Kaës (1993), Kaës, Faimberg, Enriquez, and Baranes (1993), and Losso (2000, 2003),[4] who describe a 'transpsychic' modality of transition in which, lacking transitional space, the mind cannot transform and appropriate what it receives from the other.

In transpsychic transmission, which takes place in a narcissistic dimension, the intersubjective space is very limited or even absent; the receiver's transformative mental apparatus is bypassed and the contents are not worked through but are often pervasive and disturbing. This pathological relational level is certainly involved in the overall phenomenon described by Grinberg as 'projective counter-identification' (1967). Communication does not take place 'between' the subjects, but 'through' and 'beyond' them (or a good part of them), and the receiver's preconscious is deactivated or flattened.

Moreover, Luciana's mental movement was for the most part self-determined and relatively little co-determined.

---

4 More recently, Faimberg (1998) has specified that the process of intergenerational transmission passes through unconscious identifications, which can be analytically reconstructed.

Here, by contrast, is a brief clinical vignette of a 'mixed' type, with the intra- and interpsychic both quite significantly present. It may serve to make the jump to the next configuration less dramatic: a short transit corridor.

After a few sessions, my third patient in analysis (a young woman of 25) said she felt very reassured at being in the care of 'an expert analyst of about 57 to 58 years of age,' as she apparently thought I was. At the time, I was actually only 32.

Without entering into the merits of the clinical case, I will only say that, on the spot (clearly also to reduce the effect of the narcissistic affront that this assessment provoked in me), I thought I had found proof of the blindness and overdetermination of transference projection. I also managed to reflect on the patient's need to feel herself in the capable hands of someone with experience – someone who I clearly was not.

Only much later was I able to discover other, deeper aspects of the issue – for example, that my process of de-identification with my analyst and supervisors was, at that time, far from reaching an acceptable, relative conclusion.

'Whom' had my patient seen that day? And 'whom' or 'what' had I unconsciously wanted her to see? Me as I was, so inexperienced and full of doubts, or 'someone else for me,' preferable and more reassuring, not only in the patient's eyes but also in mine?

I thought back to this episode when I happened to read an article by Searles (1986) in which he asks to whom do the expressions on the therapist's face belong – to the therapist or to the patient? He adds that it is as if the patient has prematurely claimed the therapist's face as his own. And I would add, in contrast, that not everything is the patient's projection alone; sometimes what manifests itself in his communication has complex origins, and we should bear this in mind precisely because our work revolves around the patient himself.

Perhaps, without our knowing, there was a draft, a door left ajar between our mental apparatuses, or a small opening, almost invisible, like in the great wooden doors of Italian houses in medieval times, at the bottom of which was a swinging flap (a 'cat-flap') through which the house cat could come and go unheeded, unseen, and without disturbing its owners, intent on other pursuits. Years later, and given the successful outcome of that analysis, I think that the cat-flap also carried out a useful, regulating function, allowing 'intake' between a frightened patient and an inexpert analyst.

I would like to pause briefly on this element of the cat-flap. In my opinion, it is a good symbol for a structural (it is part of the door) and functional (it was specifically designed so that the cat can carry out its function of catching mice inside and outside the house) device that is not only intrapsychic but also interpsychic. The cat-flap is quite distinct from the door, which allows the passage of people, and from incidental cracks, which allow the passage of mice, clandestine, parasitical guests that harm the community/interpsychic–relational apparatus.

I conjecture that the cat-flap device corresponds topically to a preconscious mental level, and relationally to an interpsychic level; it does not imply a total and 'official' (interpersonal) opening of the door, and at the same time it does not correspond to the unconscious cracks and 'transpsychic' transmission levels on which the 'mice'/projective pathological identifications carry out their actions. Analysis 'constructs a cat-flap' and coaches the 'cat' (the preconscious) to use it.

In the interpsychic exchange, with a saving of energy, we often implicitly – but also instinctively and consensually – accept that the 'cat' comes in and goes out, that it goes back and forth between us and the others. At times we see and notice it; at others we do not. Its passing is a natural, noninvasive, and nonparasitical event that is not subject to rigid control and that generally does not disturb us.

The interpsychic side

It is extremely difficult to pinpoint the criteria for defining an analyst as 'a supporter of the interpsychic,' precisely because, as we said before, no one nowadays denies that there is interaction in analysis. Rather paradoxically, to find indicators of an analyst's effective orientation with respect to his recognition of interpsychic co-participation in analysis, we should take as our basis highly empirical elements, such as, for example, the absence of an annoyed reaction on a colleague's part when we speak of interpretation as a potential vehicle for the patient to indicate the analyst's mental state, or of the subjectivity of the analyst's choice in selecting the material to interpret, and similar issues.

I say this because, generally speaking, no one likes to present himself as theoretically anchored to a limiting view of the analytic work, such as an appreciation of the intrapsychic without sufficient integrative attention to what the interpsychic might appear to be.

But over and beyond the official declarations of principle, each of us functions and works in his own way, though we are often partially unaware of it (I owe this observation to my having taken part in the study group of the European Psychoanalytical Federation's 'Theoretical Working Party' on the implicit theories of analysts). Therefore, all indications of belonging to one school of thought rather than another should, in fact, be tested in the field.

Notably, however, the 'interpsychic' area is quite cross–party and finds support among a fairly wide range of schools: many neo-Kleinians (such as Pick, Spillius, and Steiner) pay great attention to the readiness of the object to receive projective identifications and, as a result, to the interpsychic work of the analyst with the patient. Among Kohut's followers, alongside the somewhat old-fashioned provision that the analyst should concentrate syntonically on the patient's experience with an appropriate attitude, leaving aside the rest of the self, there has been a gradual functional recovery of a broader front for the psychoanalyst's self, as in Goldberg's (1994) article with the significant title 'Farewell to the Objective Analyst' (see also Ponsi, 1999). Even the interpersonalist followers of Sullivan have moved from a tactic of 'participant observation' to one of 'observing participation' (Hirsch, 1996).

In the area we are now investigating, there is no doubt that the Barangers have accomplished a milestone with their concept of the unconscious fantasy of the analytic couple (Baranger & Baranger, 1961–62), founded on the reciprocity of unconscious experience: a bridge, as De Toffoli (2000) notes, between relational and intersubjective theories, on the one hand, and the field theories subsequently developed by Italian authors.[5]

For an intersubjectivist, on the other hand, the interpsychic can be

---

5 In Italy, the concept of *field* began to assert itself in the 1990s and 'arises from the inadequate description of psychoanalytic events in terms of simple relational processes and the need to integrate them into a more complex model, which should be capable of accounting for the interactions between analyst and patient, but also between conscious and unconscious, mind and body, internal and external, present and past' (Riolo, 1997, p. 55; translation by Malcolm Garfield).

a limiting and relatively little-known category since it concerns phenomena of superimposition or coalescence, of exchange and at times of cooperation between areas and functions of two minds, which do not necessarily correspond to two subjects in the strict sense. The interpsychic concerns a basic functional physiology in the relationship between two mental apparatuses, which does not necessarily entail constant involvement of the more structured levels of subjectivity (which, as I will mention below, can be simultaneously present in a regime of highly complex psychic functioning).

Therefore, it is by no means the case that the analyst, in an analytic phase of significant interpsychic contact, can answer intersubjectively 'in a highly personal way' (Greenberg, 2001), interacting as a person. Rather, the interpsychic concerns a regime functional to the pair at work which entails coalescence and facilitating exchange between two mental apparatuses, but which does not entail categorical and precise consequences on the level of technical theory (e.g., in an intersubjectivist sense).

A distinction must be made, therefore, between *interpsychic, interpersonal*, and *intersubjective*: interaction is the phenomenological common denominator among these three concepts, but the interpsychic is a more extended psychic dimension compared to the other two. The interpsychic is a level of 'wide-band' functioning, in that it allows the natural, uninterrupted, and not dissociated coexistence of mental states in which the object is recognized in its separateness, alongside others in which this recognition is less clear. This does not occur for pathological reasons but is due to a temporary and transitory condition of companionable, cooperative fusion (Bolognini, 1997a, 2002a, 2004e; Fonda, 2000), which is part of the normal, good mental cohabiting of human beings.

In this sense, the image of the cat-flap is once again useful, symbolizing something different and intermediate between the opening of the 'interpersonal' door and the clandestine breaking-in of the 'transpsychic' cracks exploited by the mice.

The interpsychic is a universal, ubiquitous dimension, but it does not presuppose that in that moment only the functional level belonging to separate subjects capable of recognizing others is working, even if it is clear that this level must have been achieved by the subject, as an advanced point of its general psychic development. Teicholz (1990) points out how mother–child or analyst–patient interactions entail constant reciprocal regulation, but not necessarily constant reciprocal recognition, which, on the contrary, can sometimes be avoided thanks to this regulation. The interpsychic can thus also pertain to levels of presubjective functioning; in any case, in the interpsychic, the patient usually maintains a central position in the analyst's mind. Conversely, Goldberg (1994) emphasizes that in intersubjectivism, the accent often ends up falling on the analyst's feelings, ideas, and fantasies in the encounter.

Mention must also be made of another of the most important gateways to understanding the interpsychic: the concept of transitionality, which makes it profitable to visit the intersubjective 'common spaces,' the antechamber and 'day-area' of the self, while protecting the nuclear self from traumatic encroachment by the non-self, and allowing sustainable interactions between the two psychic apparatuses, without experiences of reciprocal violation. By not citing them individually, I will inevitably do a disservice to the numerous authors who, from Winnicott on, have focused their attention on the intermediate area, because we all consider them the chief and most accredited representatives of the exploration of interpsychic dynamics.

It goes without saying that 'most relational models integrate the intrapsychic approach with the interpersonal, regarding the analytic process as an encounter between internal object relations and real experience in the here and now of the analytic situation' (Fiorentini et al., 2001).[6]

Significant – and by no means predictable – openings to new horizons concerning the interpsychic have been seen especially, in my opinion, in Italy and, more recently, in France. There seems to be growing interest among French psychoanalysts in interpsychic functioning, the fruit of the meeting between two psyches in the analytic space, which produces psychic changes (Minazio, 2002). The Botellas' work on *figurability* (Botella & Botella, 2001), intended as a form of prelinguistic symbolization, describes an *état de seance* during which, in the treatment of serious cases, conditions of very primitive hallucinatory mental functioning come about, are recorded, communicated, and worked through in a work regime involving the interpsychic.

Moreover, the 2002 Brussels Conference of French-Language Psychoanalysts emphasized an appreciation of the interpsychic. Of particular interest along these lines was Haber and Godfrind-Haber's

6 Translation by Malcolm Garfield.

contribution, *L'expérience agie partagée* (2002). According to these authors, when linguistic symbolization is not yet possible, *figurability* and *acting out* are the two ways of psychic functioning that retain and transmit elements of experience that cannot yet be symbolized by secondary process; they contain the emotion and meaning of lived experience – they are 'images of action.' 'Shared acted experience' constitutes, in their concept, an 'interpsychic entity' that prepares us for change. Concepts of this type have precedents among the French as well – for example, Perron-Borrelli's 'representation of action' (1985, 2001), Le Guen's 'motorial representation' (2001), or even, concerning the analyst, 'talking action,' which Racamier (1992) maintains may be used by the analyst.

What interests us most here is not the possible 'scandalous' reevaluation of acting out, which does not correspond to these authors' ideas, but the quest for analytic meaning and function even in elements that appear to be unusable in analysis but become potentially transformational material when considered and worked through in the interpsychic sphere.

Of course, those who have frequented international psychoanalytic forums will recall other authors who have previously described substantially similar configurations and processes (e.g., *enactment*, stemming from the work of Jacobs, 1986, and Ogden's *interpretive action*, 1994b). Nevertheless, it is important to recognize that the French works have been rigorously developed in a research context characterized by specific theoretical and methodological assumptions following a scientific path enriched by its own continuity (Squitieri, 2002).

Despite its remarkable scientific diversification – calling to mind the patchwork of city-states in medieval Italy – Italian psychoanalysis is strongly characterized by its great attention to the relational dimension in which work with the patient is carried out. This dimension is regularly included in the field of observation and analytic work, while not exhausting the subject in itself and not reducing the importance of the intrapsychic. In our tradition, the relationship is regarded as an unavoidable factor, which should be analyzed and its complex implications used with a view to interpsychic exchange.

In this sphere, the following works are specifically pertinent to the interpsychic area:

1   Ferro's (1996, 2002) and colleagues' work on the *modulation of the field*, *narrative derivatives*, and *functional aggregates* represented

by characters who enter the scene in analysis as expressions of an ongoing process ('oneiric activity of wakefulness'), 'with the two members of the analytic couple tending to dream and communicate with each other what is happening between them almost second by second' (Bezoari & Ferro, 1992, p. 390).[7]

2   Those on the theme of the analytic relationship as a complex system, by Vergine (1981, 1992), Chianese (1987, 1997), and colleagues.

3   Works on the physiology and pathology of fusionality by the Rome group of Neri, Pallier, Petacchi, Soavi, and Tagliacozzo (1990) and, more recently, Fonda (2000).

4   Those – in the Winnicottian tradition – on *shared mutative experiences* by Giannakoulas (2000), and on the dialectics between individuality and relationality by Bonaminio (1996).

5   The contribution of Nissim Momigliano (1984) in search not so much of an 'unveiling' as a recovery of what could not be developed in the course of previous relationships.

6   And, finally, I would like to include works on empathy as a complex phenomenon (in contradiction to certain North American ideas), presented by Bolognini (1997a, 1997b, 1998, 2001, 2002a, 2003b, 2004a, 2004b, 2004e), Pasquali (2001), and Di Benedetto (2002).

Clinical material predominantly in support of the interpsychic

In the clinical fragment that follows, which might intrigue those fond of paradoxes, the interpsychic work is in part expressed and in part carried out through a shared event/experience: a burst of laughter. In this exchange, the analyst functions first as object and then as co-subject for the patient.

In this session with Franco, he keeps silent for 25 minutes. During this time I first wait with interest to listen to what he has to say, then I wonder as to the possible significance of this silence in view of the last few sessions (without reaching any great conclusions), and then I lose myself in my own thoughts. Franco says, 'You think that I'm silent;

---

7   Translation by Malcolm Garfield.

in actual fact I'm telling you the dream I had last night, which I can't remember.'

Instinctive laughter from both of us. There and then, the reason for the laughter is not clear, but it is certain that both of us share the feeling that the patient has managed to say something remarkable. From the patient's tone as he makes his comment, I gather an impression of surprise on his part for what has occurred to him and, at the same time, a pleasant self-irony.

Gradually, the meaning of the patient's intrapsychic 'outburst' becomes clearer (his successful verbalization of a split internal reality, his conveying it to me as the start of reintegration; but here we are still, in the strict sense, in the area of intrapsychic resolution, and the analyst is used as an object by the patient). The significance of the spontaneous and hearty laughter that instinctively brought us together also emerges: we shared both amazement and amusement in discovering together the secret existence of a split dialogue within him, which made sense of his previous silence; with a few words, the patient also showed he was aware of my awaiting something from him.

Certainly, at this point, I would also have liked to know the content of the patient's (presumed) dream, but what Franco managed to say to me and to himself is interesting enough. Besides which, the way in which he told me is also rather significant: through his choice of communicative form, Franco shows he can rely on our tried and tested common space in which even a paradox may be welcomed and listened to, with the hope of being understood and made use of. In a sense, Franco shows in this fragment of a session that 'he can place his trust analytically in the two of us,' calling upon me as a co-subject in a condensed and syncopated working through (so fleeting as to be almost an intuition), which is partly carried out and partly expressed as laughter.

Moreover, the interpsychic, as can be seen, is not principally concerned with confusion: Franco and I shared a pre-subject and co-subject area of impressions and thoughts while retaining, at the same time, on other levels and with nondissociated continuity, individual ways of psychic functioning, characterized by appropriate separateness.

This description, which might appear contradictory (when all is said and done, is there or is there not separateness?), attempts to show the complexity of the relationship between subjects, whose effective functional level – in terms of fusion/contact/separateness – is hardly ever unequivocal. Rather, it is based on a complex, contemporary presence of various organizational modes of the individual and the pair, alternately more or less invested and activated by developments in the relationship.

Widlöcher's (2001) concept of *co-thinking* does not imply the loss of individuation. And empathy by no means requires a substantial loss of reciprocal boundaries but, rather, a targeted, respectful readiness for contact in specific areas of the self, suited to the aim (Bolognini, 1997a, 2002a, 2002b, 2004e; Fonda, 2000). Regarding relationships between the *interpsychic* and closely linked concepts that in my opinion are not exactly coincident ones, such as *empathy* and *projective identification*, I believe that they describe different aspects of the same homogeneous relational reality.

In brief, I consider the 'interpsychic' to mean a functional level of high permeability shared by two psychic apparatuses, which encourages situations of complex empathy by means of exchanges based on so-called normal (Klein, 1955) or communicative (Rosenfeld, 1987) projective identifications.

Empathy is a complex psychic condition of the individual or of the pair that requires functional interpsychic levels, but not only these, in order to be practicable (Bolognini, 2002a, 2002b, 2004a, 2004e) – figuratively, it needs both the cat-flap and the door.

Projective identification – in the conceptual context we are exploring – is a specific mental and relational operation, which in its communicative forms extensively uses the interpsychic levels of exchange (the preconscious cat-flap) and contributes to eventual empathy. In evacuative or intrusive-parasitical forms, it contributes to pathology and figuratively corresponds to the 'cracks for breaking in' exploited by the mice (unconscious clandestinity).

An example of specific appreciation of the interpsychic in technique

I am convinced that most analysts are aware of developing, with experience, their own personal style – although in many cases it is not officially theorized – in using techniques at an interpsychic level in collaboration with patients.

Over the last few years, I have been particularly impressed by clinical reports by certain child analysts (I would mention, among others, Herzog's at the 1999 IPA Congress in Santiago [Herzog, 2000], and

Schacht's at the 2000 Milan Congress on Winnicott [Schacht, 2001]). What I found striking was the ability of these colleagues to allow their young interlocutors to get deeply in contact with them while working 'within the relationship' on several levels, sharing very primitive experiences and communicating in a transformative way, without losing their admirable conceptual clarity. They show a remarkable capacity for realizing situations of complex empathy, using, naturally, the functional interpsychic levels as well.

A feature that these clinical studies have in common is their faith in the practicability of dialogue with internal worlds; the analytic dialogue, experienced interpsychically 'from within,' is particularly effective, first in containing and then in symbolizing – what is exchanged may often be experienced as experientially 'true' (as in a dream), even though not real.

As for the intentional and specific technical use of the interpsychic, I think this can be verified relatively rarely. Usually, it needs an analyst well tuned to himself, above all, and then to the patient's internal world and dynamic organization, so that it is possible to transmit combined verbal/sensory elements from within the analyst to within the patient.

So that the words are not merely sounds, or poor signifiers of representation and affective evocation (Racalbuto, 1994; Di Benedetto, 2002; Bolognini, 2003b), the analyst must know how to open himself up and be receptive, with a spatial and functional internal readiness – 'projective pro-identification' (Di Benedetto, 1998) – for communication and relational exchange. This should not happen by way of suggestion, but in a regime of 'informed consent' toward the patient – that is to say, by collaborating with his conscious ego, which should opportunely become gradually aware of the transformations in progress. To make the process more natural and livable, the working pair can occasionally use a 'service door on the ground floor,' whose key the patient has trustingly given to the analyst.

The clinical example I now present does not, of course, concern 'the' form but one of the many possible forms of appreciating the interpsychic in technique, defined moreover, in this particular case, in a decidedly and admittedly personal way.

Clinical fragment on 'incurable inconclusiveness'

Rita, a 38-year-old patient suffering from an overall creative block, is an intelligent woman who has so far achieved very little in life in relation to her potential. She asked with conviction for analytic help only after many personal and professional failures. In this particular session in her third year of treatment, she carries on for 30 minutes in complaining that she has not yet finished a job she was entrusted with at the office where she works. She has to compile a list of customers, selecting them on the basis of certain commercial characteristics.

I think that Rita is talking to me indirectly about her poor associative productivity here in analysis, but I deliberately limit myself to a vague exploration, asking her to explain the specific situation to me a little more clearly – for example, how long would it take to complete the list? She replies that, in fact, it would not take long, no more than an hour or so. The problem is 'making up her mind' to start.

There was a sense of stagnation in the air, of stultifying immutability.

After a pause, I ask her in a very loud voice, 'Well? When do you intend to do it?!?' She is obviously rather surprised. Then I ask her again, still in the same way, 'Well? When do you intend to do it?' She laughs.

I am speaking as if I were not addressing her, but someone a little way off or hidden somewhere, to make myself heard. In fact, at that moment my fantasy is: I am standing on the doorstep, speaking loudly to the maid so that the lady of the house, who is in the drawing room and does not show herself, can hear. The Rita who laughs is, at that moment, the laughing maid; but how the lady of the house reacts, I do not know. I let myself communicate in this way, here, because I know that Rita was previously able to trust my discreet and respectful use of the 'service door.' I take steps, however, to formulate the sense of my intervention in a comprehensible way, making it available to the patient's ego. I am careful to do this without completely emptying my message of its aspect of intentional summons: I limit myself to enriching it with a representational contribution that can be shared.

> Analyst: I am addressing another part of you that is in another room and wants to carry on sleeping. In our dialogue, you send ahead a reasonable and aware part of you, with which I can speak more softly, but which is powerless. I'm addressing the other part, down there.

Patient (*laughing*): Well, in fact, it makes me laugh because I feel it's true. (*Pause. Then, more pensively:*) It now occurs to me that, a few nights ago, I dreamed *I needed someone's help to move some objects in a sunken ship.*

There has been an unblocking; the stream of associations has started up again. I think this association reconnects the patient with 'needing someone's help,' and that drawing up a list of 'customers' also has something to do with becoming aware of the self-'customer'/patient in analysis. In her family, Rita, her mother, and sisters tended to form an alliance to keep her father – who was rather authoritarian and not very cooperative – out of their plans and problems, with some advantages, but at the cost of having to do without possible support. I feel that I am better able to understand the fantasy I had when I raised my voice: her internal father 'asks' to be allowed back on the scene and for the 'women of the house' to stop this obsessive witchcraft that makes him an outcast.

Analyst (*feeling that the stream of associations has begun again and that Rita has taken up the task of 'completing the commercial list'*): To put things in order in the depths . . .

Here again I keep things deliberately vague, because I am actually reflecting on the fact that there has been a 'sinking,' something has been shipwrecked, and I wonder what Rita's shipwreck was. The answer emerges, in a natural way, from the subsequent association.

Patient: About that list of customers: the bosses in the office should see that I'm good at my job, but I'm afraid. In fact, perhaps I want to be *the best*, but at the same time I have doubts about myself, that I'm not capable, not up to the mark.

And so the patient's stream of associations is on the move again, and there emerges in Rita a rather sorry, hidden 'lady of the house,' whom I warm to: the firstborn, once in competition with her two younger sisters, as she is now with her colleagues in the office (and in analysis), who struggles desperately – and so far unsuccessfully – to defend a narcissistic experience, which has 'sunk' like that ship, choked between omnipotent ambition and fear of impotence.

I will go no further into the analysis of the content that emerged, or its development in the session, other than to summarize that the 'women of the house' cut out the father not only because he was authoritarian, but also to avoid, at least partially, the impact of their feared rivalry; and that the paralyzing effect of the maternal oedipal superego blocked Rita's desire and creativity. Correspondingly, it is clear that the initial interpretive line would have to be subsequently integrated by a further recognition of the structural intrapsychic: the superego aspects call for further representation in the patient's ego. The line chosen here is a line of 'access.'

What interests us in this material is the entrance on stage of a spectator: the analyst 'enters' into the patient's intrapsychic by intentionally using the interpsychic. In this case, the conscious drama- tization concerns an internal scene, illuminated paradoxically by an external visitor who has found – not altogether by accident – an open door through which to peep and produce some kind of change.

The term *interpret* is extended, in this case, to its theatrical meaning of *playing a character* – one who enters the scene with technical know- how and a mandate to change things – and here the analyst uses the interpsychic to gain access to the oneiric (Bolognini, 2002a, 2002b, 2004e). It is up to the analyst to employ this tactic, one close to the area of play, with moderation and according to specific criteria. It can be used only rarely since it requires a fortuitous, harmonious inspiration. Conversely, if it is used as the result of a histrionic or perverse tendency on the part of the analyst, it would be forced and forcing and would occur decidedly more frequently.

I could continue with the previous associations by saying that, clearly, if you want to go into 'someone's house,' you have to stay on the doorstep and send significant messages inside (otherwise you risk 'acting out the transpsychic').

On the other hand, Rita's laughter also reveals her pleasurable surprise: the 'maid' could no longer bear having to face reality by herself, and the 'lady of the house,' despite all her anger and fears, must have felt somewhat liberated by being located and contacted – albeit only, in this case, in that rather bizarre way (but for her, an acceptable one).

In order to 'move the objects in the sunken ship,' the patient had to recover this much-needed father (representing a mobilizing internal function) once and for all, by putting the intrapsychic in contact and in cooperation with the interpersonal through means of the interpsychic.

Conclusion

By using the natural currents fostered by the setting, regression, and a certain familiarity with the transitional area, the analyst can gain access, neither furtively nor traumatically, to the interpsychic and can therefore – on rare and privileged occasions – enter the 'dream vault,' 'engine room,' 'black box,' fantastic scenario, 'heart' of the relationship shared with his patient.

Through this internal mental coexistence, the analyst may produce changes more effectively, by reactivating or, in some cases, generating and bringing to flower the necessary functions – containing, representational, symbolizing, narrative, communicative, and elaborating – initially lacking in those who entrust themselves to his care.

We are indebted especially to the work of Bion, and in particular to his extraordinary concept of *reverie* (1967, 1970), for the best description of analytic, maternal, and in general interhuman functioning, which makes changes understandable and reproducible and which involves considerable use of the interpsychic.

Clearly, this ideal picture of the analytic situation should also take into account endless negotiations with the defensive ego of the patient, who often fears interpsychic sharing at least as much as he desires it, as well as the internal resistance of the analyst himself, who, though more practiced than his patients in contacting his own preconscious and that of others, is still fearful of the new and unknown – as is only human.

The ability to frequent the interpsychic with an acceptable degree of awareness and technical know-how, to reduce the random nature of analytic developments and open up new access routes to the intrapsychic, therefore requires constant self-analysis. It also requires a sense of respect for and continuity with the work of those who have gone before us in a century of psychoanalytic research, as well as 'trustful resignation' in the extraordinarily paradoxical nature of our work.

The latter condition is an everyday one, which we undoubtedly feel more comfortable with if it is somehow shared (culturally, but also on some occasions interpsychically) with our colleagues. As a result of this coexistence made up of periodic meetings and exchanges over time, I believe we are comforted, in the reserved intimacy of our offices, by the established intrapsychic presence of a highly differentiated, but substantially supportive, community.

And so, in the belief that I have been able to share with you at least a modicum of thoughts and affects, and that we have now to go our separate ways, I would thank you for patiently hearing me out and conclude with the help of my patient Luciana, the university researcher who will have to leave analysis for six months (the 'little leaf detaching itself from the tree').

One month after the session I reported, Luciana was much better; she was working through the prospect of this temporary but significant detachment, and she brought in a dream that shows, I believe, the intrapsychic transposition of the interpsychic work carried out together in analysis:

'I find myself at some kind of assembly, facing a stage on which there is a little boy of about two, still wearing a diaper. The child runs onto the stage; he's "a little love." Suddenly he decides to run toward me; I'm directly below the stage and I feel terrified. I watch myself watching him and think, "You'll drop him, you won't catch him." In my mind's eye, I already see myself dropping him and him falling. But when the little boy really does jump, I instinctively catch him and hug him close to me, saying, "Well done! That was a good jump!" – and he's happy. I am amazed; I didn't expect to be able to react so instinctively.'

I think that Luciana, surprised at her capacity to hold and contain her own self, needy of containment (the child in a diaper), is bringing me the representation of a profound intrapsychic change: the function represented in her dream now appears to be sufficiently introjected and has become her own. The dream dynamically condenses various aspects, among which the interpsychic work carried out by the analyst's mind with the patient's mind must not be ignored, in an atmosphere progressively moving toward the 'being able to trust us' in analysis. Luciana's self, from the leaf in the first dream, changed first into a puppy and then into a child.

5

'INTERPRET-ACTION'

We are not 'merely an interpretive function.' Perhaps we would have wanted to be that, pursuing an idealized image of psychoanalysis and, above all, of the psychoanalyst; but the concepts of countertransference, the analyst's transference, enactment, and intersubjectivity have worked to our advantage in disillusioning us about our way of being coldly antiseptic in sessions.

In the history of psychoanalysis, I have always been quite struck by analysts' progressive capacity to transform, where possible, their obstacles into resources. This has been the case for the dream and for transference and countertransference, and something similar is happening for enactment, too, despite much resistance. Certainly, the transformation of obstacles into resources is possible when the analyst's awareness of the dynamics at play improves. This seems to set in motion what I call the 'ecological tendency' of psychoanalysis: a masterly process of singling out, selecting, and recycling the theoretical and technical byproducts of a sort of 'chemical breakdown,' transforming them into something potentially fruitful – obstacles that become tools.

The dream, transference, and countertransference were not 'royal roads' in the beginning; they became such with the advancement of our scientific knowledge. I believe that enactment is following the same theoretical–institutional course. Given shape by Jacobs's brilliant intuition in 1986, the concept met with opposition at first and was then rediscovered, and for some years its international clearance through customs has been underway. In the end, it will be an advantage for everyone to conceptualize within a theoretical context endowed with meaning an entire class of clinical situations that are damaging if not understood and, instead, can become profitable if revisited analytically and utilized in making a good interpretation. Enactments often witness the analyst *tumbling down into the shared unconscious in spite of himself.* Let me be clear: *it is not a choice.*

Typically, the analyst doesn't do this on purpose. Rather, he finds himself caught up in it against his will, in opposition to his own technical and theoretical ideals, not understanding anything – at the time – of what is happening. All in all, he undergoes a series of developments that he would have preferred to monitor and guide with full awareness, in an orderly way and with a certain mastery of the situation.

The analyst's great resource, however, is the possibility of recognizing, at least in retrospect, the event itself, of reflecting on it, and – when things go well – of drawing from it a useful meaning, even if at the cost of some narcissistic bruising to his ideal self-image. At times this emerging meaning is extremely valuable because it is connected to the patient's unconscious scenes, which the meeting with the analyst has powerfully reactivated.

In this chapter, I would like to explore some rare moments of intentional analytic utilization of enactment situations. It should be understood that I am referring to situations in which the scene was proceeding in the direction of a rather sterile repetition of a script that had already been written and recited many times, and in which the analyst did not limit himself to furnishing an interpretation from outside, with an intact selfish component dissociated from his real working self.

In the clinical example that I will relate, the analyst works from inside this scene, exploiting an intuition and intentionally interpreting (in the sense that an actor interprets) the role of one of the patient's internal objects, deeply experienced – but not totally – by the analyst in his real self. I have already anticipated this in the previous chapter in describing Rita, the patient affected by 'incurable inconclusiveness,' whom I addressed with the voice of one of her internal parts. Here I will develop this technical course.

Let me immediately be on the safe side: I do not believe I am describing things that are completely new (I will cite the work of colleagues who have already explored this territory). Rather, I would like to contribute toward giving citizenship status in psychoanalysis to a series of technical operations with which every analyst has had occasional experience, perhaps without dwelling on the theory of it more than a little. Nor would I want to encourage an intentional setup of this type; these moments happen when they happen, just as with empathy, and if one tries to voluntarily reproduce them, one can be certain that the game will not work.

So then, one may ask, why describe them? My answer is first to appreciate them when they happen, and then to understand something more in regard to the delicate and complex interpsychic game that underlies them.

I have the impression that in those moments, some particularly precious secret passages become functional, passages whose existence it can be extremely interesting to become aware of.

Two sessions with Alba

Alba is an almost professional patient because of her psychoanalytic culture, in that she is a pedagogist and works as a scholar in a nearby city. She is 36, has been married for seven years to a white-collar worker, and has an 11-month-old baby girl. She has been in analysis for two years and two months and comes four times weekly. Alba was previously part of an analytic psychotherapy group for three years, but she had a strongly ambivalent experience (which was entirely reciprocal and made explicit) with the leader, an analyst of some reputation with whom she never 'let herself go,' and whose functioning and structure she defensively tended to imitate during sessions. The therapist had pointed this out to her with a certain amount of annoyance, and, a couple of months later, Alba decided to leave the group.

She asked for individual treatment so that she could 'better understand the adult–child interaction,' and she had only a beginning awareness of her personal difficulties, which led to limited adaptability to cooperation in general. She is partially aware of the relationship between her request for individual analysis and the failed experience with the other group. She has a brother five years her senior with whom she does not get on, who is her parents' favorite, despite the fact that Alba was always better at her studies, and the atmosphere is one of mutual competitiveness.

Her father is described as strict and self-centered, phallic and despotic; her mother, as a housewife who is mostly noncommunicative and lives for him alone; and the patient portrays them as an excluding couple, devoid of empathy. Alba is not really ugly, but she dresses and does her hair in such a way that she comes across as an undifferentiated being; she wears trousers and athletic shoes, has short hair, and carries a unisex bag. She arrives punctually at sessions, respects the setting, and expresses herself slightly nasally with a schoolteacher's tone of voice. She describes her personal affairs with the air of one who is certainly in analysis, but who has already found her own 'mature' internal order, which should assure her of great consideration on the part of others (she does not say this, but it is understood from her demeanor).

We are starting our third year of analysis, and Alba is coming increasingly into contact with the annoyance and difficulties produced by the asymmetry and dependence of analysis. She does not openly challenge me, but her dreams, minor lapses, and occasional shifts to peripheral figures, as well as to atmospheres that are often boring and heavy, presage negative transference developments.

At home, Alba would tend to be somewhat directive with her husband, and she handles her child with attention but with a competence that is a little too self-confident, with never a doubt.

One final detail: on arrival, she never says '*Buongiorno!*' but instead uses a semi-informal, nonspecific greeting ('*Salve!*'), which blurs our age difference and takes no account of personal distance.

Monday's session

She enters, greeting me in the usual way. Her face seems rather inexpressive. It's difficult to tell how she is; I think she's slightly detached, but then she starts talking energetically.

Alba: I had quite an interesting dream.
(I notice she says this with a compliant air; I am curious.)

Alba (*in a slightly 'knowing' tone*): Well . . . *there was this hill . . . and then, after a while, this ship . . . and this chief . . . obviously, the chief of the ship . . . I decide to go and nose around. I was helped by the fact that I could leave my 11-month-old baby with a warm, maternal babysitter, who held her in her arms.*

(While she's recounting her dream, I feel rather annoyed by the strange opening of the narration: 'this' this . . . 'hill' ship . . . 'this chief' . . . 'obviously,' etc.)

84

Alba (*continuing her narration*): *I wanted to nose around because this ship was . . . not exactly notorious . . . but famous, almost mythical. In fact, inside the ship, this chief directed a room full of drugged people, lying lifelessly on the floor. So − I thought − is this all there is? . . . (A brief silence − naturally, I begin to think that the 'chief' is me) Ah, no; I also observed that there were five women warriors, five Amazons, tall and black. One was behind me, beautiful and wicked; she bent down and brushed against my hand. There was contact. I drew back and thought: I'm not one of you!*

At this point, Alba pauses for a rather lengthy period, without producing associations.

I become aware of a kind of functional split inside me: part of me sets to work on the dream with an initial impetus that is usual for me when the dream is somewhat elaborate and complex. This impetus consists of observing the dream as a whole and the elements of which it is composed, like a painter who takes a step or two back to take in the whole canvas, or as if I were observing the background with a wide-angle lens.

This enables me to begin considering the patient's adventure. Because she has begun to substantially trust me (i.e., she entrusted the '11-month-old baby to a warm, maternal babysitter who held her in her arms'), the patient can 'nose around' in other, more disconcerting areas of the transference (i.e., 'the ship . . . not exactly notorious, but famous, almost mythical' − the world of analysis), where there is a crushing servitude of patients who are regressive and dependent ('a room full of drugged people lying lifelessly on the floor'), to which the patient reacts by denying her fear with an attitude of superiority and challenge (i.e., 'So, is this all there is?').

I think that, in this scene, the patient is repeating a similar configuration regarding her childhood dependence on her father and the parental couple experienced as a (phallic) monolithic object, wishing to redeem herself by freeing herself of it, even on a concrete level as she did with the group analyst.

I am also struck by the presence of the five Amazons, tall and black; they call to mind the problem of her relative sexual undifferentiation (Amazons cut off a breast and carried weapons), and they were also characterized by their extreme, impenetrable group cohesion (a parental couple that was too compact?).

I go no further with my thoughts and communicate nothing of this to the patient, because in the meantime another part of me has remained heavily involved in and intrigued by the feeling of annoyance at the strange form of Alba's opening remarks: 'this hill . . . this ship . . . this chief . . . obviously, the chief of the ship . . .'.

I feel irritated: 'This, this, this. . . .' I begin to think angrily: This *what? Which* hill? Which ship, which chief? They are *this* to you, but not for me: I don't know them, I didn't dream them, I've never seen them. It was *you* who had the dream, not me!

Still thinking to myself, I reflect that the appropriate and, in some sense, the 'intersubjectively respectful' way to tell the dream would have been: 'There was *a* hill . . . there was *a* ship . . . there was *a* chief . . .,' informing the other (i.e., me), and, as it were, placing the object halfway between the two of us – not keeping it so complacently close to herself, and for herself, with narcissistic self-sufficiency.

At this point, I feel doubtful: perhaps I'm concentrating too obsessively on this stylistic detail; perhaps Alba's way of expressing herself is not so important.

Yet it's true that it irritated me, and I can't help reflecting on the reasons for this irritation. I feel that this way of telling the dream makes the interlocutor feel excluded (the word *parvenu* comes to mind).

'This, this, this . . .': Alba launches into her story at an already advanced stage, recounting something her interlocutor is hearing for the first time and about which he knows nothing, and she does so ostentatiously, as if it were already known to both. Thus the listener feels excluded, inadequate, and impotent. She also openly demonstrates that she is not doing anything to bring him up to her level of knowledge.

Alba the narrator is delighted that she is already familiar with the material, which she relates in a hyperadult tone of voice, from on high, without bothering to fill the gap in information/experience. Even her relaxed way of telling her story seems to accentuate the difference in a subtly provocative way.

I realize now as I write this that I may seem too meticulous in my account. I also find myself again in the unmistakable atmosphere – experienced during the session as well – of going through a little of my own childhood neurosis, recalled during analysis: digging my heels in when faced with exclusion from the world of grown-ups, who 'know,' who 'can,' and who at times exaggerate in their complacent exhibition of 'knowing' and 'being able to,' even to the point of producing more humiliation than admiration in their children.

This is a pronounced effect that I feel cannot be traced back entirely to primary envy on the part of the child, but which is, rather, it seems to me, the fruit of transgenerational transmission of a certain amount of suffering, in the form of an actively sadistic administration of an experience of inadequacy, indignity, and exclusion.

When an adult 'shows off' in front of a child, emphasizing beyond measure his superiority and narcissistic completion, he does not lay down the basis for inspiring admiration, nor does he give the child an opportunity to grow up to be like him and to emulate him. Rather, he inflicts on the child the suffering that was his, getting pleasure and reassurance from this.

I am attempting to convey to my colleagues not only the 'phenomenological' description, as it were, of this clinical fragment, but also the apparently disproportionate phantasmatic and emotional echo that was provoked in me by Alba's *way of expressing herself*, which was also her *way of doing things* – that is, a complex interpersonal action.

At this point in the session, I was somewhat conscious of all this, and I wondered if the echo I felt could be attributed, theoretically speaking, to a transference from the analyst to the patient (i.e., to a problem that was predominantly mine, resurrected by an interaction of no great significance for the patient), or to countertransference stirred up in the analyst by the patient's transference. The answer to this question, as we shall see, was beginning to take shape in me.

So, taking advantage of the long pause that Alba allowed herself after recounting her dream, I decided to question her 'from below,' toning down but not completely suppressing my irritation.

Analyst: 'This hill . . . this ship . . . this chief. . .' – excuse me, Alba, but why 'this'? I don't already know the things you dreamed about; they cannot be 'these' for me. I know that you know this and that you don't confuse me with yourself. Correct me if I'm wrong, but it seems to me that you delight in your superior knowledge with respect to – and because of – my lack of knowledge. Perhaps in the past, someone has behaved like this toward you, making you feel like I do now.
(Privately, I have two other thoughts – two theoretical formulations – that I don't communicate to her, but write down: first, 'the narrative form may contain the problem'; and, second, 'identification with the excluder.')

(The patient is dumbfounded, surprised, and suddenly pensive, associating. As I said, she is a very intelligent person, capable of letting herself go to this working passage, and she answers me.)

Alba: My father is 6 feet, 3 inches tall, and keeps to himself when he's with Arianna [her 11-month-old baby]. He doesn't get down to her level. (*Pause.*)

Analyst: So he stays 'up there'? (*I feel I can 'play' on the concrete and symbolic register.*) (*Pause.*)

Alba (*She suddenly stretches her arms down, touching the carpet with her hands. I think she is* making contact with her own 'ground floor,' *the basic level of her own feelings; there's a sensation of movement, though physically we are both completely still*): I'm very, very angry. Dr. X [the group analyst] pointed out something similar about my behavior, but he was nastier. He said I was 'high and mighty.'

Analyst: Always something to do with 'high' and 'low' . . . By the way, the five Amazons in the dream were also tall . . .

Alba: Yes. One was behind me, she had light-colored eyes, beautiful and wicked. She bent down and brushed against my hand; she also made contact. I was appalled and drew back, saying, 'I'm not one of you.'

(I think that the number five usually brings to mind, perhaps a little scholastically and often with regard to masturbation, the fingers of the hand, but in this case it seems rather to refer to the conflict of 'need–fear–rejection' concerning 'getting someone to give you a hand.' But I want to hear what the patient has to say, and I wait for her associations.)

Alba: Five makes me think of the three years of therapy with Dr. X and two with you . . . In this time, I've 'brushed past' analysis without ever really being touched by it; besides, you've got light-colored eyes.

Analyst: I believe you're afraid that if you trust me in analysis and let me 'give you a hand,' you'll end up like those drugged people, at the mercy of the chief of the ship/analysis. You desire this analysis (*as a pedagogist who is well informed about psychoanalysis, which is for you a 'famous, almost mythical place'*), but it is also feared, so your dream would appear to tell us. . .

Alba: You're right. It's not easy to trust.

Analyst: But you trusted the babysitter . . . You left Arianna with her. . .

Alba: Yes, I trusted her.

(I think this final emotional closing of the gap is preconscious and should not be emphasized; otherwise, Alba might feel obliged to make a pacifying end to the session, which would not do justice to the complexity of her experiences with regard to me. I limit myself to saying, 'Let's stop here,' the formula I normally use.)

(Alba gets up from the couch with great difficulty, as though she is trying to regain her inner order.)

I think I'm a good babysitter for her, but that I still scare her a little and definitely make her very angry. The problem of 'high' and 'low,' of he who knows and he who does not, and how to make knowledge 'fall from on high' to those 'down there' who don't know, or how instead to offer knowledge in an acceptable way without causing humiliation, is very important in this case, I feel.

I am struck by the idea of the grandfather who looks 'down his nose' at his 11-month-old grandchild. 'Grandfather' and 'babysitter' seem to be two split elements of the parental object.

Then I remember how angry I was during the session with 'This . . . this . . . this . . . ,' and I think that I 'was' Alba, and Alba 'was' her father.

Tuesday's session

Alba arrives with her usual neutral expression, but as soon as she lies down, she starts talking.

> Alba: I've been thinking about what you said yesterday about the way I recounted my dream. There's some truth in it. But I felt angry and sorry when I was told this. I have to admit that it is my father's style. I also have to say that my mother backs him up every time, in every way. She always sides with him.
>
> Analyst: She is solidly behind him, just like the Amazons were united among themselves and against others . . . (I think the patient is picking up contact again with the exclusion she made me experience; from being the excluder, she goes back to being excluded, after the active reaction to 'abandoning analysis' over the weekend. She seems more authentic to me.)

I cannot relay this part of the session exactly, because a discourse arose that required me to make very rapid mental movements.

I could summarize by saying that Alba described an experience involving an 'excess of exclusion'; her associations touched on themes such as castes, social classes, and 'giving people the opportunity to learn' versus 'being complacent about the gap' as a source of pleasure for those 'up there.'

As she brought these themes into our asymmetrical setting, which provoked aggressiveness in her, it emerged that anal configurations in object relations (such as 'me on top, you underneath'; 'either rule or be ruled') and in phallic relations ('being firm and tough' like the Amazons) did not seem so narcissistically invested.

I mean that Alba's tendency to identify with her father's behavior of superiority and that of the hyperexcluding parental couple seems to be due more to a defensive need than to the desire for narcissistic complacency, or to a fixation with a perverse pleasure. It seems to be strongly linked genetically to severe doubts about the effective willingness of the other to allow her to grow up, to convey a sense of possible development. The patient does not seem to be irredeemably enamored of her father's style, which consists of confining and despising one's own excluded, immature parts in the other – the parts of one that 'don't know.'

This enables me to have some faith in the future development of this analysis.

Yes, that's fine, you will say, but what about the text of the session?

I can supply the final part, which I remember better and can faithfully reproduce. I relate it with a little apprehension, since there is a variation of technique that is rather personal and might be hard for some colleagues to accept. Anyway, here are the last lines.

> Alba: Something of the sort [we are talking about the hope that the other will 'lend a hand' to help with growing up, or not] came to mind when, while studying Lacan for an exam, I came across the expression 'the analyst as a subject who is presumed to know.'
>
> Analyst: In the dream, you didn't want to make contact with the Amazon's hand and, from the associations you made, we can infer that you 'did not want a hand' from the Amazon/analyst because, rather than a 'subject who is presumed to know,' the analyst [Dr. X at first, and now me] might be a 'subject who delights in the other's ignorance.' [I omit to say: 'like your father, more or less, who looks down his nose at his grandchild,' though I think the connection is clear to Alba. But she is puzzled.]

> Alba: I don't understand. [She says this as she gets up off the couch, as the session is over.] You will explain it to me next time.

I sense that Alba is reliving in anger a feeling of exclusion from being able to understand, from being in the know. My reworking of Lacan's phrase, adapted to describe the phantasm of a sadistic object that does not want her to grow up, is too intellectual for her, though it was not my intention to speak from 'on high' – quite the opposite, in fact. I am sorry I did not find the right words to describe her fear of having to deal with a parent who wants to 'keep her down' so that he can 'stay up there.' I mentally run over her words again: 'I don't understand . . . You will explain it to me next time.'

By now we are both standing, both 'up.'

I have an intuition and decide to give it free rein: I assume an air of superiority, presumptuous and complacent, and I say in a totally nasty tone, articulating each word, 'We shall see whether I feel like explaining it to you. . . .'

Alba immediately catches on to my playing a role, my intentional 'turning into' the feared object and giving it voice, and we both laugh.

At this point, the session really does end, and our leave-taking is noticeably relaxed.

Conclusion

I believe I used a moment's fleeting but precious perception 'on the fly': Alba's ego, which had just regained an erect position, was still hurt and humiliated at not having understood; but it was also regaining a recognizable state of relative and painful adulthood, not so different from my own. At the same time, she was still immersed in the last few phrases of our dialogue and therefore highly receptive with regard to it. She was in a state of passage between 'up' and 'down,' between inside and outside, which can perhaps be compared to the phase of reawakening in which a dream may be either wiped out in a few seconds by the censor, or 'saved' and written down on a sheet of paper, or fixed in memory.

This was a moment when the young Alba, dependent and narcissistically humiliated, is present alongside the grown-up Alba, who, in order to distance herself from her wounds, loses contact with her true self and identifies with the aggressor/excluder, forcing the other to experience the suffering part. There I felt that I could play the role of her superego not by describing it, but by intentionally interpreting the part, with a slight caricature so that she would experience the fear induced for a split second, recognize it, and then discharge it, faced with proof that it was fiction, once insight had been gained.

In Italian as in English, the word *interpret* applies both to translators and to actors who bring a character to life. In this case, it came to me naturally to take advantage of favorable interpersonal circumstances to make visible an intrapsychic object and, more generally, a dream sequence, which had been repeated who knows how many times deep down within Alba, but always with the curtain down. A dream that previous generations must have literally administered – more than transmitted – from one to the other, in undigested form and more or less traumatically.

At the right time, maybe we will be able to imagine, one day, Alba's father as a child, and even farther back his grandparents, wrestling with the same injuries and humiliations: all gradually inclined, in the absence of alternative solutions, to find the illusion of relief in freeing themselves from this internal weight, unconsciously 'passing it' to their own offspring, in a potentially endless chain that the analysis has the goal of putting to an end. If we ever arrive at making it possible to imagine a similar sequence (the 'three generations' of which Faimberg, 2005, speaks), at that point, a transformative, liberating assumption could finally be realized, but also a calming one, complete with a sort of retroactive sympathy that would close the circle.

Let me return to the technical aspect of this type of 'interpretation,' of which, moreover, one finds innumerable examples in the psychoanalytic literature, and of which – it should be clear – I do not often make use, because I believe that very rarely does one experience a situation with a real 'poetic sense' that is both useful and shareable. I consider it rare for an analyst to intuit with sufficient precision the simultaneous presence of suitable conditions both in the patient and in himself. Like the blooming of a flower in the desert, this privileged joining is unpredictable, and it is difficult to succeed in catching on the fly the possibility of creative play in analysis.

Analogously to what I have written about empathy and empathism, it is highly probable that the analyst who believes he can intentionally create these situations will end up forcing things and becoming a caricature of the creative analyst. In short, this way of proceeding cannot become a 'style.' One must take into account the possible inconveniences entailed in the breaking of the analytic frame by adding a fragment of analytic dialogue after getting up from the chair and the couch, respectively.

Undoubtedly, the debate on the distinction between 'acting out' and 'action' in psychoanalysis has many illustrious precedents, like Ogden's (1994b) conceptualization of *interpretive actions*, or those of Racamier (1992) on the 'speaking action'; perhaps in the case I have presented, we could speak of 'interpret-action,' if the type of work that I have tried to describe can be of analytic quality, and if one can recognize a harmonic coexistence of thought and communicative action capable of involving the ego as much as the self.

Running through the configurations and developments that emerged from our dialogue in the session, it is then evident how the asymmetry of the analytic setting enhanced transference repetition of the patient's neurotic problems. To reach a certain degree of empathic comprehension, I was obliged to travel, *malgré moi*, through an 'inverted complementary countertransference' in which I felt first-hand the patient's deep experiences in contact with her internal object – impersonated through identification, in the session, by Alba herself. From my point of view, this is confirmation of how the interpretive function of psychoanalysis cannot really be carried out without a partial experiential immersion in the patient's inner world.

I would also like to point out that the analyst's 'dis-identification' from the role he had been quietly assigned by the patient (identification is – strictly speaking – an unconscious process) requires an internal trigger, a reaction made possible by perception of experiences by our working self, which signal the presence of extraneous elements. That is, when faced with Alba's 'this, this,' I felt an instinctive annoyance, which I believe paved the way for our shared transformative work.

Finally, a further consideration – the most important one.

In the clinical scene I have described, the intrapsychic is gradually brought out, explored, and modified with the use of meaningful interpersonal exchanges. I spoke as a person, at times impersonating an internal character of Alba's who was to her like an internal person, engaging in dialogue with her central ego (Fairbairn, 1944, p. 71).

But I think that this was possible also because, a little at a time, through prolonged living together and the analytic cohabitation, Alba became accustomed to sharing – at least at times – a functional interpsychic dimension in which the perception of the meaning of things, of exchanges, of relational movements slightly precedes the conscious and logical registering of these same things on the part of the central ego.

This is nothing extraordinary, I would like to make clear; we are all familiar with this dimension, and we have all experimented with the possibility of implicitly retaining a working 'cat-flap,' provided we have acquired a certain familiarity with our house cat. But this relative familiarity is not an obvious fact, already given: one must profit from it, construct it together.

To gain access to secret passages, familiarity is necessary.

6

MY DOG DOESN'T KNOW DESCARTES

The disenchanted analysis of the 'interpsychic' man–dog

> If one wants to know a man in depth, one must first read what he writes, then observe how he behaves when he eats and when he plays, and finally one must see his dog.
> A man's dog speaks for him.
> If a man tells you that he doesn't have dogs and perhaps even detests them, then you will have defined him.
>
> Piero Scanziani, 'The Mystery of Man and Dog,' 1978[1]

> If dogs don't go to heaven, I want to go where they go.
>
> Anonymous

The dog loves to live, play, and work with people.

To do so, he has been accustomed for thousands of years to co-constructing and sharing a basic interpsychic area with us, just as he has, since the dawn of his origins, cooperated syntonically in the pack with his fellow dogs.

Only some humans, however, know how to recognize and utilize this common area, responding 'sensibly' to the animal's explicit

---

1 Translation by Gina Atkinson.

convocation and creating meaningful situations of understanding and rapport.

As in the much more dramatic cases related to child-rearing, between dogs and masters, too, a prevalence of the human 'intrapsychic' in relation to the shared 'interpsychic' opening interferes with the couple's creation of something enjoyable and profoundly sensible and produces unproductive and frustrating situations for at least one of the two. The projection of the foolish and incompetent 'master' (as we will call him) reveals his pathological tendency to take the place of the other's reality, and to suppress a possible shared intersubjective reality.

As is known, dogs lend themselves very well to representing projections of people's internal images, both positive and negative. In his text, Scanziani (1978) – who was not a 'psycho-something,' but a great expert on dogs – presents an interesting historical panorama of the propensities for dogs of famous figures from the past, with rather convincing reconstructions about the underlying motives of some chosen individuals. Recall, for example, Alexander the Great's preference for giant Molossus dogs, which obviously fulfilled in him a fantasy of prevailing power; and, by contrast, Frederick the Great's passion for little, slender greyhounds – at first inexplicable in a king who challenged his enemies in wars over seven years, and who made Prussia into a formidable war machine. This predilection on the part of Frederick the Great, however, is ascribable to his having been born to a coarse and oppressive father, while he himself was a delicate, frail youth, lonely and in need of warmth. Interestingly, the supreme narcissist Gabriele D'Annunzio displayed for this same breed, the greyhound, an affected desire that was more declared than felt, since he valorized these dogs as the contemporary equivalent of the strong and fast, tracking and hunting dogs of medieval times, while in reality making sure they were not underfoot. Scanziani (1978) writes:

He who loves himself too much cannot love dogs.

Napoleon and Mussolini did not have dogs.

Bonaparte always detested the infidel Josephine's little dogs, and they repaid him in kind, to the point of following him and biting the imperial heels. . . . Napoleon, indifferent to the deaths of men, did not even notice the dogs' exploits.

One evening, on the field of Bassano, which was covered with dead bodies, the tyrant heard the desperate cry of a dog next to the body of his dead owner. Many years later, at St. Helena, the ghost of that dog still haunted the sick and imprisoned emperor, who confessed to the Count De Las Cases: 'I calmly ordered the initiation of 100 battles, and I looked on with an impassive eye as thousands of men died. But I still remember an evening in Bassano when I felt my soul pierced at the cry and the pain of a dog.'[2]

Today, after a century of psychoanalysis, we could say that a neglected and renounced part in the interior of the self of that cruel and megalomaniac leader had found a secret passage through the network of narcissistic and split defenses that so strongly characterized him, finding a way to represent itself in an unexpected creature, in an affectivity and expressiveness that had been torn by pain.

The title I chose for this chapter ('My Dog Doesn't Know Descartes') is actually a citation. There was a book of this title by Mario Girolami (1967) in which the author (a prestigious doctor and clinical chair in Rome, and at the time also president of the Italian Society of Gastroenterology), on the basis of his observations about the mental life of his dog, firmly rejected the Cartesian distinction between body and mind, between 'res extensa' and 'res cogitans,' and especially between the animal psyche and the human psyche (usually upheld by excessively emphasizing presumed qualitative differences rather than quantitative ones between them and us). Furthermore, and quite significantly, the counsel of the then-very-young Giulio Cesare Soavi was cited many times in that text; he was a Roman psychoanalyst who would later become well known at the national level for his studies on interpsychic 'fusionality' (e.g., Soavi, 1989; see also Neri et al., 1990).

The book's thesis was not so innocent from a cultural–political point of view, when one recalls that Girolami was the personal doctor of the pope (Pius XII), and that the book thus brought some trouble to him in his Vatican visits. As a result, he assigned responsibility for it to the top management of the National Board for the Protection of Animals, of which he was president for a long time in subsequent years, having made a very definitive choice of field . . .

I cite this book and that person in order to describe a possible ideological conflict of principle that could have created then (and

2 Translation by Gina Atkinson.

could even create today) some 'blind spots' in considering, with a sufficiently liberated spirit, the relationship of human beings with animals, and also something that interests us more as analysts: the relationship of the ego with the self, of which the animal can become the natural representative at an internal level.

Political–cultural problems of this type did not exist, on the other hand, in Freud's home. Those who have visited Berggasse 19 and lingered attentively in the room where a video runs continuously – showing images of the family that are commented upon by Anna Freud on the occasion of her historic return to Vienna for the International Psychoanalytical Congress of 1971 – will have noticed that Anna's voice, always deeply but composedly moved at the replaying of family scenes, breaks down into uncontrollable tears when, just at the end of the video, the household dogs appear. She calls them 'these marvelous creatures,' and she reacts, not more and not less, as though she has once again seen family members; and in effect it was so.

According to the testimony of his patient Smiley Blanton (*Diary of My Analysis with Sigmund Freud*, 1957), Freud, who took great account of his dogs, thought that: 'The feeling for dogs is the same that we harbor for children: it is of the same quality. But do you know how it differs? . . . One gives nothing ambivalent in it, one does not notice any resistance.'[3] And further, in a famous letter to Marie Bonaparte, Freud makes reference to the fact – in addition to the absence of ambivalence – that the dog gives us a representation of the 'simplicity of a life free from the almost unbearable conflicts of civilization, the beauty of a perfect existence in itself' (in E. L. Freud, 1960, p. 434).

As Anna Maria Accerboni (1990) wrote, Jo-fi, the chow given to Freud by the Princess Bonaparte,

. . . was so dear to Freud that he separated himself from her only with difficulty, and he held her close to him even during sessions. The testimony of Freud's son Martin maintained that, with the little dog present, he never needed to consult his clock in order to know when the analytic hour was finished: 'When Jo-fi got up and yawned, this was the sign that the hour had concluded; she never surprised him in announcing the end of the session late, though my father maintained that she was capable of an error of perhaps a

3 Translation by Gina Atkinson.

minute, at the patient's expense.' Evidently [concluded Accerboni], Jo-fi, like any good dog, sided with her master![4]

Cohabitation and *collaboration*, to my mind, are the two key words for understanding the interpsychic dimension that can unite man and dog in some situations.

The interpsychic (Bolognini, 2004a) is for me that dimension of cohabitation and cooperation in which the sense of the self is extended – naturally, and not in a pathologically shared way – to another contiguous being, with effects that at times are reciprocally propagated at the level of the central ego (Fairbairn, 1944, p. 71) as well, with an awareness of what is unfolding, but not always and not necessarily. As I have earlier specified, I find useful, by contrast, the term *transpsychic* to designate those pathological processes in which the extension goes beyond the borders of the other in a violent way, intrusive and subtle, passing through anomalous and nonconsensual channels, with distortion and dispossession of the other's subjectivity.

Let us refer to the interpsychic without any reference to, as I think of it, telepathy or various paranormal phenomena, but as the condition of the *benign and necessary, primary physiological fusionality* that we all recognize as legitimate and even 'a duty' in the mother–baby couple, and thus one that is practical for growth and for the transmission of life and competence, until the maturity that leads to a progressive detachment has been set in motion. In it, too, in fortuitously natural situations, an attribute of cooperation can be recognized, from the first intake connected to mouth–nipple suction.

As everyone knows, the canine capacity/necessity to live together psychically as well was originally connected to the life of the pack, of the group, and to the natural propensity for 'common work' in hunting and in the defense of territory and the biological heritage of their community (the 'guard'). But it is also connected to the game, perfectly congruent with the natural system, of teaching and learning. Wolves, too – the ancestors of our dog – have their own formative 'training'!

Jo-fi and Freud, during their daily cohabitation in the microcosm of Berggasse 19, formed a proven 'operative unity' in which Jo-fi seemed to have modest duties, but well-defined ones: to be there, to

---

4 Translation by Gina Atkinson.

be patient with the guests, and then to say 'enough,' not by chance but based on a fixed and controlled protocol, day after day. We do not know what idea Jo-fi formed of the contents of the sessions, but we can imagine that in the case of violently acted-out negative transference, she would not have remained indifferent, and that she would have arranged, perhaps in her own way, to reestablish the setting that she knew was correct.

As I am attempting to show in this book, the intra- and interpsychic dialectic is one of the recurrent themes of contemporary psychoanalysis. Unfortunately, starting with an observation of the human–animal relationship, one could furnish an infinite string of examples (mostly rather tragic ones) of the prevalence of the human intrapsychic with respect to the perception of others' psychic reality. By now I am trained to recognize the signs of disappointment and mortification in a dog that is not minimally understood by someone, either in his needs or in his offers to play, to exchange, to collaborate, or simply to cohabit.

But rather than citing one among an infinite number of piteous cases capable of tearing the hearts of dog lovers, I want to recall for you a happily ironic representation of this type of human–dog mismatch. In the famous film by Aki Kaurismäki, *The Man Without a Past*, the absent-minded protagonist finds himself facing an improbable Nazi-like character from whom he rents a cottage near the sea. The landlord, to give a firm idea of his own terribleness and to subjugate the interlocutor by terrorizing him, arrives dressed in paramilitary fashion and brings with him a dog harnessed like a ferocious attack animal (calling him 'Ursus' or 'Brutus' – I don't remember which). The landlord threatens that he will set the dog on the unfortunate and bewildered protagonist in the event of any default in rent payment, but the dog, affectionately wagging his tail, goes to lick the poor man's hand, curling up at his feet (later, in the film's credits, the viewer finds out that the dog belongs to the film's director and was engaged as part of the cast on this occasion).

One could comment on the *human intrapsychic* and *human–dog interpsychic* aspects of this interaction as follows: there was much of the human intrapsychic, and all of it deposited in the foolish aspirations of the landlord, and there was zero human–dog interpsychic interaction between the dog and the landlord's conscious aspects. There was considerable interpsychic exchange, however, between the dog and the undefended 'man without a past,' and, probably, with an underlying split part of the Nazi–like landlord, evidently not as bad as he consciously desired to represent himself.

Several years ago, I observed a real clinical situation in which a patient's transference expectations did not correspond to canine reality, when I had a young man in treatment who at that time displayed markedly narcissistic and solipsistic traits. He strongly devalued his dog, an affectionate mongrel who was always ready to play and cuddle, precisely because of his dependence and friendliness. He considered the dog to be weak and, instead, dreamed of having a proud and distrustful dog of a type that he had vaguely heard talked about: the Mali greyhound. The patient explained to me that, in the desert areas of that African country, groups of semi–wild greyhounds followed the nomadic tribes, collaborating in the hunt, and receiving in exchange a part of the kill.

What greatly seduced my patient was the fact that these dogs were not really domesticated. They followed the tribe, it was true, but remained at a certain distance (literally, some ten yards from the caravan) and maintained a collaborative interdependence, but avoided direct contact. This seemed to me a 'talking metaphor' of his unconscious relational plan within our analytic cohabitation.

This idea worked extensively in the patient, such that, on his return from the summer break, he announced that he had succeeded in procuring a Mali greyhound puppy, who now trotted exuberantly around his house. In a certain sense, the patient expected from the puppy the personification of his longed–for, ideal style of relationship, arrogant and proudly reluctant to engage in affective contact.

But he had counted his chickens before they were hatched – that is, without taking into account the extremely warm–hearted mongrel he already had, who in the course of a few weeks had, without difficulty, turned upside down the patient's plan and in good measure the genetic mandate of his African cohort. Through play, the call for connection, and naps together, the Mali greyhound ended up firmly ensconced on my patient's bed, together with the other dog, in a climate of blessed fusionality.

My patient gave himself no peace, and was profoundly disappointed.

But when, some years later, he terminated his long and tormented therapy, with the modifications in object relations that analysis can permit, he surprised me: at his last session, he brought his dogs to my office. They entered, I have to say, in their own ways: the mongrel came directly up to me, wagging his tail cheerfully and sniffing my

101

hand (to 'register' me), showing no sign of distrust. The other dog did not do this; he traced the boundaries of the large room, exploring the perimeter, and only a little at a time did he approach me, cautiously, and then curled up a few yards from us. His face, his expression characterized by those horizontal and enigmatic eyes, was effectively very different from the mongrel's.

Still, the Mali greyhound cohabited with us for the entire hour, calm, in representation of that part of my patient that, though marked by a traumatic history that could not be denied, was at this point integrated into his conscious sense of self and rendered tolerably co-livable with me and with his internal objects. The patient was no longer the victim of the sabotaging demands of an ideal ego, one that was both hypernarcissistic and desperately defensive.

In contrast – and rightly so, in the spirit of equitable justice – here is a strange case of the clear prevalence of the canine intrapsychic with respect to the unfolding of an interpsychically consensual relationship. Professor Casolino, an expert at the ENCI[5] and a judge of the international contest, is an elderly gentleman with a zest for narrative. (Incidentally, he was the official discoverer/savior of the 'Cane Corso,' the thirteenth Italian breed to be officially recognized, which was recovered *in extremis* at the border of extinction in the 1970s.[6]) During one of our long conversations in the public park in which our dogs were used to gathering, Professor Casolino recounted a curious episode to me of which he had been a direct witness.

Some years earlier, he had found himself accompanying a well-known breeder of St. Bernard dogs to a competition. During the trip, made by car, they stopped along the freeway at a coffee shop, and allowed the two imposing animals bound for the competition (a male and a female) to get out of the back of the station wagon, in order to water them and let them warm up a little in the flowerbed behind the coffee shop. The two big dogs had done their regular business, roamed about in the green area, and then had unexpectedly run off, in unison and at full speed, in the direction of a nearby machine shop. From there human screams of terror were heard a few seconds later, and the breeder and Professor Casolino ran inside to catch the animals.

---

5 *Translator's note*: The ENCI (*Ente Nazionale Cinofili Italiani*) is the National Society of Italian Dog Lovers.
6 *Translator's note*: The 'Cane Corso' is a medium-to-large-sized guard dog of the molosser or mastiff type.

The scene was this: the two dogs had seized by the overalls, at shoulder height, an unsuspecting mechanic who was busying himself with the oil pan of a car, lying on the floor under it, and they had extracted him by force from underneath it. The man, who appeared terrorized, had felt himself caught from behind and had then seen just a few inches from his face the two huge nonhuman heads, and he nearly had a heart attack.

At the arrival of their owner, the two St. Bernards, in contrast, appeared happy and certain of praise; in fact, *they had rescued an unlucky man who had ended up there as though in the case of an avalanche,* and so the dogs would certainly have been rewarded for the excellent work they carried out, as in the age-old tradition of human–dog collaboration. Psychoanalytically speaking, the two 'rescuers' had thus proceeded according to a regime of clear predominance of the overdetermined intrapsychic, producing a *transference* (in this case, in playing with terms, we could even call it a 'rescue transference') in relation to that man. In perceiving the other's terror, the dogs would probably have ascribed the experience to the risk run by the human being under the oppressive mass of the car, but luckily they had arrived, and then the poor man – thanks to their well-timed intervention – would soon be calmed down.

Let us move now to the city center of Bologna, the European capital of 'Punkabbestia.' Hundreds of 'alternative'-type young people arrange to meet – and often end up firmly ensconced – under the porticoes of the historical center of the city, together with their dogs, with whom they form a structured psychic unity, rich in meaningful implications. The Punkabbestia are a phenomenon of youth that is widespread in Italy, and I don't think they exist elsewhere in the same characteristically militant way (in Brazil, for example, there are 'Pit boys,' who keep the regulation, *de rigueur* pit bull, but they are a completely different phenomenon in that they are at the extreme right and their dogs are openly considered weapons).

Those local figures are boys and girls who are adorned and dressed in a plain but bizarre way; they distance themselves from their homes and their own cities, each having a dog as his only regular companion (they are, therefore, 'punks' *con una bestia,*[7] or 'Punkabbestia'). Usually, they are not delinquent, but they live in a sort of parallel world with

---

7 *Translator's note*: This translates as 'with a beast' or an animal.

respect to society, though they locate themselves for the most part in the historical center (they are the 'excluded,' 'eccentric' ones) of the city. They make the most of their assets, receiving money from their families; they usually do not steal. They refuse every type of commitment and dependence on others.

Through piercings and tattoos, these young people condense a complex representation of their unmentalized – indeed, narcissistically invested – internal wounds in the service of defense, which I will not describe at length. They form a group, and their dogs are together but do not form a pack, because each depends on his own master.

The Punkabbestia actively and narcissistically try to sustain an idea of themselves as *intentionally 'eccentric,' to deny an originary experience of de-centralization and exclusion*: they avoid depression through narcissistic overinvestment in an idealized, self-sufficient self, and they may *project their needful and dependent self onto the dog*, who follows them like a shadow and who in effect depends on them. They seem to take reasonable care of the dogs, but overall the dog must fulfill two basic functions:

1   It must represent and confirm an 'ideal self' who is liberated and ostentatiously instinctual, who does not bend to society's conventions and does not suffer the disgrace of a leash.
2   It must, however, impersonate the dependent self as well, toward which – through the medium of the dog – the Punkabbestia display a sort of affectionate condescension; the dog serves to reassure the boy, in fact, that *the one who is afraid of being alone and of feeling abandoned is not the boy himself.*

But let us return to the interpsychic.

With that concept, I intend something very modest: nothing to do with amazing intuitions or lectures on thought, and not even with who knows what moving instances of the dog's understanding of the master (which in some rare cases are in fact verified, in a totally natural and explicable way). I refer to the habitual cohabitation of being together, very often the result of a sort of reciprocal tuning, which is the product of one's reciprocal investment and progressive entry into the other's reasoning and feeling, which can be accomplished between a trainer and his dog-student just as between a retired person and his mongrel. I am thinking of the kind of cohabitation that permits them not only to know each other very well, but also to felicitously take for granted a host of functions that have come to be carried out together, often without noticing this: perceptive functions, whether directed toward the external ('who is arriving?'), or reciprocal signaling ('we are calm,' or 'we are alarmed,' etc.).

I have often been struck by the facial expressions of dog and master while they are going about their daily tasks. A classic example occurs when they ride together in a car, truck, or cart. I lived in the country for many years, for entire summers, and I was always surprised by the fact that, between the master who was driving and the dog seated by his side, there was always a model identity of expressions and intentions. In short, I marveled that the master left no doubt about the fact that, in spite of the rules of the road, the obvious place for his cohort was there, on the passenger seat (after all, the dog wasn't riding in a taxi!), not in the trunk that is used by – significantly – hunters, many of whom seem to see their dog as a biological device that is more or less efficiently directed toward the goal of catching game.

Furthermore, I was equally struck by observing in the dog/cohort/passenger an analogous certainty of his own role, and an obvious way of sharing the meaning of the mission that was being undertaken. This often seemed to be the case on trips to pick up or deliver fruit or vegetables, or construction materials or other goods, presumably from suppliers or warehouses already known to both dog and master. There was a firm certainty of the necessity for both to be present in order to achieve a good result of the entire operative maneuver.

It was not completely clear to me how far the detailed mentalization of all these processes reached (with regard either to the dog or to the master, who seemed equally mentally organized along the implicit procedural register). I noted, however – and, I must admit, greatly admired – a dimension of healthy self-evidence and of *mental energy conservation* due precisely to the fact that man and dog proceeded in evident accord, assuming a shared directionality and, all in all, assuming very similar expressions.

At this point, a long series of coincidences is clear enough, coincidences with a fusional dimension that we psychoanalysts hold to be (especially from the time of Mahler on; see Mahler, 1968) one of the necessary stages of the formative coexistence between mother and child in the development of the human being. And we well know the ruinous consequences that the lack of this physiological phase of upbringing can involve, with the desperate search in subsequent phases for equivalents to what was missing, and with others' consequent incomprehension of the meaning of this search, which seems pathological and incongruous if one does not know how to understand it correctly.

What psychoanalysis has not been very interested in, by contrast, is precisely this *widespread dimension of the basic, necessary interpsychic,* which in fact the majority freely provide for themselves through family and work, in social gatherings or in other daily situations. In this way, people 'function in attunement' with others, without knowing it, satisfying a *basic quantum of microfusionality in cohabitation* that is beneficial to the self – stabilizing it, confirming it, and often conserving energy for the perception of a sense of existence, unity, and cooperative contact in being there with others.

The dog shares with us in these needs, and he is overjoyed to coparticipate in our existence.

Descartes and many others like him who 'know' – people who may be categorized according to various beliefs and narcissistic presumptions about the ennobling existence of a 'beautiful soul' of elevated spirituality – do not consider the dog our relative. But those among us who have really tested themselves in a dimension of cohabiting and reciprocally searching for understanding cannot usually support a conviction of radical, substantive difference for long.

One can agree, paradoxically, on only one point: we cannot realistically define dogs as 'our relatives.' In fact, if we live together and truly observe their profound way of being with us, the definition of dogs that we will find more correct and true will be different: it will be 'our family members.'

7

THE PSYCHOSEXUALITY OF
MUCOUS MEMBRANES
Inter-body and interpsychic

Among the many possible areas of reading through which the history of psychoanalysis can be considered, one of the most fascinating and at the same time most specific is that relative to psychosexuality.

Especially in 'Fragment of an Analysis of a Case of Hysteria' (1905 [1901]) and *Three Essays on the Theory of Sexuality* (1905), Freud described the gathering and fixation of the libido, with major and minor erotization and with more or less pathological defenses, around the zones progressively experienced and invested by the subject in the course of his development. The oral, anal, urethral, phallic, and genital zones have been studied in relation to drives, sensoriality, unconscious fantasies, and modalities of object relations that characterize the various moments and levels of self-organization.

Of particular interest to us analysts are all the psychic and relational derivatives that are the result or the equivalent of the experience and sexual organization of the subject in his own self, and then in the relationship with the object. Psychosexuality has thus come to be considered, researched, and interpreted in a complex way – ever since Freud's time – in close continuity with the bodily.

Interesting, in this sense, are the notes of Ernest Jones (1961) on the fact that, in this sphere, he maintained two unfaltering points for his entire life: one was that no psychic process unfolds apart from physical ones; the other was that the physical process must precede the psychic one. 'Both opinions would argue a certain priority for physiological processes' (p. 368).

The mucous membranes

The mucosal epithelium covers the interior of the hollow organs of the human body. In particular, the mucous membranes constitute the epithelium of the organs that regulate the entrance into the organism of external elements, their nutritive or fruitful absorption, and the subsequent eventual expulsion of catabolites of waste and/or of indigestible contents because they are structurally unmetabolizable or excessive.

The mucous membranes also cover the border areas of the passage between inside and outside, delegated to the interchange between the internal spaces of two individuals who intimately unite with the transmission of liquids, as in the suction of nursing or in genital coupling. The kiss is the intermediate sensorial and relational moment, celebrated in infinite figurative and literary productions by artists of every era, who connect primary nutritive intimacy to loving intimacy; the kiss constitutes a sign of possible potentially fertile genital coupling in the future.

Freud spoke of this in the first chapter of 'Fragment of an Analysis of a Case of Hysteria' (1905 [1901]), which is the text in which he explicitly cites at many points the mucous membranes, more in terms of fixative evocations than of somato–psychic–relational equivalences. He takes up the argument again four years later in *Three Essays on the Theory of Sexuality* (1905), in which he states that 'the skin, which in particular parts of the body has become differentiated into sense organs or modified into mucous membrane, . . . is thus the erotogenic zone *par excellence*' (p. 169).

Freud is especially interested in the erotic excitement produced during contact between the mucous membranes, and to that he connects the sexual meaning assumed by these particular tissues. I intend instead to privilege the fact that *through the bodily openings coated in mucous membrane, the 'inside' of an individual is placed in direct communication with that of another individual.*

Because of their anatomical–functional characteristics, the mucous membranes can facilitate co-penetration between two individuals and the transfer of substances from one to the other. Through mucosal secretion, the co-penetrating organs make good use of lubrication that reduces reciprocal frictions, mechanical impediments, and irritating frictions; and the materials of exchange (milk in suction, sperm in insemination) flow in an interliquid, facilitating medium (saliva, prostate, and vaginal secretions). The entire process of co-penetration and of transmission and exchange thus finds a complex facilitation, and two human beings harmoniously blend into a couple, creating an intimacy and a sensorial, somato-psychic continuity that contributes to the intertransmission of contents.

It is interesting to note that desire corresponds to the realization of these facilitating physiological conditions, while its absence blocks mucosal secretion; from a potentially excited condition, the subject who is forced into an undesired co-penetration then passes into an irritating situation, or even one of express refusal through a further muscular closing of the areas of potential co-penetration (vaginismus; closing of the mouth; spastic gastric contraction).

In *Three Essays* (1905), Freud discusses at length the fact that vaginal lubrication had a specific meaning as preparatory to the sexual act. And again in *Three Essays*, Freud, in a footnote, remembered Moll's thesis:

> We are reminded at this point of Moll's analysis of the sexual instinct into an instinct of 'contrectation' and an instinct of 'detumes-cence.' Contrectation represents a need for contact with the skin. The instinct of detumescence was described by Moll (1898) as an impulse for the spasmodic relief of tension of the sexual organs, and the instinct of contrectation as an impulse to come into contact with another person.
>
> (p. 169)

Moll's conviction, in which the 'contrectation' drive would subsequently arise in the course of individual development, is interesting, I think.

Physiological equivalents of the primary areas of bodily co-penetration, through the mechanism of functional displacement, pertain to the gaze, to hearing, and to attention. The desiring subject will facilitate, will 'fluidify' in a receptive sense, a disposition toward relationality, investing and facilitating the functions and processes that make possible the coupling of visual and auditory processes and of thought. By contrast, he who does not desire 'will not even want to see' the other, 'will be deaf' to his entreaties, and absolutely 'will not want to know.' The continuity between bodily functioning and the psychic and relational is thus evident, unconsciously and preconsciously constant, and all in all is extremely interesting for us analysts.

The area that I am interested in emphasizing is that of the *inter-bodily, interpsychic equivalent* in relation to areas of passage. For the principle of equivalence, which is crucial in psychosexuality, inter-bodily events and interpsychic events can be identical deep down and can assume subjective meanings and intersubjective analogues, trans-migrating from the bodily to the psychic and vice versa, while the individual's conscious ego is only partially aware of this.

More particularly, I maintain that the interpsychic may have to do with the equivalents of an intimate coupling, desired or accepted, while the transpsychic is the equivalent of a forced and traumatic desire to break the bonds of personal boundaries. Words – their content and what they evoke – often substitute, on the basis of this equivalence, for substances that are the object of exchange.

In general, various interpsychic phenomena reproduce the originary model of primary mother–child interchanges and can be found, then, in the phantasmatic aspects of the individual's subsequent life, as they had been experienced in both qualitative and quantitative senses. These considerations are in line with those of Ferro (2010) on various types of interpersonal coupling, and on relative 'mental sexuality' that is more or less productive (setting aside anatomical sex) as a generative font for something new in the interchange between two individuals.

Returning now to a discussion that I initiated in the past (Bolognini, 2004e), pertaining to the mucous membranes as 'transit tissue' and to their interpsychic equivalents:

A communication, in common language, can, after all, be 'dry,' 'poor,' 'chilling,' or on the contrary 'hot,' 'rich,' 'fluid'; a person can 'loosen up' or 'rigidify,' or more simply 'open up' or 'be closed'; contact can be 'soft' and 'enveloping,' or 'bristly' and generate 'friction'; thought can become 'flowing' or can 'dry up.' One could continue at some length with this series of examples, but although initially 'stimulating' (on the side of the life-enhancers), it could become 'over-exciting' (tending toward the manic), until it was actually 'irritating' (when the stimulation is too much an end in itself and does not issue into something satisfying and conclusive).[1]

(p. 158)

---

1 Translation by Malcolm Garfield.

We are well aware that, in psychotic malfunctioning, these equivalences become symbolic equations (or, rather, strictly speaking, *asymbolic*), and, as a result, the subject who is regressed or fixated at that level of malfunction interprets all the relational and/or subjective effects of these sensations in a concrete sense.

But to repeat, I am most interested here in general human functioning and in those physiological and ubiquitous areas of normal daily interchange that I define as interpsychic. In those, our mental and relational life flows mostly in an implicit and preconscious way, following a principle of accepted naturalness; only in rare moments is the subject's insight increased, and he consciously takes note of what he is experiencing in himself and between himself and the other. In analysis, by contrast, that happens regularly, and we work to facilitate these processes of internal contact and subsequent self-representative mentalization, which are useful also in stabilizing the sense of self and of the relationship.

A crucial point for the analyst, in my opinion, is to have the capacity to work clinically in a non-erotized way during phases of very intimate mental coupling, which the patient may on the other hand experience as *erotized precisely because they are experienced in reality as 'faraway and impossible.'* It is understood that I am not saying that the analyst should ignore or negate the experience of inappropriately perceived erotization on the part of the patient; indeed, it is to be hoped that the analyst will be fully perceptive and will know how to efficiently represent the erotized way in which the patient experiences those moments. That will serve the analyst well in prioritizing a diminution of the patient's excited tension – containing it, transforming it into verbalizable representations, and most of all carrying it forward to more livable affects. At that moment, those representations and those basic affects are barely accessible by the subject and he can scarcely deal with them, since he does not yet have at his disposal the shared object experience that he needs. He thus remains imprisoned in an excited, frantic state precisely because his experience is not bearable and thus not resolvable.

In a certain sense, taking up again Moll's late-nineteenth-century definitions cited above, we are passing from the 'need of detumescence' to the 'contrectation,' through the relational and interpsychic forms that are equivalent, at the internal level, to those concrete movements.

Clinical example: Gianna's kiss

Gianna, a very melancholy patient in her forties, chronically disheartened and agoraphobic, initiates the session by putting forth a stream of wearying complaints for more than half an hour. She reports feelings of malaise, apathy, and not wanting to live, and she makes me in turn feel weighed down, to the point that – like her – I don't see any hopeful prospects. She adds that it seems to her this morning that, at intervals, she 'cannot feel' her right arm.

After a dull pause, she recounts a dream from the previous night, beginning in a somewhat detached manner. '*We were together, Doctor, you and I, and you held me on your knees. My mother was there in the kitchen and bustled about.*' At this point the reader must know that the patient has always had a healthy alliance with her mother, who is assertive, strong, and independent; her father, deceased for many years, is rarely mentioned in the analysis and is almost a hidden figure. '*You kiss me passionately. I feel your lips on mine. At first I am very surprised . . .* [pause]. You understand, of course!'

I think that this 'You understand,' said with a respectable air, a bit shocked, is a small strategic masterpiece: to evade responsibility for her own desire, the patient summons me into a position of ego-syntonic agreement in renouncing the misdeeds of the active, seductive analyst of the dream. '*And then the situation progresses . . . How can I say it? . . . Better and better . . . In reality I enjoy it . . .*' (I think to myself that an internal, reintrojective movement is at work: there is a gradual reassumption of desire as her own) '*. . . until I wake up.*' Silence follows.

Deciding at this point to comply with the distribution of theatrical roles, accentuating the characterizations to emphasize them, and assuming, therefore, a very serious and reproving air, consonant with the superego representative summoned by the patient, I say: 'An untenable situation!'

The analyst, already engaged at nighttime in the dreamlike direction of a contradictory role as both an object of desire and an active seducer, chooses, then, to 'interpret' a third role in the here and now of the session: he decides, that is, to knowingly personify, in the interpersonal scene, the patient's superego, proposing such a personality application in a way that is explicit and perceptible, and that can be confronted. This lightly applied 'plastering' of a caricature, with a consequent ironic streak, goes a fair way to neutralize the danger.

Here an adjustment of the emotional tone takes place, changing the atmosphere of the session.

What I want to emphasize in this case, however, is not the 'interpret-active' choice (of which I have already written in the chapter on so-called interpret-action), but the fact that, through such a technical action, the internal/external contact symbolized by the mucous/kiss contact becomes possible. This takes place in a sensorial, almost concrete form in the dream, almost a presymbolic equation, as though the kiss were really a kiss – in the form of symbolic equivalence in 'speaking together of internal things,' in the dialogue in the session, in which a functional, symbolic consideration of what appeared concretely in the dream can be actualized. And I indicate that exactly this 'possibility' (as opposed to the 'impossibility due to superego prohibition') causes erotization to diminish in favor of true internal contact – satisfying, creative, and not hyperexcited.

Gianna says, laughing, 'Yes, I wonder where we would end up!' A warm and joyous atmosphere is emerging, one that is not maniacal; it is libidinal, but not eroticized. She continues, 'You enjoyed it very much, like me . . .' She pauses. 'So! You know that sooner or later, I won't wake up and I will continue the dream through to the end!' Gianna laughs with pleasure, calmly: the self has been recontacted, reassembled, refreshed, and libidinally comforted, no longer excluded and invalidated by the superego's prohibition and by the anxious strangulation of the unconscious defensive ego.

At this point, the work of psychoanalytic reconnaissance can begin in the light of ego work on both what happened here and its antecedents. In this endeavor, an understanding of the partial anesthesia of the right arm can also be included – as the bodily equivalent of not being in contact, of not feeling an internal part of the self.

There is a point of distortion in human relationships that marks the passage from excitement to overexcitement, and from there to a pain 'without meaning'; that point is probably situated in the area from which – because of the perception of a lack, the potential generator of desire – one moves on to the perception of the impossibility of contact and of coupling, and then on to desperation, without being able to organize the corresponding renouncement and mourning. Stubbornly (and desperately) insisting on an unsatisfiable fantasy that will not be actualized, the subject proceeds in a state of overexcitement, straining himself to the point of a period of impotent painfulness.

That pertains to the kind of defenses that we define as manic, in which we could say that the subject does not surrender to evidence of an absence of the object and its functions and insists on *maintaining a highly excitatory level, as though the object were there and coupling could be realized*. At bottom, the maniacal register seems to have something in common with the hallucinatory attitude; in both cases, the defense seems to consist of 'making something exist' that in reality is missing.

Broadening our area of observation a little, I like to define (a little provocatively), for example, wine and alcoholic drinks in general as 'maniacal milk' – as equivalents, that is, self-manageable ones (in the sense that the subject experiences a narcissistic sensation, already in and of itself intoxicating, of being able to procure it alone), of the maternal nutrient that 'will make him immediately well' and that takes away sadness. This has the added corollary – for men – of a vein of reassuring masculinity in the act of drinking, of the apparent confirmation of a proud independence from the maternal object (which is powerfully tinged in the unconscious fantasy, like the true object of need). The narcissistic reinforcement of a 'twinning' element (the sense of friendship and of a sort of confused social 'brotherhood' – *you and I are equal* – induced by alcohol) reinforces, then and there, the sense of cohesion of the self, which is otherwise missing.

In making these remarks, I would not want to be read as censoring the pleasures of the table: to enjoy good wine is one of the pleasures of life, of course! I am describing, however, an underlying psychic condition in which, from the initial desire, one tragically latches on to the protective barrier of a frantic defense in facing an unpleasant reality. Based on this defense, directed toward the denial of desperation, the subject 'raises the stakes' of the game through hyperstimulation, and through the creation of substitute 'anti-objects' (e.g., wine instead of milk) of a maniacal quality.

But let us return to the mucous membranes and to their interpsychic equivalence. What are the analyst's 'psychic mucous membranes'? That is, what are the mental equivalents that can function in analysis as those parts of the self that permit a nutritive or creative interchange between two persons?

Analysts have long been accustomed to hearing themselves disparagingly analogized to prostitutes. And if we consider the mucous membranes, it is pretty much inevitable that the discussion will lead to references of this kind, which take off from an unconscious base of desperation (i.e., of an absence and of the loss of hope of finding relational correspondence in an external object).

The prostitute agrees – for payment – to simulate a coupling that in reality is partial and unilateral, because the desire is only the client's. The prostitute provides a setting and a contact that are acceptable for the client in that they are, in a certain sense, 'better than nothing.' In contrast, she does not provide her own desire, because who knows where that lies, and anyway it cannot be mobilized on command. The prostitute is a mostly pathological subject, or at least is rendered such – emotionally mute and inert during her activities. Through the recourse to appropriate internal splits, she is rendered available to tolerate the bodily penetration in exchange for money.

The analyst, apparently, at the beginning of treatment, seems to make himself available in a not dissimilar manner, with the exception of the non–bodily nature of the contact. The analyst's 'emotional' mucous membranes do not 'moisten' on command, and the analyst deceives himself if he thinks that he can officially 'love' his patient simply by virtue of the fact that the patient is there; in this sense, I have explored in a rather disenchanted way the myth of the analyst's empathy, which remains one of the most confused aspects of the collective representation of our professional persona, and not only for laymen (e.g., Bolognini, 2002a, 2004e).

At the same time, while the prostitute is a necessarily rigid and dissociated subject from an emotional point of view during the exercise of her work, the analyst has much greater internal freedom and can react in a much more integrated way to his experience of living with the patient. For example, it can happen that he will empathize, or will be moved, or will feel sympathy or antipathy in a more or less motivated way. In short, the analyst is not a prostitute in the strict sense because he is not anesthetized as a consequence of dissociation.

Actually, I would broaden the field of possible equivalent references, introducing a more ample series of referential figures. In my opinion, patients' wounded or needy 'psychic mucous membranes' find different types of interlocutors in analysis. I think of the emergency-room analyst/doctor as a first intervention for psychic survival in the case of serious injuries or (internal) fractures; and of the analyst/nanny (or wet nurse), where the self may have been deprived of nutritive factors for the growth of the mind, and thus one may be dealing with the facilitation of a careful resumption of the capacity to nourish oneself and to assimilate. I think of the aesthetic analyst when a narcissistic, needful aspect is in play, one of reparation and enrichment; and even of the analyst/womb/incubator, when primary containment is the truly necessary condition, and the quality of the containing fabric is reflected by the psychosensorial quality of the experience of psychic contact in the treatment.

As Kestenberg (1956) writes:

> I am inclined to believe that the transitional object serves a multi-tude of needs. It represents an ideal solution for the infant who cannot cope with so many tensions stemming from the outside as well as the inside of his body, tensions which overcome him with greater force when the waking activity ceases and the immobility and aloneness of the sleep separation brings about a unique inti-macy with his own body. Oral, anal as well as genital needs seem to be met in holding on to articles of special texture which feel like mother's breast, like the tissue cleansing the anal and genital regions, all areas where the 'me' and the 'not me' meet. At that stage, inner sensations are most probably still fused with, and pro-jected to the outside, so that they too can be mastered by the method of delineation of boundaries between oneself and others. Some children indicate that a special softness of the texture is important, as if they wanted to reproduce the feel of mucous mem-branes, which are the mediators between outside and inside.
>
> (p. 262)

One could take offense at these characterizations or judge them superficial, if one did not reflect on the profound meaning of the complex symbolic equivalences; the phantasmatic and relational equivalents, if efficiently 'played' on the symbolic level, render them anything but strange or uncommon.

The crucial point – just as with the physiology of healthy mucous membranes – is whether the areas of contact, of psychic co-penetration, and of exchange that are placed at the analyst's disposal are adapted to the goal. Do the 'psychic mucous membranes' function well enough to nurture, to favor self-expression, to facilitate further approaches and exchanges from the subject's interior to the interior of the other?

At bottom, I think that every analysis succeeds more or less well in relation to the fact that there may be a desire, but there must not be erotization; exchanges will take place, but they must not be invasive or forced; a natural intimacy is constructed, but also a shelter against intrusion. There should be an appropriate warmth without inflammation, a communication as flowing and as fluid as possible but not overwhelming; a sufficient, enduring contact, but not one that is insisted upon to the point of irritation, and so forth.

Analysts, aware of the symbolic equivalences underlying various situations in the session, can at times derive some advantage by representing in this way the exchanges at play with the patient – that is, as corresponding to a contact that is qualitatively similar enough to those I have described. They can assess these relational configurations with regard to their appropriateness and potential productiveness.

I will conclude this chapter with a clinical fragment: the dream of a patient who, after some years of conflict between letting herself go toward dependence and contact, and, on the other hand, resisting conditions of detachment and self-sufficiency, is slowly settling into a beneficial regression, long desired and feared:

'*I am in a session. At a certain point, I hear you speak in a muffled way. I feel like I'm in a suspended bubble. It's a marvelous sensation; I hear your voice but your words don't register. I know that I have to listen to you, to come out of that state, but I don't want to. Then I tell this to you, and I ask you if you, too, are there in the bubble or if I am alone. You tell me that you are there also, and that for the first time you feel a positive sensation with me – that we are in exactly the same state and that this is a good sign, that it had never before happened to you with me. While you speak, I am as though suspended, floating; I know that if I listen to the meaning of those words, I will come out of this state, and I don't want to.*'

It is a textbook dream, exemplary of the purposes of our discussion, of which I want to emphasize the experiential, integrative aspect.

In the intense psychosensorial evocation of being contained in the interior of the maternal body, of hearing the voice of the other and enjoying the interpsychic 'floating,' the certifying ratification by the working ego must concede the right time to the experience of the self, before being brought to completion.

8

THE COMPLEX NATURE OF PSYCHOANALYTIC EMPATHY
A theoretical and clinical exploration

Empathy has been my major field of interest for more than twenty years now. So I believe that briefly reporting the reasons for my clinical and theoretical interests, as well as the historical and conceptual route I have traveled, is not a mere exercise in narcissism. I feel that many of you, in fact, may find something of yourselves and your training experiences in this brief description and the scientific scenarios I will outline here.

When I was a young candidate in training, grappling with the traditional difficulties of my first analytic treatments, I was often struck by a kind of intra-session experience that was rather rare – absolutely unpredictable, as far as I could see, but nevertheless remarkable. What characterized the experience was effective emotional contact and a propitious representational clarity, during which the patient's conscious experience was shared and deeply felt, though patient and analyst retained their separateness and personal individuation.

It sometimes happened that not only the analytic 'glance' (the intellectual understanding, the ability to explain, Jaspers's idea of *Erklären*),[1] but also the total experience of 'understanding and feeling' (in the well-integrated form of comprehension or *verstehen*) penetrated a little deeper into less ego-syntonic areas. It was as if the links in the chainmail of the defensive ego were at these times temporarily

---

1 For an explanation of Jaspers's *Erklären*, see Campbell (1940, p. 347).

enlarged, allowing our internal sensors to gain greater access to our own preconscious and that of the patient.

When I say 'a little deeper,' I am not referring to heaven knows what heightened powers of introspection, a frenzied moment of clarity, or a hypervisual phenomenon. I am merely reporting a state of overall good functioning that unfortunately takes place all too rarely.

Perhaps the best metaphor I can provide is that of certain beautiful days, when the air is crystal clear and the eye can see for miles with nothing to block its view of the horizon. From my hometown, the Alps are clearly visible four or five times a year, when by some happy coincidence the air currents sweep away the clouds, humidity, and mist (the symbolic equivalents of internal defenses and the usual difficulties in getting the interpsychic relation under way).

On those rare occasions, the mountains are there to see in all their very moving beauty. Yet the real distance from them is not belied; they are and they also appear to be distant, and therefore separated from us, but they are perceptible and every detail can be savored as the scenery changes from woodland to upland pastures, right up to the highest rocky peaks caught in the sun's rays.

This metaphor is not limited by its connection with the visual to the concept of insight exclusively, because the experience I have described is almost always shared, moves more than one person, and facilitates further development in relationships between those present. This perhaps opens up the prospect of a possible connection between insight and empathy, as phenomena associated with, respectively, the intrapsychic and the interpsychic (Bolognini, 2004a).

What struck me on such occasions was the way this privileged condition enabled me to work with the patient in a very natural way without great exertion. Thus, the patient's rhythms and subjective difficulties were respected, since the fears, impediments, and defensiveness of the interlocutor were properly perceived and consequently given instinctive respect.

At the same time, to a great extent the patient would also share this momentary atmosphere of contact and representability of his inner world. He would usually allow himself to open up in regard to his relationships and the self, at least until the inevitable return of the mist and clouds, when analysis would go back to being an uphill grind, made up of obscure and fragmentary associations, long silences, and unbridgeable gaps, contained by the setting and by a basic trust in the effectiveness of the method.

Convinced that I had in some way or other discovered the trans-formative nucleus of analysis, where knowledge and change were possible, I naively thought that if I managed to successfully study the techniques for deliberately creating empathic situations, I would have found the equivalent of the philosopher's stone for psychoanalysis.

I also observed with a certain amount of embarrassment that I was unwittingly cultivating within myself the fantasy of a special, innate 'empathic competence,' as if I could count on some hidden talent for tuning in to my patients. I was able to recognize this narcissistically rather pitiful delusion, however, when I realized how widespread these fantasies were among my young colleagues; they seemed to be almost a universal prerequisite for would-be analysts. As the years of clinical practice went by, so my investment in such fantasies faded. Alas, how many days of mist and fog awaited me, instead of the crisp, clear air I had so desired at the start of my training!

The first section of my book *Psychoanalytic Empathy* (Bolognini, 2004e) contains a detailed investigation of the psychoanalytic litera-ture on the subject from Freud to the present day, and I will not make a scholastic summary of it here. Suffice it to say that my illusions about being able to somehow predetermine empathy were preserved and protected for some time thanks to my reading of the works of Kohut (1971, 1977, 1984), for the simple reason that this author – who is in many ways very interesting and has been too readily dismissed by his detractors – conceives and describes empathy as a method and not as a fortunate eventuality, which is now the way I regard it, after many years of reflection.

For similar reasons, I cannot agree with Modell (1990) when he calls empathy a 'voluntary act.' My own experience, backed up by discus-sions with colleagues, confirms that analysts who are determined to empathize are headed for a blind alley. They will probably encounter a closure of the preconscious and may even end up becoming almost a caricature (masterfully described by Schafer, 1983, when he ironizes about analysts who are convinced they have the 'right pace').

The unconscious cannot be tamed on demand, and the pre-conscious is intolerant of too purposeful an attitude on the analyst's part. By contrast, the literature is full of convincing arguments in favor of the fruitfulness of surprise in analysis (Faimberg & Crel, 1990; Eiguer, 1993; Smith, 1995; Schacht, 2001). Surprise is an irreducible and unplanned factor with a potential for producing creative openings; it is a factor to which experienced analysts wisely 'resign' themselves.

I would nevertheless make one concession regarding the methodical practicability of the empathic transformative area, and that concession concerns psychoanalytic training, a facilitating factor. Returning to our meteorological metaphor, we could say that although it is not in our power to decide whether there will be sun or rain tomorrow, we can move to a place in the world where the climate has strong tendencies in a particular direction. There we would be justified in expecting certain climatic conditions to be far more frequent. Thus, it is not unrealistic to suppose that good psychoanalytic training may be conducive – in a modest but far from negligible way – to a more frequent occurrence of empathic situations, provided that the analyst does not set out to empathize methodologically (and provided that he does not delude himself that he has moved from Edinburgh to Marrakech).

Over the last thirty years, frequent criticism has been leveled from Europe at the North American 'ego psychology' of the 1950s and 1960s, against some obsessively fussy descriptions that occurred in some writings (for instance, some passages from Schafer's papers on empathy – which personally I like very much, particularly when he described internalization processes: Schafer, 1972), and against the general claim to define and pigeonhole every possible internal attitude of analyst and patient in structural maps of the ego. We also know that many Europeans have interpreted the interpersonal, inter-subjectivist, and co-constructionist currents in the United States as a reaction against previous excesses of the ego-psychology school. Indeed, nowadays it might even appear 'inexpedient' or unfashionable to express the type of appreciation I feel – albeit specifically on the subject of empathy – for the contributions of Greenson (1960), Olden (1958), and, in fact, Schafer (1959).

In spite of such criticism, I believe that these authors' work has had the very positive effect of removing at least partially the concept of empathy from the almost mystical air of magical indistinction that surrounded it. Though some of their descriptions may appear rather schematic today, we should acknowledge their contribution in clearly locating empathic situations in the conscious–preconscious zone and unequivocally distinguishing them from phenomena of identification. The latter are unconscious by definition and, since they are intrinsic-ally unthinkable, are if anything diametrically opposed to empathy, with its rich capacity to be thought. Unlike identification, empathy also assumes the flavor of 'feeling oneself into' someone else (from the

German *Einfühlung*) while remaining aware of one's own identity as a separate person.

The shared experience of these areas of specific fusional contact for intimate communication (Bolognini, 1997a, 1997b, 1997c, 1997d, 2002a, 2004e; Fonda, 2000) is possible precisely when the persons concerned have attained separateness, individuation, and a sense of self that is sufficiently solid and defined within its own limits. Identification, in the strict sense of the word, is the very opposite of this condition.

The Kleinian and post-Kleinian schools have also made valuable contributions to our understanding of empathy. They are based on a very distinctive conceptualization in which the physiological vicissitudes (which are communicative and potentially pro-empathic) and/or pathological vicissitudes (involving evacuation, control, etc.) of the mechanism of projective identification are studied with remarkable finesse (Klein, 1955; Money-Kyrle, 1956; Rosenfeld, 1987; Bion, 1967, 1970; Steiner, 1993; Grotstein, 1981, 2005). Their works have helped me to further distinguish projective identification from projection, which in my opinion is also an anti-empathic factor.

I found a recent contribution by Widlöcher (2003) very interesting, in which the author takes up the Freudian concept of 'thought induction' (Freud, 1921) and connects empathy, through 'thought transference,' to the associative and representational 'co-thinking' of analyst and patient. That is, the associative process of co-thinking 'enables us to achieve the effect of empathy,' and 'the interpretation should be understood as a direct effect of the co-thinking.'

I have to admit that a good many of my observations run counter to the common statements about empathy generally put forward by non-experts. Unfortunately, these statements are echoed by some colleagues who seem to have misgivings about the concept or are reluctant to go deeper into the matter. First among these commonplaces is the idea that empathy is a sort of generic analytic 'kindheartedness,' whereby the analyst should be *a priori* well disposed toward the patient and tune in to his ego-syntonic experience, becoming concordant with it. Quite the contrary, empathy is a complex intra- and interpsychic phenomenon that requires a certain capacity for internal articulation, freedom of perception, and representation of affects and configurations of every type.

I have proposed a possible definition of psychoanalytic empathy (which goes to join those of Beres & Arlow, 1974; Schafer, 1983; and many others):

True empathy is a condition of conscious and preconscious contact characterized by separateness, complexity and a linked structure, a wide perceptual spectrum including every colour in the emotional palette, from the lightest to the darkest; above all, it constitutes a progressive shared and deep contact with the complementarity of the object, with the other's defensive ego and split off parts no less than with his ego-syntonic subjectivity.

(Bolognini, 1997b)[2]

As you can imagine, such a definition rules out both easy solutions in the clinical field and monofocal theoretical formulations. One cannot specifically and exclusively attune oneself (or even delude oneself that one has the power to do so), in a concordant countertransferential way, with the patient's 'wounded narcissistic self.' Nor can one do this with the patient's sexuality, or even, in a complementary counter-transferential way, with his internal objects – believing that one has thereby lived through an authentic empathic experience, or at least a psychoanalytic empathic experience, with him.

Though somewhat doubtful of my complete success, I would like to think that in this short preamble, I have conveyed the idea of my passage from an initial attitude marked by fond hopes and simplification regarding empathy to one that I hope is more mature – one that recognizes the complexity of empathy and respects the natural time span of the creative psychoanalytic encounter.

This is, of course, my own personal history, but perhaps it reflects some of the possible routes to be traveled with respect to this concept, which because of its very nature tends to stimulate in the analyst, on the one hand, fantasies of omnipotence or, on the other, a flat rejection. It can at first appear, in an illusory way, as the philosopher's stone of psychoanalysis, or it can provoke repudiation of something that appears to elude rigorous metapsychological pigeonholing.

A session with Monica: from 'sociability' to recognition of the self

The clinical material with which I will highlight some of the theoretical points made earlier is slightly different in nature to the vignettes usually presented – and different from what I have presented in past

2 Translation by Malcolm Garfield.

works on empathy (Bolognini, 1984, 1991, 1997a, 1997b, 1997c, 1997d, 1998, 2001).

We generally tend to report sessions or sections of treatment with rather sensational developments, fairly spectacular breakthroughs, peppered with important moments of comprehension between patient and analyst, and a strong emphasis on one specific aspect that proves to be the crux of the matter.

For this occasion, I have chosen to report a session that is not particularly exciting in its short-term developments, but proposes, I think, a less elementary image of psychoanalytic empathy, respecting its complexity. This is the aspect I wish to stress here, also distinguishing the 'natural' empathy we encounter in everyday life from 'psychoanalytic empathy,' the fruit of training and experience.

Monica has been in analysis at three sessions per week for approximately a year and a half. She is 34 years old, married without children, and works in an office. She is very 'normal,' sensible, and unhappy. She comes across as a genteel, reliable person but says she is pervaded by a sense of angry impotence that goes back to her childhood. At times she connects this with faint, fragmentary insights that come and go unpredictably and with a vague sensation of a lack of authenticity in her personal and family relationships.

Her father was in his time a public figure, very concerned for his social image. Her mother was also involved in this external representation, which extended to family life because of the need to confirm an ideal model of emotional harmony both within and outside the home. Some of Monica's memories, in fact, made me think with some sadness of the glossy family atmosphere described in Robert Zemeckis's 2003 film *Far From Heaven*. Now her parents have both retired and live in a different city. She has an older sister who left home early on and does not seem to have close relations with the rest of the family, especially since she got married and had a child.

In analysis, Monica is 'well behaved' – that is, she makes an effort to present a smiling face when she arrives, and she is careful not to create particularly conflictual situations with me, devoting many sessions to describing her relational difficulties outside analysis. My attempts to set up a connection between events internal to the analytic relationship and external ones are received by her with polite interest, like everything else I say. For the moment, it is difficult to tell for certain what she really feels and what she does not. In fact, I get the impression that most of these exchanges take place on an ego–ego level (Bolognini,

2002a, 2004e) with a tendency toward logical reasoning and little experiential contact at the level of the self. For example, sometimes when she enters – smiling delightedly and offering a kind of prepackaged a–conflictual atmosphere – I feel I am being subtly sucked into an internal and external attitude similar to hers, as if I, too, were being silently summoned to take my place in the 'glossy' family circle portrayed in Zemeckis's film.

Indeed, I feel that in most of the sessions my inner stance is an interlocutory one; it is as if I had not yet really found her emotional centre of gravity, as if I myself had still not fully plumbed the experience of this analysis. I wait, and I listen to her with a certain degree of interest, following the thread of her associations. Sometimes I get rather bored; at other times I feel more involved, but the overall impression is still of a long lead–in, like the 'approach march' of climbers to reach the foot of the mountain they have set their sights on climbing.

Monica arrives for a mid–week session in an unusually agitated state. It is just before a brief break in analysis of a few days, of which she has been given notice in advance and for which she does not know the reason (I am going to a conference). This interruption in analysis does not appear to bother her.

While on her way to the session, she met a man in the street who seemed to her to be Dr. D., an acquaintance of her husband's with whom they had been to dinner a couple of times in recent months, in a congenial atmosphere. They greeted each other cordially and stopped to chat. To her surprise, she then realized that he was not Dr. D. but someone who looked amazingly like him, almost his double. On the spot, Monica was gripped by a sensation of paralyzing panic; she was unable to say another word. In the meantime, having greeted her and shown spontaneous cordiality, the man did not look puzzled (as if to say, 'there must be some mistake'), as would have been appropriate. He merely continued with politely generic remarks. It then became clear to Monica that he thought he must have met her somewhere, but could not place her; feeling guilty about it, he was playing for time with conversational platitudes, hoping to recall who she was.

Needless to say, at this point in her story, I am greatly interested in this strange situation from an analytic viewpoint, but more generally I also feel rather involved because, at a human level, the situation becomes increasingly strange and distressing, so much so that I start 'to feel bad for her,' as the expression goes.

What comes to mind is a novel by the Spanish writer Javier Marías (*Tomorrow in the Battle Think on Me*, 1994), in which a man who has lost track of his young wife, having been separated from her for a year, picks up a prostitute who is identical to her. Unable to tell whether or not the prostitute is really his wife, he engages in a strategic dialogue, concealing his interest, to discover the truth about the real identity of his interlocutor, who in turn is darkly reticent. I will come back to this intriguing association later.

> Monica (*still shaken by events*): Embarrassed, I realized that this man felt guilty about not recognizing me, on the assumption that we had met somewhere before, and so he felt obliged to be friendly, keeping to general remarks and ending up by asking after people's health, as one generally does in such situations. He asked somewhat cautiously, making sure he kept it very vague, as to whose health exactly he was asking after, it being obvious that he thought I might have a husband and children or that I could be single. He thought that he simply couldn't remember. I was aware of the misunderstanding but didn't have the courage to admit it because of how stupid I would look if I owned up to the mistake. So when conversation flagged, I in turn asked after his health. And he replied, very briefly but in general terms. At that point, I got the impression that a vague doubt was beginning to flicker through his mind, too. The one thing I was sure about was that neither of us seemed to be able to afford to say in all frankness, 'Sorry, I don't know you from Adam!' and admit their mistake.

Listening to Monica, my mind moves in two completely different directions right from the start. On the one hand, I identify with her subjective ego–syntonic experience, and it is like living a nightmare when, on top of the sense of social embarrassment, one adds the feeling of imprisonment and the powerlessness to act in a usefully liberating manner. Side by side with this (to some extent in constant alternation with it), I cannot help but perceive in another part of me an attempt to distance myself from this identification with her. I find myself thinking that the situation is totally bizarre, as if I wanted to minimize it or make it less real.

I remind myself that, after all, it happened to her and not to me. So much so that, paradoxically, I experience a strong temptation to distance myself even further by releasing the tension with a burst of internal sadomasochistic laughter. (This is rather like what happens when we see a bittersweet comedy in which the hero or anti-hero is dogged by persecutory misfortunes, and our implicit realization that they happen to him and not to us enables us to relieve our anxiety with a hearty guffaw.)

At the same time, however, the feeling of pain and embarrassment persists since I continue to put myself in her shoes. And yet, little by little, my mind finds a clearing; there is a potential space where a rather dreamlike, timeless scene can take place: two people who think they know each other gradually realize they are perfect strangers, but are compelled to be formally polite and familiar to each other when realistically they should admit to their mistake. To make matters worse, the subsequent awareness is a source of almost insurmountable anxiety and resistance, and the desire to free themselves from the dilemma is frustrated by the compulsion to maintain an ideal facade of respectable relational 'normality.'

Monica's tale has a fitting end: with no mention of the misunderstanding, the two characters tacitly stage a painless leave-taking, reciting irreproachable expressions of mutual well-wishing in an air of false cordiality, while actually in a cold sweat for the perceived but unexpressed poor figure they cut, both seeking to get away from the physical scene of the encounter as quickly as possible.

A silence follows the end of her tale. Monica appears exhausted, having relived her embarrassing experience in the retelling.

My thoughts at this point are: 'There is a danger that we two, here in the sessions, could end up imitating them,' and then 'It's just like Monica and her parents, with their false facades, unable to bear anything that didn't fit in perfectly,' and later 'This is exactly what happens to Monica every time she is forced to relate to someone in a significant way and with some form of dependency: she bottles up her anger and hostility, which she cannot feel or express, behind a charming smile instead of a ferocious, but genuine, growl.'

My next thought brings me a sense of greater freedom and relief, gaining access to the psychoanalytic garden of the preconscious that borders on a timeless, dreamlike space, peopled with faceless figures. 'Monica's internal object, seemingly so friendly and approachable but in fact so ambiguous and alien, was incarnated only a hundred yards from here; perhaps it is approaching even now. I feel that if I offer my interpretation now in terms of a shift in the session, Monica will certainly understand and agree with it on an intellectual level, and we will again remain psychosocially perfect strangers. But if I wait just a little longer, perhaps the true significance of this internal scene will make itself felt.'

I am generally careful to regulate the patient's anxiety to a level that is tolerable, providing containing interpretations, if needed. Now that Monica has evacuated, at least partially, some traumatic elements through her narration, I feel there is a little room for thought.

While I bide my time, reflecting on our previous sessions with the occasional qualm (had I perhaps tried for 'forced empathism' by unrealistically socializing, like the Dr. D. look-alike?), Monica comes out with something that seems to open up a working space. Now less agitated, but sadder, she says, 'More than the fact that I mistook that fellow for Dr. D., what really strikes me is that I wasn't able to tell him I had made a mistake. Why not? What was I afraid of?'

I know, at least in part, what she was afraid of, since I felt this 'something' almost violently myself as I identified alternately and partially with her while she told her story. But I do not want to be the one to say it to her, because by delegating her feeling and recognition of those sensations to me, Monica tends to deprive herself of them, evacuating them into me. She also deprives herself of a mental function (feeling and recognizing) of which I believe she is potentially capable. On the other hand, her last statement shows me that she is beginning to focus on an emerging problem active in her preconscious.

There is a moment's silence between us. I feel no need to break the silence because I know that Monica does not experience it as hostile and distant. The patient knows that I listen to her and reflect on what she says. She knows I am giving her time to think. Something is moving within; Monica is 'working,' and I bide my time. By now, I am able to feel and represent things with sufficient clarity, and I can stand this waiting and her conflictual reintrojection.

I decide to help her by providing assistance with the question she asked herself.

Analyst: Now, what would you be afraid of? (*I use the conditional tense to convey an idea of vagueness and provide an unrestricted space for her search. By putting the question thus, I make sure Monica does not think that I have a precise answer in mind, but that I am concerned to hear what she thinks. This is important: my question should open up a space, rather than making her feel as if she were under police interrogation.*)

Monica (*swallowing hard and sighing*): I was afraid of looking stupid. In that situation, there were two people who would really cut a poor figure, myself and the man. It was unbearable.

Analyst (*beginning to feel a little less weighed down by an inner burden*): Well, . . . it seems like you're beginning to bear it . . .

Shortly afterward, the session ended with the feeling that a difficult task had been accomplished, a feeling not so different from the labor of childbirth. We part with the impression of having worked well, but it seems to me that there is still much to understand about the bizarre episode that the patient reported in this session.

Reflections after the session

The clinical vignette I have reported gives rise to many different observations. My choice of which to include, as well as being highly subjective, will aim at highlighting points of interest for the topic under discussion. One aspect I wish to dwell on is the very sensitive and accurate perception, which Monica clearly developed after only a few seconds, of the inner stance of the pseudo-Dr. D. – an attitude that changed in the course of the encounter. Monica recognized and described it with labored precision because, though initially different from hers and resulting from a different logical reasoning, it later became identical to her own. It seems that Monica had keenly empathized *malgré soi* with her interlocutor's inability to admit his mistake. Of course, here empathizing must be distinguished from sympathizing; it is more a question of recognizing, albeit with some suffering. Monica, at that moment, felt no sympathy toward the pseudo-Dr. D. – or, rather, toward 'that person faced with those difficulties,' the same difficulties as hers, given that Monica as yet felt no sympathy toward her own self 'faced with those difficulties.' (Her ego and her internal objects did not yet seem ready, in the initial stages of this analysis, to come to the aid of the self in difficulty.)

Empathizing in this specific situation, therefore, means a partial or sectorial sharing of the internal experience of the other by feeling and managing to represent it. In this case, there is no 'good-naturedness,' no disinterested protectiveness, no sweet atmosphere of noble sentiments; there is only confounded embarrassment due precisely to a confounded perception of the wretched and disagreeable things both were experiencing toward the other and toward themselves.

There is a 'poor figure' that Monica cannot yet bear to cut, within herself and with me. It probably has something to do with the underlying feeling that there is a lack of authenticity in our 'taking an interest in her psychological health.' As I mentioned earlier, Monica always arrives for sessions with a pleasant smile and manner and seeks to retain them throughout. Because of this, she could be forgiven for thinking that, in actual fact, I 'don't know her.' And she does not know me, or, rather, how I would be to her emotionally if I really knew her. Many adolescents, for example, are aware that much of their lives is unknown to their parents, in particular their sex lives: 'secret secretions' (Mantovani, 1989).

Would I bear the shared 'poor figure' with her if I recognized her and found the strength to talk about it frankly? How do I make out in my internal relationship with my ideal of the ego? What kind of partner would I be in an analytic episode as embarrassing and detrimental for my image, for her, for us?

So, Monica has empathized despite herself, in a limited and sectorial way, with the pseudo-Dr. D.'s experience. And from a certain moment on, she perceived that he, too – likewise despite himself – was on the same perceptive and presumably representative wavelength as she was in this distressing experience. I believe that this is a remarkable and curious instance of a rather complex form of empathy, since it is based on a perception of the other person's internal organization and some internal movements; yet it cannot be defined as an experience of true psychoanalytic empathy.

Let us go back for a moment to Monica's words at the end of her captivating narrative, the words that gave rise to these reflections. Her statement is like a fork in the road where two ways part, the path of natural empathy and that of psychoanalytic empathy: '*More than the fact that I mistook that fellow for Dr. D.,* what really strikes me is that I wasn't able to tell him I had made a mistake. Why not? What was I afraid of?'

From the patient's words, we managed to reconstruct which of the things that she could fear was nearest to her consciousness – the one she had evacuated in me, partially but not completely. In so doing, she had kept one function for herself, one that was communicative and not merely expulsive. We also saw that a deliberate silence, a kind of pause for breath on the analyst's part, was enough to bring some elements to consciousness, since the analyst had experienced and represented within himself the conflictual area at stake.

The patient regards the first part of her statement ('*More than the fact that I mistook that fellow for Dr. D.*') as an uninteresting hypothesis that can be readily discarded and passed over. The analyst, however, finds it has an unmistakable edge to it; though it lacks the classic linguistic marker of the negative, there is no mistaking a defense mechanism.

Thus, we have before us a denial, giving us the first possible representation of content with which the patient's mental apparatus is unable to cope for the moment, but which is fleetingly signaled, only to be immediately undervalued, disinvested, and abandoned. In such cases, the analyst is like a bloodhound: armed with his previous direct experience as analysand, he 'sniffs out' the denial even before the application of an intellectual methodology, such as a language expert would use to draw the same conclusions. And this enables the analyst metaphorically to open a window in the mind, a particular 'file' that allows him to probe (rather than identify with) another, deeper area of the patient.

In this case, for example, it could be described like this:

'I am terrified by the thought that I was unable to distinguish someone I know from someone I don't. The thought that I distorted that fellow's face to see in it Dr. D.'s fills me with fear of myself as having a psychic malfunction, of being a "psychiatric case." And why on earth should I have had this deep-seated wish or need to meet Dr. D.? With whom is this Dr. D. associated in my fantasies? I'd rather not think about it, or about myself in an extreme state of regression, confusion, need, and desire. All in all, it's better to think about the "poor figure" I would have cut, even though it also gives me the shudders for other reasons. Besides, I'm also frightened by the mere idea that I could unwittingly have exposed a problem of falsity that I would reencounter "in any street" of my life, by repetition – even here with you. More than being afraid of cutting a poor figure, I'm afraid of realizing that I do not really recognize myself, my family, or even you (perhaps because I don't really know them).'

I think this is profound, unconscious psychic content. However, now is not the right moment for an interpretation because the patient would only consider it weird. I mention it here because it came to mind due to her perceptible negation.

In the course of my exploration of empathic situations, I have come to the conclusion that psychoanalytic empathy is something different – more profound and more complex than the natural

131

empathy of which people with well-balanced sensitivity are generally capable (Bolognini, 2004b, 2004c). A sufficiently skilled analyst has the ability – on certain fleeting and unpredictable occasions – to identify with the patient's subjective experience and complex internal organization. This, however, differs from that of the layman in that it involves a broader spectrum, including, for example, the perception of the patient's defensive ego, its activity and force.

What is it that Monica does not want to feel or think right now? And why? How vigorously does she unwittingly oppose deeper contact with herself? Undoubtedly, the analyst possesses a theoretical conception of such problems, but I have come to the conclusion that it serves above all to formalize his choice of technique. Conversely, what happens first is that the analyst 'savors' the experience of the other (and his contact with the other's experience). He perceives and evaluates its proportions and dynamic implications by means of a form of identification that involves the analyst's self – the setting and object of his overall subjective experience. This all takes place well before the intellectual, rational interpretation by the intellectual functions of the ego.

To put it another way: what distinguishes the analyst's way of functioning from that of a psychologist, or a philosopher, or a theoretical linguist is not so much the reference to a different cultural discipline as it is a familiarity with the preconscious and identificatory contact with the psychosensorial experience of the self (Bolognini, 2003b).

The analyst recalls and associates; he sniffs out and savors. He identifies partially or temporarily at the conscious and preconscious level. He does these things because he is accustomed to doing them, because he was trained to do so in the course of his own analysis, and because someone else during his period of training made him perceive a way of using these functions creatively by working directly on him. Part of this psychic work, however, could be carried out instinctively by sufficiently healthy people who, during their upbringing, were lucky enough to have a relationship with an emotionally competent parent or setting. What is specific to the analyst, then, is his ability to maintain a field of perceptions and representations that is broader, more complex, and more mobile.

The analyst, in fact, possesses a certain aptitude for suspension. He suspends judgment while waiting for new developments; he suspends his evaluation of the clinical work; and he may even suspend representational activity (Racalbuto, 1994; Giaconia, Pellizzari, &

Rossi, 1997) in order to facilitate a more spontaneous and dynamic flow of associations after temporarily abstaining. This is one of the possible interpretations of Bion's (1970) celebrated phrase 'without memory and without desire.'

Furthermore, the experienced analyst is ready to make mental room for the emergence of new configurations, linked to a greater or lesser extent to previous ones. An incongruous detail or a split-off element may find hospitality in a 'suspended' secondary framework, before being integrated or reconnected with the rest of the context. And it is rare to find a layperson who can stand this suspended state for more than a few moments, or who is willing to do so. Just think of the haste with which, during a normal conversation, people generally hurry to give their own opinions or advice to those who are making a considerable effort to talk about their doubts and problems, or to explain a complicated personal affair or a conflictual internal experience.

Because of the first-hand experience gained in psychoanalytic training, and not just by reading about it in books, the analyst is on average less afraid of approaching the intermediate intra- and interpsychic areas of others without the reassuring expectation of immediately swamping them with stopgap contents. In addition, through practice and training, he takes care to ensure that certain areas of the professional self are not entirely pervaded by the experience of the other, however intense that might be. In this he is aided not only by his own complex theoretical framework, but also by his habit of protecting an internal area devoted to the natural and preconscious consultation with the masters of psychoanalytic thought and his own colleagues. In other words, he can count on the help of those who by means of genuine introjection (and not merely by incorporation) have become an essential part of his internal world.

This by no means guarantees complete protection from countertransference and 'emotional contagion' (Bonino, Lo Coco, & Tani, 1998), as each one of us knows to his cost. Nor do I intend here to sing the praises of psychoanalysts in an uncritical and idealizing manner. We all know only too well that hardly a day passes without our being reminded in our clinical work of our technical and psychological limitations.

Nevertheless, I am reasonably certain that Monica would have been unlikely to find sufficient patience, willingness to listen, room to maneuver, resonance, comprehension, and maieutic techniques outside the confines of our consulting rooms. Otherwise, her interlocutor might be well versed as far as theory, but untrained in preconscious contact with the self, or, on the other hand, sensitive and responsive, but not methodically trained in suspension and complexity.

At this point, let us return to Monica and the session described earlier. There is another fundamental clinical element that emerges from the material, by which I mean not only Monica's narrative, but also the analyst's shared experience while listening – an experience recognized, thought out, and integrated only with difficulty, as it took place. That element is a countertransference detail: my last bastion of defense, my thought that 'well, in the end, this distressing incident *happened to her and not to me!*'

I do not frequently resort to a device of this nature to neutralize my discomfort in identification, my shared anxiety. I have good reason to think that in this specific situation, there was unconscious defensive contagion, something similar to what Anna Freud (1936) called *defense transference*. Indeed, projective rejection – that is, ridding oneself of a painful experience by attributing it exclusively to the other – might at first sight appear a realistic choice in this case. The pseudo-Dr. D. bumped into Monica, not me, and the two of them created the scenario described.

But it is also true that, on a psychological – rather than a logical – experiential level, the episode also happened to me as I identified with Monica. My attempt to defend myself from the discomfort I felt when I identified with her could depend on the specific aspects of Monica's defenses, a possible object of unconscious identification on my part. The classic expressions are: 'I don't know what you're talking about,' 'It's got nothing to do with me,' 'It's none of my business,' etc. They are used to assert one's total and absolute extraneousness with respect to an unacceptable situation. We sometimes hear people say, 'he dissociates himself from it,' when describing the extent of someone's involvement or, rather, noninvolvement with an object or a situation. Without being aware of it, one can also dissociate oneself from one's own feelings, perceptions, thoughts, and memories, from vast parts of oneself, remaining awake and vertically split in one's ego. At times, 'the left hand knows not what the right hand does,' as the expression goes. At other times, it knows but this does not necessarily mean that it can feel and move in an integrated manner with the other hand; incomplete dissociation exists when there is splitting.

I remember the way a patient of mine described sexual intercourse with the husband she hated. She said that she 'left her carcass at his disposal' and observed the scene without emotion in an alienated way from the outside, as if 'she' were two or three yards away from 'them.'

Run away fast, distance the self physically, escape, 'dissociate one's self from': Monica has perhaps exposed me – and this is my thought on quiet reflection after turning the events over in my mind – to the trial of internal splitting. It is the same thing that she herself, terrified, shared with the stranger, when she unwittingly transformed the intra-psychic into the interpersonal with the pseudo-Dr. D. (as happens when the unconscious overflows from the individual psyche and becomes shared), and then back to my intrapsychic in the session. These events, which are not usually located at the conscious and/or preconscious level, cannot be fully understood immediately.

In my view of empathy, sharing by no means corresponds to empathy but is only a potential precursor (Bolognini, 2002a, 2004e). A great deal of countertransference work (Di Benedetto, 1998) still remains to be done before sharing (which may be a traumatic event, not integrated by representation and working through) can lead to an authentic empathic comprehension. Sharing, or the summons to take part in the interpersonal extension of an intrapsychic scenario, very often has more to do with repetition than with empathy.

Clearly, most of my reflections concern the intrapsychic disposition of Monica's ego, superego, and ego-ideal toward the self. But there are other elements in the analytic field of the session I reported that enable us to consider a further possible development in this analysis. The analyst's association to Marías's novel opens up various scenarios. For example, the subject of sexuality came to mind through the prostitute in the novel. Might not Monica's great concern for the poor figure she cut have something to do with the fact that, though she thought she recognized in the pseudo-Dr. D. a socially impeccable interlocutor, she actually stopped a strange man in the street?

What parts of the transference, or what fantasies, are prefigured in this aspect that was hardly touched upon in our subsequent explor-ation? And what is the connection between this episode and separ-ation? Perhaps the preannounced separation (the analyst's upcoming absence) might have something to do with the patient's failure to recognize the object. Might it not be linked to a possible defensive attempt to disinvest the object itself? And the missing wife in the novel, who also came to mind, may perhaps be obscurely linked to the patient's sister, who left home early for reasons connected with love and sex.

Thus, my intuition is that sexuality and separation, love and genuine mutual recognition appear to be closely linked in Monica's internal world. All this will probably prove useful in the future.

For the moment, this is as far as I will go in the analysis of this session with Monica, not wishing to claim to be able to see more than is really there. Let us give the analysis time to unfold and develop Monica's transference in all its rich complexity, which is far greater than the matters discussed here. I have chosen to focus on certain specific elements, since my interest is to highlight some fundamental points that I can briefly summarize as follows:

1   *Empathy is a complex state* that is not limited to concordance with the patient's conscious, ego-syntonic experience (the hypothesis of gross 'simplifiers'), nor with a specific conscious or unconscious part privileged by a particular theory (such as Kohut's 'wounded narcissistic self'). On the contrary, it requires space and suspension for an elaborate identification with the patient's various internal areas and levels.

2   *Empathy cannot be planned,* because it comes about through occasional, undeterminable openings of the preconscious channels of the analyst, the patient, or both.

3   The analyst's training gives him on average an advantage over most other people in being able to create the intra- and inter-psychic conditions suitable for the development of empathic situations *with greater ease and in a more elaborate way.*

4   *Empathy has nothing to do with kindheartedness or sympathy,* because it may come about through a type of identification that in itself is not particularly flattering or gratifying, sometimes made possible by the specific resonance with corresponding 'undesirable' areas in the psychoanalyst or his negative feelings.

5   Psychoanalytic empathy includes the possibility to accede over time and *through the working through of the countertransference to the reintegration of split-off components,* whose existence is not only hypothesized – in the manner of engineers grouped around a drawing board – but experienced and recognized by the fully aware analyst.

6   *If the conscious is the natural seat of the organization and formalization of experience 'in the light of the ego,' the preconscious is the place for the exploration of the experience of one's own self and that of others.*

To my thinking, analysts may be compared to skin divers who, equipped only with natural instruments, are able to explore the marine environment to a depth of a few meters. This possibility is rather modest compared to the abysses that open up below them. However, it is invaluable when contrasted with the vain efforts made by many of our patients who have never been able to set foot in the water.

9

THE GLASS HALF EMPTY OR HALF FULL

Dream work and oneiric working through

'*Träume sind Schäume*': 'Dreams are froth.' Freud, in his essay 'The Unconscious' (1915b, p. 168), referred thus to the generally widespread opinion of the senselessness attributed to events in dreams.

Popular opinion regarding the dream often oscillates, as is noted, between idealization and complete devaluation: dreams either 'do not mean anything' or else they contain great truths, if not amazing premonitions.

If, on the one hand, Freud (who by nature was not at all favorably disposed to the 'magical') had loudly denied the idea of a 'lack of meaning,' on the other hand, he certainly had not lost sight of the opposite risk – that of an idealization of the dream as a psychic product of highly functional quality. In fact, he had expressed a balanced position between these two extremes, in line with his well-known way of proceeding between two polarities.

In 'Remarks on the Theory and Practice of Dream-Interpretation' (1923), for example, he pointed out to analysts the danger of idealizing 'a mysterious unconscious,' even stating: 'It is only too easy to forget that a dream is as a rule merely a thought like any other' (p. 112).

Regarding dream work, already in 1901 (*On Dreams*) he had expressed himself in a disenchanted way, bordering on the reductionistic:

> Dream-work is not creative, . . . it develops no phantasies of its own, . . . it makes no judgements and draws no conclusions; it has

no functions whatever other than condensation and displacement of the material and its modification into pictorial form, to which must be added as a variable factor the final bit of interpretative revision. It is true that we find various things in the dream–content which we should be inclined to regard as a product of some other and higher intellectual function; but in every case analysis shows convincingly that these intellectual operations have already been performed in the dream–thoughts and have only been taken over by the dream–content.

(p. 667)

When I read this passage, what struck me was the fact that, immediately afterward, Freud cites – almost associatively – mathematical calculations as a possible example of that 'high and more elevated intellectual activity,' evidently characterized by abstraction and conceptualization. Today we understand such abstraction in a more absolute way as the uniquely meaningful and noble activity among many possible high–level, integrated activities. (See, for example, the current valorization of the not-so-banal concept of 'emotional intelligence,' or of 'harmonic fine tuning of the ego-self,' and, more in general, of the explorations into creative thought, and into artistic creativity in particular.)

The *dream work* consists of the process of transformation of latent content into manifest content, through the four fundamental mechanisms of condensation [*Verdichtung*], displacement [*Verschiebung*], considerations of representability [*Rücksicht für Darstellbarkeit*], and secondary revision [*Sekundäre Bearbeitung*].[1] With regard to this last component, secondary revision or elaboration, the quantity will be greater in 'daydreams,' very often unconscious ones (Freud, 1900), and lower in actual dreams.

In 'Dream Work and Working with Dreams' (Bolognini, 2000), I cited the contributions of some authors who in various ways, over subsequent decades, have attributed more complex functions to the dream work, almost as though they noticed a sort of relative conceptual restrictiveness in the rigorous limits established by Freud.

---

1 *Translator's note*: The English translations of these terms are taken from Laplanche and Pontalis (1973).

Andrade de Azevedo (1994), for example, noted that: 'The anti-thesis between distortion and representation was never totally resolved in Freud's work on dreams. Emphasis on distortion tells us of defensive aspects and functions, while representational aspects suggest working through' (p. 1188).

With contributions that have not always been convincing – but interesting if only for the trend that together they gradually came to form – many authors have suggested the idea of dream work that is more complex than a dedication to the covering up of deep contents. This has occurred to such an extent that it would perhaps be philo-logically correct to preserve the original Freudian meaning of 'dream work,' according to a historical perspective, and to propose that of *oneiric working through* for the further functional attributions later suggested by various other authors.

I will briefly summarize, picking out authors and intentionally not entering into the specific merit of their works. Adler (1911) spoke of the dream's 'functions of premeditation'; Maeder (1912) spoke of a *fonction ludique* [playing function] of the dream, as a preparatory exercise to subsequent operations in external reality; Grinberg (1967), describing 'elaborative' dreams in phases of integration, highlighted the patient's growing reparative capacity as he begins to know how to take care of himself; Garma (1966) outlined a 'broad' way of thinking during dreams – an archaic-type thinking, intensely visual, but one in which judgments, reflections, criticisms, and other mental processes exist, belonging to the same type as those of being awake; the theoretical line that starts with Winnicott and extends to Bollas placed value on the experiential dimension of the dream; De Moncheaux (1978) hypothesized a reintegrating function of the dream with respect to trauma; and Matte Blanco (1981) reexamined a possible aspect of displacement in dreams, like an opening – at times, a creative one – onto possible new places, times, and representations, and saw condensation as an attempt at integration of different spatiotemporal categories.

There are still others: Kramer (1993) was concerned with the effects of dreamlike activity on the mood-stabilizing function, and Greenberg and Perlman (1993) with the increase in REM sleep in situations of complex learning. Fosshage (1997) brought out the generally synthetic function of primary process, which emphasizes, through highly intense sensorial and visual images, the affective coloring of the experience.

At the summit of these contributions – in a comprehensive vein, in my opinion, based on some consonant directions – we can place the great contribution of Bion (1962, 1970) on the dream's metabolic function, taken up again and later developed in an original manner especially by Ferro (1998, 2002, 2010) and Ogden (2003).

Also in the same work (Bolognini, 2000), I brought out the prospect of *a potentially and occasionally creative area of dreaming* (with all Freud's cautions and limits about not falling into the previously mentioned idealization of the dream), based on the possibility of representation, of decomposition and recombination of the elements at play in the subject's internal world, thanks to the beneficial and reconnective effects of primary process and to the reorganization permitted by secondary process, which alternate in varying degrees. In this perspective, it is possible to conceive of *aspects of the dream work that are not only defensive*, so that one can speak of *a process of oneiric working through of experiences and probably – sometimes – of thoughts.*

Here is an initial, brief clinical example that can be considered according to this perspective.

A patient who has arrived at a rather advanced stage of her analysis – and who is coming to grips with an occasional depressive state (later overcome) on the occasion of the departure from home of her 25-year-old, economically independent son – referred to 'feeling down.' Immediately afterward, a dream from the previous night came to her mind: *She put 'the heart of a metal wire' into a vase of flowers in the living room, 'to hold them up,' after which she took apart and reassembled the petals, changing them around, 'in order to find the right combination.'*

The dream clearly brought in the patient's need for support, but also the beginning of her internal project of working through. As in the vase of flowers and also in the family suffering from pain – even though this was natural – changes were being brought about inside herself, in the operations of replacement and recombination of the elements at play, in order to find a new life arrangement.

The area of research on *figurability* (Botella & Botella, 2001), which has characterized a particular aspect of French psychoanalytic explorations in the last decade, has further highlighted the function of mental representation as a progressive event 'in itself' – that is, the very fact that the patient is capable of achieving such a function, after a certain amount of work, appears to be in itself a dynamically positive fact of the environment of the analytic process. The patient succeeds in *giving representation* to experiences and contents that it is not taken for granted will be representable by him, and indeed, important analytic work is necessary in order to arrive at that result.

We have already witnessed in passing the theoretical–technical recovery of other negative analytic 'waste products.' An example is the value placed on the implicit positive aspects of negation (which is, at any rate, even with 'non-' in front of it, a representation that causes a thing to exist mentally, even if it is denied at the time) (Freud, 1925). More than any other, Green (1993, 1998) has studied this specific aspect of mental functioning.

In the same way, today we note that the representability of something is not an insignificant event, which in fact causes the represented thing to exist in the subject's mind, awaiting possible further elaborative transformations. In this sense, here are two very simple dreams from two different patients, dreams that can clearly be related to their transference implications.

1. Some time ago, a patient, who was markedly disappointed that her childhood needs were not met, had the following dream after a month of analysis: '*My father, completely dressed, put on my blue coat. It was too tight for him; he couldn't button it.*' The blue coat is what the patient puts on in coming to her sessions. She fears that her analyst here today, like her parents at one time, doesn't know how to, and cannot, 'put himself in her shoes.'

We can consider this dream production according to two different dynamic perspectives, which I would categorize in a very simple way: the perspective of the 'half-empty glass' and that of the 'half-full glass.' From one point of view, the patient is not yet capable of thinking and communicating her fear of not being understood directly to the analyst, so the dream work camouflages the underlying scenario in order to smuggle it past the censoring process. From another point of view, the relationship between patient and analyst is beginning to become representable, though in a figurative way, and with recourse to a curious, 'mixed' solution that involves an image as much as a play on words.

Both these things are true: from a certain point of view, the patient is defending herself; from another, she is making progress. According to these two different points of view, *the subjective experience of the analyst at work changes:* in appreciating the patient's progress, the analyst will work with a greater feeling of being useful and, all in all, with greater satisfaction.

2. Another patient knew that I would be going away for a professional meeting. *'In the dream, my mother was in bed, alone, with curlers on her head. I felt very angry.'* I told the patient that she probably felt angry because her mom (at one time) and I (at present) have 'something else on our minds' (or heads). Our 'heads are full of other things' (the patient's mother had dedicated herself wholeheartedly for a long time to the patient's very ill younger sister).

From the associations, it then emerges that the patient is angry with me because she thinks that, indeed, I *do* have other things in my head, but not nonspecific things: rather, I have in mind precisely the things that 'will make me beautiful'! The 'curlers,' the patient says openly, are seminars, meetings, etc., that feed the analyst's narcissism, and so the analyst is ironically represented as similar to the famously inhuman mother of a 1929 song, *Balocchi e Profumi* [Toys and perfumes], the lyrics of which include the following: ' "Mamma!" cries the little girl, her eyes full of tears, "You never buy toys for your little girl; you only buy perfumes for yourself!" '[2]

Here, too, as in the preceding clinical example, we can adopt one of two different perspectives and see the glass as half empty or half full. Do we assign more importance to the camouflaging function that we call the dream work, or to the representation and the pre-thought that asks to be thought and that is then, in the exchange in the session, relayed more directly to the present recipient, the equivalent of that deep-rooted internal object?

If we observe these two brief dreams, then, from the point of view of dream work understood in the historical Freudian sense, we see primarily creations of the well-known mechanisms that camouflage deep meanings (through the four fundamental operations described earlier).

This perspective will furnish us mainly with valuable indications of the intrapsychic formulation and the functioning of the patient's defensive ego.

Conversely, if we take from it the progressive gradient of representation and intra-analytic communication, we are then capable of appreciating the patient's positive functional progress, especially in the relationship with the self and with the analyst-object. The patient is

2 Translation by Gina Atkinson.

succeeding in mentally representing for himself the experiences and contents that are difficult to think because they are unpleasant and painful, and difficult to communicate because they are unpleasant for the interlocutor, and thus are potential triggers of fearful negative relational developments (if not contained and worked through by a good-enough analytic situation).

This functional advancement is not at all to be taken for granted, and the capacity to appreciate these mental and relational events allows the therapist to form a different dynamic perspective, increasing his keen perception, his faith in and satisfaction with the evolving analytic process.

The experiential aspect of the dream, important in itself – like that of representability – to the outcome of these theoretical–clinical considerations, has been considered and found valuable by various authors of different traditions: for example, Winnicott (1971), Bollas (1987), Atwood and Stolorow (1984), Andrade de Azevedo (1994), Fosshage (1997) and Ogden (2003). This experiential aspect permits an operation of getting to know the self's capabilities that until that moment had not been contacted and experienced, and it creates a special psychic condition that allows human beings, even in retrospect, to feel the representations of the dream as 'true,' even if they are not 'real' (Bolognini, 2000).

This sensation of the dream's experiential 'truth' is not uncommonly transmitted to the analyst as well, the one to whom the dream is narrated, and it puts him in the situation, in turn, of sharing the patient's experience 'live.' This condition of a 'shared dream,' or reverie, permits the 'dreaming of dreams not dreamt and interrupted nightmares' (Ogden, 2003).

Clinical aspects

Building on the framework provided up to this point, I will present material from two clinical cases in which, on several occasions, I again found important evidence of a partial elaborative activity that was already present at the level of dreams.

I would like to clearly reaffirm that the goal of this *reportage* is not that of identifying and 'discovering' new facts or psychoanalytic concepts, but to highlight and place particular value on facts and concepts that have already been noted, proposing them, however, according to a different perspective. That is, I will bring out some beginning elaborative aspects, rather than those of defensive 'work' (although the latter exist). This perspective can allow the analyst to grasp the progress of his work in sessions *in a subtle way*, even where it appears that the patient seems only to be resisting, hiding, and confusing the waters, to the therapist and to the patient himself.

First clinical case: Enrico

Enrico was a young man of 19, very stubborn and belligerent, when he began an analysis at three sessions per week, which became four sessions per week after two years. The analysis lasted a total of six years, during which his initial paranoid mistrust in the relationship with the object underwent deep, meaningful transformations. The two dreams that I will report are relevant to, respectively, the period immediately preceding the shift to four sessions, and the final period of the analysis.

The end of the second year of analysis

Only for a short time had the patient begun to bring dreams into sessions, and in recent weeks he was bringing in many of them, consistently the more 'colorful' ones.

Enrico is an inveterate film buff, and he often makes verbal slips during his narrations, saying 'film' instead of 'dream' and vice versa. A fantasy of mine – that if he dreams more he will have less need to see so many films – is doubtless theoretically debatable and, furthermore, not very realistic, but it is connected to my impression that, if he has greater trust in me, in himself, and in the analysis, he will end up having a greater facility for *his own* 'films'/dreams – original, homemade, and personal ones.

He dreams, then, that *he loans some videocassettes to himself, and he notes them down in a notebook, as he does in reality when he loans videos to his friends.* I tell him he has begun to 'loan to me' (i.e., to bring to sessions) his 'videocassettes'/dreams, but that he still feels the need of 'noting this down in a notebook' – that is, of controlling this oneiric offering. Can he trust the situation? Will I ruin the videos? Will I 'give them back' correctly? In telling him these things, I do not concretely emphasize 'he began to . . .,' but, inside

145

myself, I reserve a specific thought for this particular developmental element.

In this brief vignette, it is difficult to unequivocally limit Enrico's progress to either the intrapsychic register or the interpsychic one, since in reality both are present in a complex way. In every treatment, both the intrapsychic and the interpsychic predominate alternately, one over the other according to the moment, but they are always interconnected (Green, 2000; Bolognini, 2004a). If, on an inter-personal level, he brings me his dreams, it is, however, just as true that on an intrapsychic level, his defensive ego is relaxing its censure and allowing him to look over his 'films'/dreams, provided that this hap-pens under adequately supervised conditions of exchanges with me, on the one hand, and between different areas of his mind, on the other.

In the following associations, in the course of the same session, the idea of a possible transition to four sessions appears for the first time. In the next two months, that project gradually takes shape and in the end is accomplished.

Three years later

Enrico is much better, many things have changed in his life, and sometimes the fantasy briefly surfaces in my mind that sooner or later he will begin to think of terminating our work together.

He brings in a dream that surprised him very much:

He dreams of simultaneously betraying his own girlfriend and his own best friend, having a secret meeting with a young Japanese woman who, in the same dream, would seem to be officially making love with his friend. In making love with her, he is struck by her voice: she emits delicious, extremely sensual moans.

After some pauses and an initial disorientation, he associates to the fact of having at last achieved a dream in his life: against the advice of his parents and girlfriend, he secretly bought a motorcycle, a Honda, and was very enthusiastic when the salesman started the engine and he heard its roar – it was marvelous!

We both begin to laugh, and in the exchange that follows, a com-ical pursuit starts up: in the dream, who represents whom? Given that he is from the Italian province of Romagna (and people there are

146

known for their passion for motorcycles) and is a compatriot of the well-known motorcycle racer Valentino Rossi (who is his idol and who drives a Japanese motorcycle), does the motorcycle represent the girl, or does the girl represent the motorcycle?!? Which is the real, overall, powerful object of desire?

As it happens, what follows in the session takes an unexpected turn, a decidedly less frivolous one.

For Enrico, a motorcycle has always been a symbol of freedom. It is a different freedom from that provided by a car; it is a more individual freedom, more playful, more connected to the pleasure of 'going out and about,' than to the duty of having to go to an exact place to fulfill an established duty, perhaps with a briefcase or some other necessary baggage.

I do not need to go to great lengths to tune in to these feelings; remembering my own adolescence is enough to locate the taste of that independence and a freedom without time, without obligations, without tasks that are too goal-oriented or precise.

I think that, over the course of the analysis, Enrico has gradually learned to wander rather freely through his own thoughts, traversing the equivalent of urban alleys, side streets, and mountainous dirt roads, with a growing sense of reappropriation of his freedom and his mental capacity. I think, too, that he has slowly started to explore and con-quer sexuality as a personal experience, in which he now moves in his own way and with satisfaction, *driving* with his own individual style.

But what is that 'betrayal' represented in the dream? Why does he betray his girlfriend and his best friend? Which configurations, which fantasies, which internal movements are expressed, utilizing deep cur-rents? Which eternal aspects of the Oedipus complex are at play, in which the 'best-friend' part of the father/rival, ambivalently loved, or the 'regular girlfriend' of the mother come to be betrayed, in attune-ment with the secret acquisition of the Japanese motorcycle?

I understand it toward the end of the session, when the thought comes up of being able to terminate the analysis in the not-too-distant future, unexpectedly and with some embarrassment, among thoughts of growth, of knowing how to drive, and of leaving. Sooner or later Enrico will go away, he will go beyond me/the father/the best friend, and beyond the analysis/the mother/the regular girl-friend. He begins to feel that he has the means and the desire to do this – and also, in a way, the guilt.

In a certain sense, it was I who sold him the Honda, piece by piece, and we constructed it together in the analytic workshop, over the course of several years. But the guilt is there all the same – the guilt of growing up and of making the parents grow old, going away from them and leaving them behind to become part of the past.

Enrico's dream can certainly be seen in the light of its aspects of camouflaging deep content, a camouflage aimed at permitting the dreamability and remembering of that content to slip beyond the nets of oneiric censure. But I am also struck by the communicative richness of the dream, which not only brings into the picture the underlying concept (= to go away, having acquired the means), but also transmits the emotional and sensorial experience of the desire, and depicts the experience of betrayal as connected both to separation from the basic maternal object and to the oedipal conquest – to the detriment of the paternal rival – with a plan and an announcement of further working-through passages.

To return to this dream and its intra- and interpsychic implications: as a typical Italian father who is somewhat apprehensive, I must have thought that the exciting aspects implicitly present in a competition motorcycle like the Honda, with many 'horses' perhaps experienced as indispensable for going beyond the parental objects and winning a personal contest, called for a certain reassurance.

A little analysis was still needed in order to pack the suitcases calmly, to transform 'Enrico/Valentino Rossi' into a more relaxed 'Enrico himself' (perhaps endowed with a reassuring Vespa . . .), and in order to be able to separate from each other in a less elated and 'roaring' atmosphere, but also a less exciting one. That then happens in a rather natural way, without heroism and without particular incidents, in the course of about a year.

Second clinical case: Giovanna

Giovanna is a 39-year-old woman of pleasant appearance characterized by a sort of 'mixed' elegance: some typically feminine attention to detail (including an expert touch when it comes to accessories and jewelry), blended with frequent use of masculine elements (a short, 'energizing' haircut, the fact that she always wears trousers, and her quick and practical attitude, as well as her man's watch). In any event, the overall picture is quite harmonious.

Her physical history is notable for the fact that she has balance problems, which have been the object of thorough clinical investigation, and she has undergone vestibular tests of all kinds – CT scans, repeated MRIs, etc.

She is reasonably happily married to a rough but affectionate man – by whom she feels loved and whom she, by and large, cares for greatly in turn, above all for his authenticity and frankness, Sexually, she is rather reticent; she never thinks of initiating sex, and when he – as often happens – makes an advance, her first reaction is to oppose it strongly, not finding any desire in her own self; then, however, 'having gotten over the initial block,' she participates with great pleasure.

She has two children in primary school, whom she loves but for whom she is extremely apprehensive, with excesses in fusional attachment (their nightly presence in their parents' bed, etc.).

Her mother, an affectionate housewife and 'safe base,' died when Giovanna was eighteen, unexpectedly, while her daughter was on vacation. The grief does not seem to have ever been adequately worked through; the patient remembers never having cried but having been in a prolonged state of detachment and relative coldness, which she overcame at that time by busying herself with practical tasks. She recalled that she left again two days later for the seaside, almost as if nothing had happened.

Eight years later, she turned to analysis – with a female analyst – in relation to her initial problems with balance, after exhaustive clinical investigation failed to solve the matter. Her treatment lasted four years, and the situation improved a good deal, 'even if not completely.' Giovanna has a partially positive memory of that experience: the analyst was professionally flawless, but she found her somewhat cold and not very creative.

Two years ago, at the same time as her father suffered a severe stroke, the patient contacted me and began treatment at three sessions per week. In addition to the same balance problems, she presents an aspect of marked hypochondriasis, convinced that she has an incurable disease.

Giovanna does not go to visit her father in the hospital for the first weeks of his stay, believing that she needs to protect herself from emotions that would be too strong to withstand. Her husband and her older sister end up facilitating her position of self-exemption, although with ill-concealed annoyance, and they stand in for her in all the upsetting circumstances.

Actually, after a few months of analysis and of progressive acknow-
ledgment of these defensive evasions, Giovanna manages to visit her
father in the hospital and to withstand her fear of seeing him in those
conditions. Five months later, her father dies. Giovanna faces this
second bereavement in a somewhat more integrated way than she
faced her mother's death, but she tends to close off the experience of
pain very quickly.

Two sisters

After the death of her father, a contentious legal battle begins between
the two sisters over their inheritance. The father, who had a preference for Giovanna – thanks, in general, to her more affectionate personality, compared to the grumpy and contrary sister – left more in
material goods to her, and the sister won't stand for it.

Giovanna brings in a dream:

> *'I see in the mirror that I have two enlarged pupils, but one is much larger
> than the other. My God! – so there's something that doesn't work in my
> head! . . . And this confirms it, the sensation of being incurably ill. How is it
> that this thing won't go away?!? . . . It's not normal!'*

She makes the association that when she talks about other people, she
would like to be able to see them, to put a face to them. Not comprehending, I ask her to what she could be referring, and I try to make
things more fluid:

Analyst: For example?

Giovanna: After the death of my mother, I had an appointment
with a psychologist who asked me to show pictures of my
family. So, today I brought pictures of my mother, my father,
and my children with me: could they be helpful, or is this
useless?

Analyst: I think that you may have in mind what I said two sessions
ago when I asked you to 'help me imagine your mother'
because you never talked about her. Today it seems that you
want to help me 'imagine' these other family members, by
bringing me their concrete images.

Giovanna (*approvingly*): Yes, that way you can understand. I simply
said to you, to describe her, 'She is a mother.'

Giovanna takes the picture out of her bag and holds it up to show me. I look at it: it's true; it is a mother. Then, in the same way, she shows me her husband and children, then her father with the grandchildren.

Analyst (*consolingly*): It's true; she is a mother.

Giovanna (*reflectively*): I didn't bring any pictures of my sister. I didn't even think of it. I don't think about her.

Analyst: In the dream, the two pupils are widened – that is, they're highlighted in a way, but one is much larger than the other. You were 'the pupil' of your father, who 'saw' you more and who left you a larger inheritance. The word 'pupil' comes from '*pupa*,' which means *doll* or *girl* in Latin and Italian: the father's favorite doll/child. As for your sister, today you won't let me see her at all . . .

(This is followed by a few minutes of silence.)

Giovanna (*She is struck by this*): In the film *Joe Black*, the main character talks separately with his two daughters before he dies. It gives you the shivers. The older daughter has a secret love for her father, but she's always felt second best. But with the little sister, who is the light of his life, the conversation is similar to a dialogue between lovers.

Analyst: Did this touch you?

Giovanna: Yes. There's a closeness. There, in the film, it's an honest-to-goodness dialogue . . . and it says things. . . . I have always received, I never . . .

I have the feeling of disconnected speech that can compose itself only with difficulty.

Giovanna: Because I couldn't quite . . . (*She makes a gesture with her arms of 'giving' or of 'going toward,' creating a sense of being stuck or of impotence*) As opposed to the second daughter in the film, who crouched down near him, I absolutely wouldn't. Oh no, I even remember the deep embarrassment on the two-seater couch in the living room, he and I sitting next to each other, alone. The fear of being complimented, as then often happened – even if in fact his words were very measured – the discomfort. He would call me 'my baby'!

Analyst (*with an exploring tone*): Just discomfort, or pleasure, too?

Giovanna: I would say just discomfort, if I answer straight off. There was a similar relationship between him and my daughter. I thought he would have preferred the boy, as he hadn't had a son:

to go fishing with, and so on. He did like him, it's true, but he really had eyes only for my daughter; maybe she was a 'me-when-I-was-little.' She is a very sweet girl.

Analyst (*amused*): Another pupil . . .

Giovanna (*laughing*): Yes.

I reflect: here, then, in the father's pupils, there is a secret passageway. It is a passage the patient is familiar with, which she has gone down more than once, but which also frightens her greatly, as if she does not know precisely where it may lead.

Dad and Mom

In a session a month later, Giovanna brings in another dream. *The street in which her house is situated is visibly closed at the end, and there is no way through. She is standing beside her car, which is stopped on the road with the door open, with her father sitting inside in the passenger seat; she is talking to a female child-neuropsychiatrist she knows, and while she is talking, she notices that beautiful red cherries begin coming out from under the car's hood.*

I think that there are many new elements in this dream: the oedipal 'secret passage' does not appear to be an open passageway any more, given that the street is 'closed at the end, and there is no way through.' And it is no longer secret: the child neuropsychiatrist is there, talking to Giovanna, and is there for the appearance of cherries out from under the hood of the car.

It seems that a maternal para-excitatory function provides some sort of assistance to the daughter; it is not yet clear whether this is in a predominantly protective sense (as it would seem to me) or an inhibitory one.

Regarding the cherries, Giovanna says she likes them very much; the ones in the dream were really appetizing. In the course of the session – with Giovanna's great effort – new connections and fragments of memories emerge regarding her father's love for her and hers for her father, as a girl and as a teen. This relational channel is later blocked when she realizes that he was really 'as if in love' with her, and this upset and embarrassed her, as was seen in the earlier session reported above. Since then, she has stayed away from him and from these thoughts.

In analysis, the patient had already let very timid signs of amorous transference (Bolognini, 1994) emerge here and there, although barely perceptible and immediately disappearing. I tell Giovanna that the 'beautiful red cherries,' which unexpectedly 'begin to come out' of the hood of the car (that is, out of the transferential 'motor' of our relationship and of her treatment), seem to symbolize, with color and taste, the unexpected appearance of something that is sweet and desirable, here and now – like at that time with her father.

My countertransference is spontaneously affectionate: I believe I am reliving faithfully enough the complementary countertransference pertaining to the paternal object, without any particular difficulty and without disturbing excitatory components. The patient is nice, and she inspires a certain tenderness. It comes naturally to attribute a certain genital working-out to her that she effectively manifests with her husband, even if with reticence and in the conflictual manner that she had previously described.

The analyst – in his role as listener, as direction-finder, and as container of excitements – is also represented by the 'child neuropsychiatrist' in the dream: a reassuring female figure who can give room to 'childish' parts of Giovanna.

The subsequent associations (which I will not set out here, for the sake of brevity) lead Giovanna to moments of contact and emotion in thinking about her father and mother, evidently now both present on the internal and transference scenarios, and the session ends with a warm sense of having refound mislaid objects and feelings.

In greater depth

In the following session, Giovanna seems to have surprisingly and solidly regressed to hypochondriacal fixations. She had been to an emergency room as a result of her vertigo, and she does not believe that she is not suffering from some physical pathology.

I feel a sense of total disorientation with respect to the emotional and relational climate of the day before, with the alienating sensation of finding myself in some sort of 'other' reality, which is incongruous and disconnected from what I had expected, as if some important things have happened about which I am totally in the dark. I am bothered by something in her tone, which is very distant and stiff, and I feel I am being openly accused of being at fault for the lack of progress or, rather, for the worsening of her subjective condition.

Furthermore, I am also bothered by the fact that Giovanna seems to want to put me up against a strong sense of the 'objectivity of her subjectivity,' as if to say: 'You see, Doctor, you traced my experiences to psychological things, but, instead, who knows what physical conditions there may be behind them?!' (That is: 'Let's be clear – all that stuff that came out in yesterday's session was drivel!')

In fact, a long interval of complaining and then outright accusations follows, and then another dream, from the previous night:

Giovanna sees her dog digging a hole in a field that Giovanna cares about a lot. (The dog, in fact, dug holes as a puppy and yesterday evening had actually dug one, for unknown reasons.) Giovanna yells at her and runs to stop her, but she slips with her foot ending right into the hole, thus falling backwards so that she ends up under the dog, who starts to pee. Giovanna tries to shield herself with her hands, but the liquid ends up partially in her face; inexplicably, even without wanting to submit to this, she does nothing to avoid it.

I am quite struck, above all, by the presence of the dog in the dream. I think that dogs, these incomparable companions in our lives, are often cast by the dream's director as representatives of parts of the self and of instinctual aspects of the dreamer.

Here there is an activity (the digging) that the patient (representative of the ego in the dream) does not want to be carried out; perhaps yesterday she and I had begun digging a little too much, ruining a 'meadow'-cover that she needs to keep in order, so that she may keep the surface of things pleasant (the 'meadow' seems to be, that is, an emblem of a personal style of defense). Furthermore, by digging, one 'unearths' things and people who are dead and buried.

The 'hole' seems to well represent a sudden and unexpected 'hole in her mentalization,' and it calls to mind the 'dizziness' of which Quinodoz writes (1994). 'Falling backwards' in the dream testifies to the patient's regression in the course of analysis, with her ending up lying down, as she is here on the couch.

I am also struck by how, even though she doesn't want to do it (conflict), Giovanna stays there, under her dog, to experience contact with a warm, organic liquid, coming from within, bathing her face. The urinary nature of the liquid is linked to a disparaging qualification, 'disgusting,' which highlights the conflictual contact with elements that are at the same time desired but rejected by the superego. In the scene described, it is the humiliating aspect of having to 'be under'/ 'be subjected to' the physical–emotional contamination that is represented. The problem of incontinence also comes into play, of knowing how to hold oneself back or not (from the point of view of the ego–superego relationship), but also that of knowing how to express oneself or not (from the point of view of the ego–self relationship).

Yesterday, in talking about her dead parents, Giovanna had clearly been one step away from crying, and my own eyes had filled up, out of a sort of visceral consonance; but she had stopped herself immediately, not allowing herself to be moved. I think that the dream reopened – conflictually, as always – this situation, which strongly begs to be experienced, lived, communicated, and shared.

> Analyst (*slowly, with pauses, to give space to thinking and to go over the patient's story sensorially*): That warm liquid . . . that runs down your face, you didn't avoid it, in the dream . . .
>
> Giovanna (*faster than I, with a less reflective rhythm than mine*): It's strange: I didn't want to, but I stayed there. Then another very strange thing happened: I stuck my finger into the dog's anus, as her stomach was bloated with air, and she let out the air and the bloating receded.

I interpret that Giovanna feels a great deal of anger, which creates a lot of inner tension for her, which in turn needs to be gotten out in some way, and it seems that she needs help to do this. I believe she is resentful toward me because of our digging, because at times she would rather 'cover it up' and 'leave the meadow untouched.'

She makes the association now that she is trying to help her sister-in-law's daughter, who is a 'hermetically sealed' young woman, suffering from depression. She closed up after the death of her father, and Giovanna had said to her: 'I saw you as human, as yourself, when you cried out as they lowered your father's coffin into the grave. You need an analyst's help.'

I reply that, while she is talking about that young woman, she is also talking about herself.

> Giovanna: I think you're right. Last night I saw a television program on the life of St. Rita. When the saint's mother died, I was overcome by desperation. I cried a great deal, too much. . . . It's not balanced.

155

Analyst: You are in the same state as your dog: you have a lot to cry over, and you need to do it. But you fear that it is not balanced to do it; and you also fear that if you feel the pain and cry, then you will lose your balance.

Subsequent reflections

You cannot empathize (in a strictly psychoanalytic and nongeneric sense) with this patient unless you can relate to both the parts represented in the dream: *the dog*, representative of the self that offers contact with basic experiences that are strong and necessary; but also *the Giovanna of the dream*, the conflicted representative of an ego that would like to keep intact the covering meadow–field of its own mind.

There is still a long path to follow in order to recover a sufficient portion of her memories and to integrate, in an acceptable way, the parts from her own humanity that have been cast away. This is true today for Giovanna, as it was true in the past for Enrico and for the other two patients whom I mentioned very briefly.

If I look behind, as one does on mountain hikes, taking note of the disequilibrium between current knowledge and comprehension and that of some time ago, I notice what a long road we have traveled together, the patients and I, and with how much hard work and how many uncertainties – three steps ahead and two backward in the best of cases.

Dreams have often tried to confuse us, divert us, or sidetrack us, but they have also given us a big hand. They have helped us share the experience of colors and atmospheres; to unexpectedly call onto the scene past or distant figures, or simply possible ones; and to fit in among them with a sort of creative 'casting,' these figures and feelings that were previously 'unthinkable,' now in a spirit of combinability. The analysis is implicitly asked to pursue and to complete, together with us, what the subject alone would not have been capable of accomplishing.

The dream is a wish to represent. Thus, dream work and working through in dreams seem to proceed together in turn, variably intertwined among themselves, and we do not know how much in conflict and how much in parallel with each other. It would seem that there are alternating phases, from what we are given to observe in sessions.

All in all, we must recognize that a certain part of the work is done by them, the patients, on their own, by night and far away from us, with an obscure, already studied (but perhaps not yet well-enough valued) type of working through: resavoring, symbolizing, putting together, and rehandling in the dream that which moves chaotically and conflictually inside of them.

It is clear that this nocturnal intrapsychic activity does not leave out the analysand's capability of coming into contact with a potential recipient, with a complex parental equivalent who is available to try out the interpsychic paths of reverie and to engage in *co-thinking* (Widlöcher, 2001), and – when things go particularly well – to draw on psychoanalytic empathy. But the analyst often finds himself served up on a silver platter of novelties and opportunities for comprehension, yet again, which are anything but obvious in the way they present themselves. In my opinion, it would be appropriate for the analyst to make use of an internal attitude of appreciation for these developments (and sometimes – with proper parsimony but without meanness – an external appreciative attitude as well).

There remains, of course, a wide margin of the unknown with regard to the intra- and interpsychic systems that regulate these events during an analytic treatment. For example, I myself could feel that I was wearing the blue jacket described by the first patient; I thought again about the curlers that were pointed out to me by the second one; I joined Enrico in fussing with his motorcycle in the workshop; and I dug in the garden with Giovanna's unrestrainable dog. Certainly, something was born of all this; but 'what' or 'who' placed at my disposition all this 'unreality' that was so true?

PART THREE

From the Transpsychic to the Interpsychic

10

PELEUS'S HUG

Survival, containment, and con-viction[1] in the analytic experience with serious pathologies

Like many psychoanalysts of my generation, I come from psychiatry. I worked as a psychiatric doctor for many years in public institutions, first in a psychiatric hospital and then in a specialized ward of a general hospital and in a regional psychotherapy center. I maintained a continuing relationship with them as an advisor, even after having dedicated myself to psychoanalysis full-time.

I continue my supervisory activities of psychiatric teams, with pleasure and passion, using the classical method of periodically working through shared experiences in groups. Judging from the ongoing request, it seems that supervision in the field of adult and adolescent psychiatry may be useful to the workers who participate; it is certainly so for me, in an atmosphere of companionable awareness that permits contact and continuing revision of our knowledge on the subjects of psychotic and borderline functioning, primitive basic defenses, and group and institutional dynamics.

In 1992, I was among the founders, together with some very fine colleagues, of the Committee on Serious Pathologies of the Italian Psychoanalytic Society, and I think that for a psychoanalyst, it is truly invaluable to have cultivated a certain professional familiarity with those levels of psychic life and the pathology connected to them. This pathology, in fact, can be transmitted – as we know very well, by

---

1 *Translator's note*: The author splits the Italian word *convincimento* [conviction] into *con-vincimento* ['co-winning'].

161

now – both transpersonally and transgenerationally, in what Money-Kyrle (1951) described as the traditional trading of unhappiness among human beings. As I have already noted earlier in this book, Kaës (1993), Kaës, Faimberg, Enriquez, and Baranes (1993), and Losso (2000, 2003) have described a modality of 'transpsychic' transmission in which, lacking transitional space, the mind cannot transform and give back exactly what it receives from the other.

In transpsychic transmission, which is accomplished in a primarily narcissistic dimension, the intersubjective space is extremely limited or absent, the transformative mental apparatus of the recipient is bypassed, and the contents are unelaborated and often pervasive and disturbing (Bolognini, 2005b). One could say that in these cases, communication does not take place *between* subjects, but *through* and *beyond* them (or a good part of them), and the recipient's preconscious is deactivated or flattened.

In this chapter, I intend to point out two relatively undervalued aspects of the containing function of the object: that of the *capacity of the object to survive*, which was explicitly discussed by Winnicott (1958) and then taken up again, more implicitly, by Bion (1959) with the concept of *attacks on linking*. However, in my opinion, this capacity has not been emphasized enough in the study of treating seriously ill patients. The second important aspect of the object's containing function that I will discuss is *internal space* – studied, for example, by Meltzer in his work on autism (1975) and on the 'claustrum' (1992).

In recent years, the transformative function of the analytic container through reverie has been privileged (in many ways, justifiably so). The Bionian contribution in this regard has been developed in highly original studies by authors like Ferro (1996, 2002), Ogden (2003, 2005), and Grotstein (2005).

My contribution is instead aimed at the importance of an antecedent *formative phase of the container*, in a certain sense *more primitive* (even though it is certainly not correct to speak in strictly temporal terms about these complex processes), with respect to the initiation and development of the functions of reverie.

As will be apparent from the situations described, I am taking particular account here of primary basic functions connected especially with evacuative needs, with the investigation, that is, of a container that – even before giving a shared and representable meaning to the elements of the experience – accepts and tolerates the containment of tensions and excesses, and that first of all permits the experience of a 'hospitable space.' I consider the study of this very primitive phase a necessary integration of the important recent studies mentioned above, which in my opinion describe further, more evolved interpsychic passages.

I will begin by presenting a brief sequence of psychiatric work, then move on to observations pertaining to more strictly psycho-analytic work.

Psychiatry: from the transpsychic to the interpsychic

This clinical vignette took place at the Day Hospital of Venice for young psychotic patients, where I worked for some years. (Currently, I continue this activity as a supervisor in the affiliated Day Hospital of Bologna.) This vignette consists of an exchange between Alfredo, a 21-year-old, seriously psychotic patient, and Ester, an expert nurse, very maternal and capable of good contacts with patients.

Alfredo is collaborating with Ester in the kitchen to prepare the midday meal, as usual. But it is evident that today he is feeling particularly bad: he is nervous, tense, has a dark expression, and seems more absorbed than usual in fantasies that visibly take possession of him, though he doesn't talk about them, and it is unclear how much they may possess him in a persecutory way. Ester's usual affectionate cordiality seems to produce a contrary effect, since she increasingly irritates him.

We know that Alfredo's father died when the son was 9 years old; but we also know that, even before that, he was rarely at home because he was a sailor by profession. Furthermore, Alfredo's mother was rather seductive, making him sleep with her for long periods both before and after her husband's death. She is an impulsive woman, hot-tempered, who uses very strong expressions and communications in all senses, both erotic and aggressive, which have produced apparent incestuous anxieties and violent rage reactions in her son.

The evident lack of a containing experience on the mother's part did not promote the creation of an internal space in the son, who in turn tends to massively evacuate his inner tensions in an urgent way. Alfredo doesn't seem to have benefited from adequate para-excitatory protection (of a protective barrier against excitatory stimuli that are too strong for his psychic apparatus) – either from his mother, given her temperament and very exciting, concrete, and invasive ways of communicating and expressing herself, or from his father, due to his absence both in reality and in the mother's mind.

His father (or at any rate, *a father* in the mental symbiosis between Alfredo and his mother) could not then fulfill the separating and structuring function necessary for his development as an individual. Alfredo is currently in the throes both of anxieties of incestuous guilt and of anxieties stemming from internal pressures to separate – potentially healthier ones, but conflictually experienced.

Today the medical doctor did not come to work for family reasons.

Suddenly, without apparent motive, Alfredo grabs a basket of vegetables and hurls it violently at Ester; and immediately, without giving her time to recover from her surprise and alarm, he screams at her: 'Alfredo!!! What are you doing?!? Have you gone crazy?!?'

Ester, upset and in a state of internal confusion, runs away, terrorized.

An hour later, the usual team meeting among colleagues takes place.

Ester, calmer and comforted by the presence of the group, gradually succeeds in thinking again. She tells what happened and focuses on the fact that what most confused and disoriented her was not the throwing of the basket, but to see and hear the patient in a 'crazed' state – shouting words that *she* should have used, with the expression that would have come to her spontaneously if he had not used it: 'He had become me, and he made me hear as though I were him. I felt that *I* had become mad!'

The 'transpsychic' bypasses the individual's mind, with violent elimination of borders and of normal functions of thinking and internal regulation. While a basic level of physiological fusionality can be shared in the interpsychic – economically advantageous, with areas of calm coalescence, and with neither the subject nor the object feeling invaded, negated, or 'substituted' by the other (Bolognini, 1997b, 2003a, 2004a; Fonda, 2000) – the transpsychic 'enters' into the other in anomalous ways and in a traumatic manner that cannot be elaborated. It occupies the other like a foreign body that can also enter into the host's 'control room,' becoming a parasite, substituting for the self and inducing it to repeat the traumatic action, this time in an active form, to the detriment of a new victim.

Repetition (Freud, 1914) of micro- and macro-traumas is here directed not only toward what is not remembered, but also and especially to what has not been mentalized and metabolized. The most primitive defense mechanism is based on *identification with the object by transforming active into passive,* and evacuating into the other the parts of the self that are experienced as intolerable. Alfredo has identified himself with the object, which in this case reunites within itself, in a paradoxical way, the characteristics of a symbiotic object, of an object of partial incestuous desire, and of a judgmental superego object.

Alfredo cannot manage to completely abandon a reassuring and unconflicted fusional regression, because it is crisscrossed by pressures of evolving separation (and he is guilty of conflictually wishing for a rupture of this symbiosis); he cannot confront oedipal anxieties if he doesn't feel protected by adequately limiting objects (the father/medical doctor); he is not capable of bearing the guilt of his own aggression, for fear of ruinous retaliation, and thus he *becomes* the other, with intimidating and repressive functions. In allowing ourselves to play with a neologism, we could define this occasional transformation from passive into active as an 'identification with the screamer' (i.e., essentially, identification with a specific type of aggressor).

Alfredo is not perverted; he has not erotized or libidinized this projective maneuver, and he does not wield it with skill. This massive evacuation is not his habitual strategy; it is the result of one of his internal ruptures (a split) and of a spasm, an expulsive contracture. His interpersonal action asks to be contained (Ferro, 2002) in a 'concave' object capable of resisting without breaking and of working through the trauma. This object was not, though, to be Ester, but the work group.

I will not elaborate here on the concept of 'the collective container' (the ward, team, or institution), nor on the dialectic 'construction (pharmacotherapy, hospitalization) container,' often confused in psychiatry for reasons that pertain as much to the ideology of the workers as to the deep fear, on their part, of contact with the more regressive and needy aspects of seriously ill patients. I am more interested in examining the concepts of 'endogenous persecutory pressure' and containment from the analytic point of view, and I will do so after a brief mythological digression.

From clinical work to mythology and back to the clinical again

The legend tells us that the hero Peleus, in love with Thetis – daughter of Poseidon, king of the sea – after having seen her enveloped by the foam of the waves, asked for her in marriage. But since she was a goddess and he a simple mortal, Peleus had to undergo a very difficult trial in order to win the right to join himself to her.

The goddess, initially not inclined to accept him and endowed with the capacity for metaphor, challenged him to hug her and hold her tightly while she transformed herself in different ways, in a long and silent struggle.

In order to have her, he must never release the hug.

According to various versions of the myth, Thetis transformed herself while in his arms first into fire, then into ice, then into arrow-heads, snakes, and many other forms, the last of which was, curiously, that of a cuttlefish (maybe because of its slippery and thus evasive surfaces, I imagine). But Peleus, who was secure of his love, never let go, until the goddess – defeated but, we might think, overall 'con-vinced'[2] of the certainty of his desire for her – abandoned herself to him, to marital bliss, in his arms.

It is very difficult to imagine a more romantic and more intense love story than this one, and there is a surprising analogy that connects this event with the type of relationship often created between analyst and patient in the treatment of seriously ill patients.

There must be an authentic passion for this type of work, for confronting the difficulties and the possible injuries – from which the therapist will almost certainly not be spared either – along the path that leads toward at least a partial recovery of the capacities to live, to tolerate upsets in the primary object relationship, and, in the end – eventually – to love.

Tenacity, endurance, enchantment and disenchantment, even the essential availability of a certain 'aspect' (in the sense of becoming – with time and for a certain period – at least somewhat internally and temporally 'joined,' almost in a family relationship with the patient, in a working area of the mind) are necessary elements in order for an analyst to truly devote himself to, and with sufficient continuity, the treatment of seriously ill patients.

In what follows, I will indicate some factors that I personally

---

2 *Translator's note*: The author splits the Italian word *convinta* [convinced] into *con-vinta* [co-won (over)].

consider fundamental to this goal, beginning with the concept of 'internal space.'

The creation of an internal space

To create an internal space if there is not already one is an absolute necessity in all cases in which internal persecutory pressure – which can be occasional and reactive, or, more unfortunately, part of a basic, structural, characterologically narcissistic-evacuative disposition – impedes any introjection whatsoever. That is, I refer to *all those situations in which the patient simply cannot take inside anything that comes to him from the object – for example, from the analyst or from the treating environment*. And the analyst's attention specifically to this functional parameter – which corresponds, then, to an internal structural organization of the patient – produces a very particular therapeutic effect. At bottom, such an effect is instinctively noted by everyone in daily life, but often one does not gain an adequate awareness of it from our psychoanalytic literature.

At a recent conference, a colleague presented the text of some sessions in a clinical group, reporting them with precision and appreciable sincerity. One session in particular, occurring near a break in treatment, presented a *pattern* that in my opinion was *absolutely typical*, a pattern that can be found in many similar situations, and that I would summarize and formulate as follows:

1   The patient vehemently attacks the analyst and the analysis, experienced subjectively in that moment as negative presences that are useless and frankly persecutory.
2   The analyst tries (usually with a mixture of lucidity and concomitant serious emotional difficulties) to connect the patient's reaction to the circumstance of separation and to the corresponding childhood experience, in order to give an understandable meaning to the current intense emotional experience.
3   The patient denies the analyst's words and gradually overwhelms her with sarcastic criticisms and a complex feeling of dark mistrust that attempts to bypass the work accomplished.
4   The analyst, after a couple of further small, unfortunate traces of exchange, deeply affected by the sense of functional devaluation and personal mortification, refuses then and there to actively

167

intervene, and she leaves it to the patient to proceed with his self–revelations.

5　After about twenty minutes of ruthless denigration, the patient's tone changes: he appears 'emptied out,' and at that point extremely depressed, even desperate.

6　The analyst, perceiving the *empty interior* and the consequent *drop in internal pressure* that have been created in the patient, hears that this is the moment to tell him 'something,' and she intervenes in a modulated way with an intentionally generic observation (almost as though to communicate: 'I am still alive! And our relationship is also still alive!' – but in an indirect and discrete way).

7　The patient immediately appears comforted and indicates mostly with a calmer and more interlocutory tone his reaction of being available now to receive something from the analyst.

8　The analyst proposes an essentially similar connection to that formulated without success at the beginning of the session.

9　The patient's associative flow resumes as he accepts and pro-duces meaningful ties among the elements presented.

It seems evident to me that in the process just described, the analyst may have had to – perhaps to her regret – accept, contain, and tolerate the catabolic, toxic, and lethal component of the patient's internal contents, of his relational connotations and his experience of himself and of the world: something that occupied the internal space and that impeded mental nourishment and transformation.

My colleague, struggling with her patient who did not listen, who did not 'take in' anything, gave space to the negative (here understood not as something that isn't there, but something qualitatively bad and painful), like a mother who has understood that *the child cannot take in any food if his visceral turbulence is not first evacuated.*

The analyst cannot and must not deny this 'negative,' expecting to force the positive into the patient's mind (either in the sense of actively 'placing' something in general, or in the sense of putting in vital and 'positive' things, like interpretations, associations, representations, etc.), if there is no space for this.

More specifically: I maintain that one can speak of an 'internal pressure' of the negative (the psychic equivalent to the somatic ten-dency to free oneself from indigestible gastric content or from oppres-sive intestinal fecal content), which must be recognized and must not be opposed. That is, the *gathering of its 'ex-pression'*[3] (as pressure from the internal toward the external – the equivalent of the fire, ice, arrowheads, and serpents evacuated by Thetis into the container of Peleus) *is part of the process of cure, much earlier than interpretation.*

On the other hand, Peleus, by creating (with his arms, in the concrete image proposed by the myth) a space capable of holding Thetis's primitive turbulence, also creates the conditions for constructing within this a containing capacity and for being able to then be accepted, in turn, inside of her, in a subsequent genital dimension that anticipates the capacity for exchange and mutual welcoming.

It is evident that this mythical metaphor, apparently dedicated specifically to the relationship between an adult man and an adult woman, may also be applied to all the stages of object relations, putting forth the theme of containment as a primary, formative need of the internal space, as well as the theme of the force of desire (in the broad sense) and of the holding and tenacity of the original maternal container, in addition to that of subsequent ones.

This analytic function and analytic space *are not a guaranteed endowment of the analytic couple as such.* Often a great deal of work is necessary in our clinical endeavors for the construction of these – in part, work that is specifically based on *sharing the experience,* when this function has not primarily been accomplished in sufficient measure by those who raised and functionally shaped the child.

Here, and not only in the interpretive arena, one sees the essential difference between a true therapist and a layperson: when confronting the interlocutor's evacuative communications/emissions, the latter tends to be *convex and not concave.* That is, he immediately begins speaking about contents, without offering receptivity to the evacuation (without listening, or listening only briefly), and instead tries to immediately provide advice, or to explain to the other the reasons for his situation, or to recount to him that which he himself experienced in the past. He tries, in short, to 'force immediate receipt' of something from the other.

Usually, that happens because the layperson, after a little while, cannot accommodate the other's anxiety, tension, or doubt within himself. But the patient, hampered by endogenous persecutory pressure, cannot receive or even emit, so that these exchanges can certainly

---

3 *Translator's note:* The author splits the Italian word *espressione* (expression) and makes it *ex-pressione* to indicate that *pressione* (pressure) is being expelled.

169

be defined as 'dialogues between deaf people.' There can be an actual dialogue only when an internal space in both is created – through a *de-tensioning process*.

The analyst who has been well analyzed, even with all his human difficulties, has at his disposal a certain internal space, achieved through experience and technique, and can allow the other the beginning of an experience of welcoming acceptance, which in daily reality is not at all obvious.

Invasions, bouts of confusion, undifferentiated sensations

Mario experienced (and brought to life in me) two sessions of hell – with tension, denigration that appeared to have no motive, associative schizoid discontinuity, and overall a protracted sensation of nameless, apparently meaningless malaise.

It is a painfully recurrent state of affairs for him; he is like this in his life as well, with people who are significant to him, and it is for this reason that he is alone.

Today, as on other occasions, he is nervously agitated on the couch, transmitting a sense of tension and of compressed and unexpressed suffering. He reminds me of a person who might have a tormenting kind of *colic* – that is, a state of tension that he cannot manage to resolve in an evacuative way due to a downhill obstacle, a spasm that obstructs the normal downward flow of contents into a hollow organ. It is only that, in this case, the 'hollow organ' is the mind, and the painful sensation is that his mind cannot transmit to me anything other than these undifferentiated sensations of tense, generic malaise, without representational correspondents.

Having known Mario for two years, I am aware that his capacity to utilize the analysis is fundamentally disturbed by a strong narcissistic, antidependent resistance, which blocks the perception of his feelings, needs, and desires toward the object (i.e., in analysis, toward me). In the third session of the week, Mario finally succeeds in producing and relating a very simple intrusive fantasy to me: he imagines entering inside me, 'from behind, through a hole in your armchair.'

This fantasy, recounted not in an innocent way but with a certain perceptible aggression, could steer the therapist toward reading the situation strictly in an aggressive sense or, alternatively, as perverse. That is, the patient could thereby express his desire to control me, to dominate me, and – in a concrete sense – to 'put it to me in the rear,' which means, both figuratively and relationally, to deceive me, to neutralize me as the analyst, to castrate me as the parental equivalent, to subvert the setting, etc.

All this is certainly true, but by now I am capable of thinking that things are not *only* like this. I am able to think, after these two years of work, that *other basic needs* are also involved:

1   The need to be *contained*.
2   To be contained, yes, *but in a relatively transparent way*, in order to avoid conscious and direct recognition of dependence – hence the intervention of his narcissistic ego–ideal, which impedes the relationship.
3   To *transform passive into active, in order to moderate and control the experience of regression*, of which he has an absolute need, but which terrorizes him.

The result of these internal deductions of mine is that, finally, I am capable of *not interpreting* (Bonaminio, 2003) reactively and prematurely and of, instead, giving him the time and the method of *being* in the relationship *without interpersonally exacerbating the intrapsychic conflict* (that of the ego torn between libidinal needs of the self and narcissistic pretexts of the autonomous ego–ideal), waiting for a possible internal resolution, one that will be simply 'witnessed' by me.

A little at a time the colic resolves, the internal spasm loosens up, and associations appear that refer to the external ('Today there was a crazy traffic jam on the bypass to get here – I thought I wouldn't make it, but fortunately the traffic started to flow and I got here on time'), but ones that describe a recovery from the internal 'peristalsis.' The patient gradually calms himself, and when he leaves, he even says 'thank you' in a fleeting but sincere way.

It is evident that this situation must be understood in a complex way: the need to be contained is only one of the factors at play, and in this case it ends up being the most important at that moment: the so-called point of urgency. The other components, the aggressive and partially perverse ones, were also present but were dynamically less significant. It is clear, then, that the analyst must have the capacity to act according to the situation: if he always makes use of a containing attitude, *a priori*, and only that, without knowing how to change registers toward other possible technical options, he would probably have to analyze his own underlying, characterologically masochistic tendency.

The analyst must essentially synthesize himself with the patient through a complex, perceptive articulation, so as to form a mental image of the various parts of the patient that are in conflict; this image must not be overly simplified if the analyst is to avoid falling into 'empathism.'

Diana on the attack

The patient's internal turbulence, injected into the transference, sometimes poses serious problems of containment through challenges to the object, which is presumed to be incompetent at containing, and which comes to be attacked in order to reverse the narcissistic and affective 'injury' suffered at one time – at a time, moreover, when infantile dependence on the object was real and almost total. The subject unconsciously seeks, then, a repetition of the traumatic event with parts of it inverted, usually via the primitive mechanism of transforming passive into active.

Even in this uncomfortable trial-like circumstance – to really say it with a euphemism – these situations at times reveal a notable potential for change; to be honest, it must also be said that one can be reasonably certain of that only after the fact.

Here is a session with Diana, a combative patient who in this period of the analysis is poorly tolerating her affective dependence on the object, and she places herself in opposition to it as much as she can.

Diana (*in an aggressive manner*): From your mailbox outside, I saw that you correspond with foreigners.
Analyst (*noting an atmosphere of attack*): What does this provoke in you?
Diana (*with an air of ostentatious superiority, and in a loud voice*): Nothing. (*Silence – tension – then, with a superego-ish tone:*) There shouldn't be any mail in the mailbox – patients shouldn't see it!
Analyst (*thoughtfully, in order to provide a respite in which the interpsychic situation can take its time, I make a rather high-sounding, generic, holding-back type of comment, aimed at creating space*): Mmmh!
Diana (*pouncing on this high-sounding element with the air of one who*

172

wants to demonstrate having discovered the other in a private, indecorous position): You're grunting!!!

Analyst (*clearly annoyed, in the moment, by the aggressive and obviously manipulative intrusiveness of the patient, who has adopted a grotesque and distorting term to mock my expression of thoughtfulness and render it incongruous*): Mmmh!

Diana (*excited and triumphant: she has the impression of having finally caught the analyst in the act and placed him in difficulty, and she reproves him with a satisfied, pithy, superego-ish tone*): Why did you do it!?! You shouldn't have done it!!!

Analyst (*still taking my time and creating space*): In your opinion . . .?

Diana (*after a pause, perplexed, with a beginning hesitation at dealing with the available space*): Am I to understand . . . that it isn't like I said?

Analyst (*noting that an internal movement of the depressive position is beginning to occur in Diana*): Yes.

Diana: I'm aggressive. I attack you.

Some discussion follows during which Diana, with anxiety, reveals the feeling that she has 'a mass in my brain.' It is a mass, she says, 'that won't dissolve.' It emerges that she cannot manage to cry – that is, she cannot dissolve her rage with pain. It seems that she may have reopened the dialogue in the session, with more livable affects and thoughts, more integrated and more communicable ones.

But here something unexpected occurs: the telephone rings and, very faintly in the background, the blaring voice of a colleague bypasses the answering machine's silent setting, so that Diana, with ultrasensitive perception, though not comprehending the content of the call, manages to catch a few words from afar.

Diana (*again very excited and triumphant*): IT'S A WOMAN! AND SHE EVEN SAID 'CIAO' TO YOU!!![4] (*There is a brief pause. Diana, visibly disturbed by that intrusion and by the subsequent exclusion, given the caller's confidential tone and perceived friendliness, seems to again adopt a defensive stance of narcissistic–maniacal–evacuative attack; then, however, she yields, and moves away with a completely different tone, somewhat alarmed.*) I'm afraid of being psychotic – insects come to my mind.

---

4 *Translator's note*: The use of *ciao* in Italian indicates a tone of casual informality.

Analyst: Perhaps disturbing thoughts or feelings . . . and in a certain sense, one could also consider that this caller sneaked into our session like an insect . . .

Diana (*worried, with a sense of internal alarm*): I have the feeling that my body is attached to the couch like glue.

Analyst (*noting the patient's anxiety in relation to the regressive experience taking place, and to her unexpected, quite strong, poorly controlled emotions, which are connected to an intense transferential conflict*): Are you afraid of 'attaching' to me?

Diana (*apparently not responding to my intervention; actually providing a useful association, produced, however, with apparent discontinuity with our discourse, as though to proudly deny the interpsychic function that I hear beginning to start up*): I got my fibroma when I began the other analysis. But I could have two children. What a lot of hard work, though! Without a mom . . . My parents-in-law gave it to me, a bit of the 'mom' treatment, but in their own way . . .

Analyst (*noting that I am in part the inevitable heir of this 'mom who isn't there,' and in part the unified representative of the 'parents-in-law who gave a bit of "mom,"' even in the ambivalence experienced and conveyed by Diana*): It's apparent that 'one can' — one can conceive of children/thoughts, together with someone else. Certainly, with 'a lot of hard work,' and they arrive 'in their own way' — that is, without our being able to control them very much . . .

To create space with a patient in an evacuative phase is a difficult operation, necessary and often fruitful, but one that requires a lot of patience. The curious thing, and in a certain sense the paradoxical one, is that to create space with a patient who has narcissistically invested — and perhaps also erotized — his own evacuative defenses and his own ways of actively attacking both the other and the work done in common can be the most refined of all forms of vengeance. Negative countertransferential currents are exploited for a technical goal, converting into technique (through the process of 'giving space') one's own instinctive reactions of annoyance and anger, to the point of gradually leading the patient to the depressive position. That is, the analyst places the patient in a position in which he can reintroject, a little at a time, that which he has expelled, making it ever more difficult for the patient to defend himself by externally projecting something that he should instead contain and recognize as his own.

It is as though the analyst is thinking: 'Now I will arrange this for you: in creating space between us and inside of you, I will help you recognize and know this part of you. You will make contact with the pain.'

There is aggression in this, without a doubt. But must we speak in terms of the analyst's sadism? No, because the analyst will be there to share the pain, with humanity, without dissociating himself from it and without 'foisting it off,' *in toto*, onto the patient.

Sharing is as much a precursor of reverie as of possible empathy. Containment is often the passage that precedes sharing, and the analyst is called upon to fulfill that basic function, whose roots extend down into the key primary relationship.

Regarding Peleus, once again

Among the various characters of ancient Greek mythology, Peleus is one of the most curiously controversial. Summarizing, more or less, his vicissitudes, we could say that he truly embodies the temporary nature of mortal beings: he was driven out of various places in which he had gotten into trouble and placed himself in one mess or another (from Aegina, for having, together with his brother Telamon, killed his stepbrother; from Thessaly, for having accidentally killed his father-in-law Eurytion during a soccer game; from Iolcus, where he was defeated in a fight with Atalanta and falsely accused of insulting Astydameia, wife of King Acastus – who, in love with him, was rejected).

In short, none of these went well for him, and each time – following the custom of the day – he had to 'purify himself' somewhere else. He redeemed himself once and for all, achieving maturity and attaining the respect of both men and gods, with the conquest of the divine Thetis.

What strikes me in reading the various versions of this conquest is the presence of a significant figure in the background: Chiron, the wisest and most knowledgeable of all the Centaurs, so expert in the arts of medicine, music, gymnastics, and prophecy that even the gods (such as Asclepius himself, the god of medicine) turned to him as an advisor. Chiron had already rescued Peleus from the other Centaurs who were about to kill him, and in the episode of the conquest of Thetis, he decisively supported Peleus during the difficult trial (Pindaro, *Nemea* IV 60).

To contain someone, one must be or have been contained, the myth seems to say. One must have had this experience, or at least one needs to have it in the course of the work.

How can we not read, in this great allegory from the past, the proto-equivalent of the intergenerational chain that transmits the capacity to nurture the immature being and the relationship, up to the point that it is possible to become an individual and to lead a separate life?

How can we not find this again in our daily activities − in analytic supervision and in group discussions in psychiatry − the 'assisted elaborative containment' of the colleague who narrates his own experience? And (giving necessary weight to the idealizing aspects implicit in this image) how can we not recognize in Chiron the analyst himself, when he supports the patient in the crucial task of learning to contain episodes of bad weather in both himself and the object, toward the coveted end point of the capacity to create with the other an intimate and generative union?

11

THE COURAGE TO BE AFRAID

Phobos and Deimos – Fear and Terror – were born of Aphrodite and her illicit relationship with Ares, god of war and of violent deaths, 'the straight-limbed, impetuous, drunken, and quarrelsome God of War' (Graves, 1955, p. 67), who in all of Greece had only one temple in his honor. Phobos and Deimos fought with him, and they were sadistic and bloodthirsty.

In 1877, when Asaph Hall discovered the two satellites of the planet Mars, he did not hesitate to designate them with precisely these names, conscious of the glacial cold, the dark, and the distance – at the time, insurmountable – that separated them from our Mother Earth and Father Sun. Separation, cold, the unknown, desperation, hate, and death are the hallmarks of the primary experience of fear in the human being.

Mythology and literature have transmitted a vast array of representations to us of our internal and external fears, and it is an arduous task for anthropologists, historians, students of religion, archeologists, art experts – and psychoanalysts, in fact – to identify the symbolic functions of representatives of fear, distinguishing (when that is possible) the symbol from the thing that is symbolized, for a cultural, 'tri-dimensional' reading of the objects of fear that is not limited to concrete facts.

The series is practically infinite: it begins with great natural catastrophes (a universal flood, earthquakes, drought, pestilence, volcanoes that suddenly explode), which can symbolize – in addition to archaic historical events in external reality – internal events as well, usually with corporeal roots (traumatic births, constitutionally disordered states of organic suffering, distressing incontinence, destabilizations of the ego, etc.). The litany then moves on to terrifying representations of the maternal figure (the Medusa with snakes for hair, capable of paralyzing victims by inducing terror; the witches in all their variations, ready to eat children like Hansel and Gretel – or perhaps to corrupt them and keep them always close, or to regressively transform them into animals, taking away the autonomy of the established order, thinking, and words, etc.). Also included among the representations are tremendous paternal images (ogres, destructive giants, werewolves, 'bogeymen,' and so on) and castrating equivalents of every type (devastating enemies who come from far away, often the ocean; in Europe, the most feared were the Vikings and the Saracens, originating respectively in the north and the south).

The contemporary arts, too, have furnished a continual representation of fear, often knowingly at the border between the internal world and the external one, with significant awareness of the possible dark interweaving between concrete objects and fantastic ones. Movies have presented a variety of spectacular solutions to the ego's fears – those of an ego in the throes of drive states, that is, and with an internal susceptibility to trauma that forms a continuous potential threat, without name or form, which demands to be represented. Here, then, are the devastating creatures of this world (sharks, giant snakes, grizzly bears) and of other worlds (science fiction, with alien invaders, 'things from another world' that engulf everything, artificial intelligence, etc.), the uncontrollable assassins of thrillers, natural catastrophes, airplane crashes, and so on.

Totally arbitrarily, I choose to cite here – for their evocative power – two scenes from among the thousands at our disposal, one from film and one from ancient literature.

In *2001: A Space Odyssey*, Stanley Kubrick portrays the endless fall into cosmic infinity of an astronaut whose cable connection with his spaceship is broken. The desperate cry that is lost in the void and becomes distant is that of absolute separation from the maternal body and, at the same time, from the self in the psychotic catastrophe: it is the cry of loss of the self, in the external world and in the internal one.

Taking a leap backward through millennia, Hector's goodbye to his wife and son – before the conflict previously predicted by destiny against the invincible Achilles – is pervaded by the mature adult's fear mixed with pain, and it therefore ends up being even more striking precisely because, in such fear, regression does not prevail over the element of adult awareness.

From maximally traumatic mental absence to maximally aware mental presence: man experiences fear in an infinite number of ways. Conversely, the possible protective supply of psychic defenses is minimal in both these last two examples, though they are very different from each other.

Fear, terror, and panic

The Italian word for fear – *paura* – derives from the Latin noun *pavor* and from the verb *pavere* [to be frightened or afraid], related to *pavire*, to hit or to fall to the ground (from which, curiously, comes the word *pavimento* or *sidewalk*), implying events such as fainting, a succumbing or giving way, or flattening oneself to the ground in order to hide.

Terror is defined by its etymological origin: the Greek *tromos* is connected to the verb *tremo* or *treo*, which means *to quiver, to shudder* intensely due to fear, *to shiver*. It derives onomatopoeically from the root *tr*, pertaining precisely to a person who shivers (Papadopoulos, 2002), and designates a further state of fear, with the initial compromise of an effective response. But terror is not disorganizing like panic, which pervades the subject, destabilizing him and breaking down his reactive functions in a distracting way.

This distinction is not trivial, nor is it intellectualized, because we know how *intolerance of the feeling of fear* can be connected to an *internal certainty of its being inevitably transformed into panic* (Barlow, 2002; Bolognini, 2004d; De Masi, 2004) and, thus, how the subject might see in emotional anesthesia – obtained through various means that range from negation to dissociation – a defense against an uncontrollable process of total disability ('panic,' in fact).

Physiological fear is a reaction in the face of a danger that, though involving the body in an important way, does not entail the acute levels of the intensely upsetting mix-up of terror, or the extreme functional disorganization of panic. It is a natural response, necessary and appropriate, aimed at preserving the life or the integrity of the subject and his objects, while maintaining the defensive and reactive potential sufficiently preserved.

He who is always without fear or physiological anxiety places himself in serious danger in external reality, and that thoroughly justifies

179

the *distinction between the courageous person*, who is capable of perceiving and eventually confronting fear, and *the irresponsible, reckless person*, who does not notice the danger. Internally, *Angstsignal* [signal anxiety] constitutes a necessary warning device in the normal awareness of the danger of massive exposure to primary anxiety, let alone to the risks of the fantastic 'danger situations' described by Freud in *Inhibitions, Symptoms and Anxiety* (1926).

Conversely, he who lives in a pathological condition of perpetual fear, leaving aside the objectivity of external dangers, is usually wrestling with internal ghosts of various types, of which we analysts are the interlocutors of choice.

I will recount a brief, enigmatic clinical experience that interrupted as it came into being: a sort of unelaborated 'clinical object' that nevertheless impresses itself on my mind like an emblematic representation of pervasive fear, observed by me many years ago in a human being whose secret I will never be able to know.

A champion of fear

Perhaps it is true, as Schafer (1983) states, that unconsciously we are all members of a community in peril, in the sense that we all share, with more or less awareness, the chronic threats described by Freud in *Inhibitions, Symptoms and Anxiety* (1926). These are the total loss of the object of love, the total loss of love, castration – the superego's archaic punishments. To these Schafer adds paranoid terror, depressive impotence, fragmentation of the self, and loss of the self in self–object differentiation. It must also be said, however, that the level of fear in some specific individuals far exceeds what is average among the population.

The most frightened patient whom I ever encountered in my professional experience was a young man of 27, who about twenty years ago began analytic treatment with me in a state of clear and persistent terror. It was not clear what he was so afraid of; he was very frightened of everything, he told me, and appeared more scared than anxious.

Even his facial expression did not bear the imprint of deep suffering or of complicated, nagging thoughts inside, but, rather, the continuous, extreme, sensorial alarm of someone who, from one moment to the next, could be run over by a car, or buried by an avalanche, or might be hit in the face with a ball thrown hard, or fall into a manhole.

He did not even seem to harbor any particular persecutory ideation, at least in the first consultation session, and his vision of the world appeared rather moderate and realistic, perhaps secured in a 'little world' adapted to his knowingly modest means. An only child, he lived at home with his parents, very protected from the vicissitudes of existence. He held a regular, routine clerk's position, about which in effect he never complained, and he got along well with family members and colleagues.

He was afraid, he told me – *he had always been afraid,* practically from when he was born. He was very afraid in every possible situation, and he didn't know what to do about it.

We had agreed – with my underestimation of the problem, and with his concealed but perceptible perplexity behind a collaborative attitude on the surface – to begin in an exploratory vein at three sessions per week; in fact, however, he came to me for a total of only three sessions.

In the first session, he immediately said to me that he had some difficulties with his girlfriend because there was a guy who bothered her on the phone in a worrisome way, and who tried to get to know her in person – something he found extremely irritating. He expressed bold intentions to react and reestablish the order of things, promising himself to intervene energetically if these disturbances continued.

The session ended with the patient rather tough and combative, while I was somewhat surprised by his courageous bristling, so different from the attitude he had exhibited in our first conversation – so much so as to make me think that maybe he had exaggerated a bit in portraying himself as frightened. I reflected on the fact that this story of the pirate-like approach by an outsider toward his girlfriend, put forth in a grand way to fill the first session, could perhaps conflictually have something to do with the desire/fear of closeness – in some ways unacceptable – between him and me in the analysis, and I prepared to await what would emerge to clarify the situation.

He arrived for his second session extremely agitated and immediately struck up with new developments in the bothersome telephone events. A phone call full of explicit sexual offers and requests for a meeting had come in while he was at his girlfriend's house. In an authoritative tone, he had asked to have the phone passed to him, and he had enjoined the unknown man to present himself in person, if he had the courage to do so, so that he could see him. Unfortunately, the other man had immediately accepted the offer and had specified that the meeting would be very simple and quick, given that he was just downstairs, at the other end of the street.

The telephone replaced, the patient had then immediately taken himself to the window to peer out, and he had identified the caller at once: 'Doctor – he was huge! Really huge! VERY, VERY MUCH SO!!!!'

Since he appeared to be still terrorized, I asked him calmly: 'So, there was . . . something to be afraid of . . . ?' I paused.

The patient hadn't a moment of hesitation: 'ABSOLUTELY! Obviously, I didn't go down to meet him – in fact, I waited a while before I even went down and returned home!'

The curious thing was that the patient didn't seem in the least mortified by that narcissistic defeat, so intense and obvious, while he appeared quite worried about again encountering that ugly fellow on the street. He said goodbye to me, still quite alarmed, and disappeared warily into the evening darkness.

The next day he arrived at the agreed–upon hour, which was the last of a dark day at the beginning of January, and I was really inter-ested to learn of the developments of his unpleasant internal and external situation, when chance contributed by complicating the situation.

At that time, I saw patients in a very small, quaint attic with a sloping ceiling, nestled among the city's rooftops; access to it was gained by first taking a narrow corridor from the front door and then scrambling up a rather precarious spiral staircase. My little office, which could hold only my armchair, the couch, and a small writing desk with two chairs, had no real windows, but just below the ceiling a piece of the sky could be seen through a 'Velux'-type skylight, which could be opened with a winding mechanism.

The patient lay down and was about to begin his account, when suddenly the electrical power was cut off and we were plunged into pitch darkness. I noticed that the patient became agitated, and I hur-ried to reassure him: 'Don't worry, it's only that the lights have gone out. I'll go downstairs to reset the electricity meter, and I'll be right back with you.' 'Doctor, I'm afraid!' 'It's all right, you're safe; just stay here, and in a few seconds we'll have light again.'

That said, I got up without delay, and in the dark I took the few steps that separated me from the spiral staircase that I went up and down several times a day, and with swift agility I reached the ground floor below. I clicked the meter, restored the light, and in 20 to 30 seconds in total, I was once more upstairs.

It was only that the patient wasn't there any more.

Disconcerted and disoriented, I glanced around under the desk and behind my armchair (the only places in which someone could have hidden), but he wasn't there. He could not have gone down the stairs because I would have run into him. Then I looked up, and I saw that the Velux skylight was open; he had escaped through it.

A chair placed underneath the skylight confirmed my suspicion. I climbed up on the chair and poked my head out, just in time to see the patient wandering about dangerously on the roof, in search of an escape route. Frozen by fear, I called to him to turn back slowly and to place his feet carefully, and when he reentered, I collapsed, relieved, into my armchair, while he parked himself on the couch for a few moments. He then said goodbye in a great hurry, adding that for that day he had had enough.

I never saw him again.

I write about this patient today because he and his devastating fear have remained inside me, like the representation *par excellence* of pervasive fear in a human being – a fear whose secret I will never know, and about which I can only question myself on the basis of the few elements at my disposal.

This patient told me little about himself, and what he did say was primarily factual and odd; he made me feel a great fear, and he could have given me a lot of trouble with his attitude that seemed to lack any sense. The unknown man who provocatively challenged him in the street, having designs on his girlfriend, appeared concomitantly with the beginning of the relationship with the analyst, and he was 'huge,' 'VERY, VERY MUCH SO!': a practically undefeatable castrator. My presence at his side, as a potential ally in the exploration of his primordial fear, had to have aroused deep homosexual anxieties: too much closeness in that tiny office, too much of an intrinsic offer of intimacy and contact in that rhythm of three visits per week.

Certainly, at first he had made a very short-term attempt at a probable adhesive identification (the assumption of a pseudo-authoritative attitude of reacting effectively, perhaps in imitation of an analyst who was 'assumed to be courageous'), but he was immediately deflated like a punctured balloon. The casual and unexpected electrical blackout had to have seemed to him like a confirmation of the fact that, when one is scared stiff, all (mental) systems shut down and are no longer useable, and in the mind all is dark: one goes crazy. At that moment he needed to escape from there, from that situation, from the two of us, and quickly find a way to return to his own home, at the cost of appearing 'outside' – or literally 'outside on the roof' as we say[1] – in the senseless rush to escape.

This patient, with the passing of the years, has returned to my mind many times, not only as a case of therapeutic failure, but also as an emblem of the *fear of living, tout court:* the separating appearance of the third – in the timeless dimension of the protracted intrafamilial symbiosis, just as in that of the pseudo-parental-couple symbiosis with his girlfriend – had to be for him an unresolved, always impending eventuality, also because, deep down, it was unconsciously and conflictually desired. His eternal damnation, I suppose, would always consist in that – damnation that required this extremely frightened man to employ 'acrobatic' solutions of compromise, internal and external, beyond those that relatively normal persons explore in a concrete sense with their steps or, in a figurative sense, with their minds.

At the same time, it must be noted that he was certain I would not be capable of containing him: his 'discharge' from the container-office corresponded to an uncontainable wandering while pursued by terror. I had been able to read his terror from his face even beforehand, from the outside; but I had had absolutely no way of experiencing and sharing his feelings together with him, if not all at one time and in a traumatic manner, on the occasion of his walk out on the roof. This would seem to represent, at the level of primary experience, a dissociated mother–child couple, in which the flow of sensations and emotions is interrupted at the beginning, subject to traumatic impacts with a further break in the relationship.

I can guarantee (and I certainly do not do so proudly) that I associated, remembered, or fantasized very little during the 'all-action' session I have just described; the facts overcame my capacity to keep myself thoughtful and receptive to a broad spectrum. In the clinical events with my patient Arturo, whom I will introduce later on in this chapter, you will still find phases of action without mentalization – integrated, however, by the possibility (though minimal) of the analyst's thinking, which, although far from eliminating the patient's

---

1 *Translator's note*: The patient was literally *fuori dai coppi*, or 'outside the roof tiles,' to use an Italian idiom.

fear, has nevertheless made it possible for analytic work to continue and develop.

The dignity of fear

We all know fear.

Not all of us, and not always, do we have *the courage to recognize it* in its various forms. Closing the eyes of the mind in order not to suffer, we have learned to do as ostriches do, to try, that is, not to see it; but it is fear who sees us.

The human being suffers from fear both for the unpleasantness of that feeling in itself, and for the narcissistic reproach that comes from one's own ego-ideal: as much from the flavor of fear, then, as from the shame of recognizing the carriers of it.

'Few are the cowards who always know all their fear,' wrote La Rochefoucauld, and in regard to 'cowardice' – certainly not an illegitimate concept in itself – I have found that many people think themselves to be cowards, when in reality they have only the very human fears that are normal. It is, after all, a universal experience that we are exploring.

In my clinical experience, then, I have often had to defend patients from the shame and guilt of being afraid. In some situations, one deals with, substantially, helping the patient to *recognize his own fear*, negated and de-negated in various ways.

Elsa, a young patient who will have to subject herself to a series of clinical exams for insurgent gastric symptoms, concomitantly with her first sessions (she began analysis just a short time ago), brings in a dream that she nonchalantly describes as 'curious':

'I was recovering in the hospital, and someone who wasn't even a doctor told me that I had something suspicious, and that it was necessary to go into greater depth. I laughed: but of course, it's my pleasure!' She giggles, smiling sarcastically as she recounts this.

The initiation of analytic regression (the 'recovery') powerfully reactivates vestiges of primary experience, with its bodily and relational vicissitudes. Elsa will have to submit to 'analyses' of her internal conditions, and she defensively leads with incredulity ('but of course, it's my pleasure!'), devaluation of the object ('someone

185

who wasn't even a doctor'), and affective detachment from the feared danger connected to the nurturing relationship with the same object, almost as though the dream (described as 'curious') did not pertain to it.

Actually, there was not much to laugh about, and in fact it was not long before Elsa's fears came to light. Noteworthy, however, was the fact that the patient forced the contrivance of laughter in a defensive and artificial way, a reaction that in other circumstances was totally natural as a liberating discharge of anxiety that could be truly overwhelming.

In certain cases, I have been able to help patients in *resizing their fears*, especially when they spoke to me of things that I, too, had experienced. They could thus perceive, in my manner of handling the material, that I knew what they were talking about, that I noticed their internal condition and respected their subjective disposition, but that I also proposed *the 'treatability' of what they were scared of and of their fear* – elements that we could touch without being destroyed.

Giovanni, a young manager with a perpetually phallic–'careerist' attitude, who proudly proclaims his 'ruthlessness' in the face of human elements that could end up being profoundly moving, is unaware that, for some sessions now, he has been grappling with the danger of experiencing pain and sadness in relation to his grand-mother's terminal illness. She cared for him as a child, and he has greatly distanced himself from her in recent years, maintaining an attitude of defensive superiority.

A memory, engendered by the present tone of the analysis, takes him by surprise in a session: his grandmother was at his bedside, caressing him and telling him stories, when he had been afraid on a night when he was ill. He cannot manage to hold himself back any longer and cries in desperation. Since the pain is mixing with shame at having yielded to tears, I intervene, placing myself in between his ideal ego and his suffering self, legitimizing his pain and the dignity of his tears.

In the subsequent session, he brings in a dream that seems to be an elaborated revisiting of what he experienced together with me the previous day.

He dreams of having completed a difficult and risky passage during a mountain excursion. He has to walk along a tenuous and slippery ledge located some distance above a sort of lake that terrifies him: if he falls down

186

into it, he feels that he will 'be lost.' Halfway along the slippery course, he falls into the water below, feeling unspeakable anguish.

But in actuality, he notices with surprise that the water is not very deep, he can climb out again, and he is coping with putting himself back together after the fear experienced during the fall, and is drying out his clothes.

'So . . .,' I comment, 'essentially, you had a nice bath!'

It is not difficult, in the remainder of the session, to recover the connection with a fear of falling into a lake of tears and pain, thereby losing the dry, controlled structure that befits a manager with icy eyes.

In still other cases, I could do nothing other than *share with patients their own pain*. It was like this at the end of 2004, when the impossibility of knowing, day by day, the names of the victims of the Indonesian tsunami kept many people anxious, and me as well, with one of them who feared for the health of a common friend of ours.

In the end, it fell to me to *be afraid for certain patients, in areas where they themselves were not afraid* – sometimes when they were right about this, and sometimes when they were wrong. For example, there were patients whom Balint and Balint (1959) would have defined as *philobats*, perhaps to an extreme degree, occupied in exercising massive counterphobic defenses and in the excited erotization of risky situations.[2] I have had many of these in treatment, and with some I really felt that I was on a roller-coaster.

Furthermore, I am not a lover of risk. Some of the accounts of extreme climbing, of the escapes of enormous spiders or poisonous snakes from terrariums or cages kept in bedrooms, of immersions in very dangerous oceanic depths with currents capable of dragging a diver so far from his boat that he cannot get back on board, of challenging nighttime car rides at 150 miles per hour, and so forth, have produced complex feelings in me: for example, an *alternation between fear and irritation* (if they had stayed calmly at home, they would have left *me* in peace, too!!!). I had to keep these feelings under control in order to avoid alarmed or moralistic externalizations that at the time could not be useful in understanding in greater depth the internal situation of these patients.

At times, *these persons clearly evacuated into me their own fear: I felt it*

---

2 According to Balint and Balint, a *philobat* is a person who avoids ties, tends toward independence, and looks for gratification in adventure – often dangerous adventure – as well as in travel and other new experiences.

instead of them, and one could catch – and see clearly – a secret pleasure in putting me on the grill, so to speak, with a knowingly given dose of information, aimed at filling me up a little at a time with an experience of which they thus succeeded in ridding themselves, at least in part.

No psychoanalytic school has described these processes as well as the Kleinian one: the theory of projective identification – founded on the *experiential substance* of what comes to be transmitted to the receiving subject who in turn becomes conditioned to it, and on the *primarily unconscious* nature of this exchange – has greatly helped us in representing for ourselves what happens.

Rosenfeld (1969, 1987), in addressing an earlier work of Klein's (1955), appropriately distinguished *communicative* projective identifications from *evacuative* ones. In the first, the object in which the projection occurs is not modified very much by the projective process; in the second, by contrast, the object is invaded, taken possession of, controlled, and traumatized by evacuative intrusions. Clinically, Rosenfeld was very attentive in particular to the fact that the analyst should be capable of perceiving and recognizing these intrusions, and that he should then be capable of rendering interpretations that have an understandable emotional meaning for the patient.

I am particularly interested in another consequence of this process: the fact that the subject who emits projective identifications may not be very much altered by the flow of his contents toward the outside – that he may not evacuate everything, but keeps at least a part in internal contact with his experience. For example, that *the patient keeps his feeling of fear even while making me share it* (Bolognini, 2002a, 2004e).

If he does not do this, and if he aims only to frighten me, the work required is much more arduous, because it will imply the necessity of a substantial reintrojection of his initial fear before it will be possible to occupy ourselves with it together. Before that process has at least in part occurred, every interpretation will run the risk of being merely *information for the patient's ego*.

The '*ego–ego exchange*' between analyst and patient, with all its traditional corollary of 'explanations,' favors the reinforcement of defenses with respect to the possibility of experiencing the self. When this possibility is missing, the dialogue occurs in an abstract dimension, a nominal and substantially dissociative one: 'the talk is about words' (Bolognini, 2003b) more than about human elements. One must be afraid as a twosome: 'two persons frightened (at least a little) inside a room,' even if one of them is hopefully a little less frightened than the other, in order to be able to say things that have 'body' and 'meaning' for the other.

A message from the beginning of an analysis

The counterphobic mechanism is one of the most common defenses against the experience of fear: with a characteristic style, many patients try to confirm to themselves in every moment that they are strong, tenacious, and healthy, cultivating fantasies of total independence and of disregard for danger, and trying to evacuate into others (usually family members, friends, or the analyst) their fears in a manner that is more or less explicit and direct. Arturo, a patient whom I will discuss again in the chapter on panic, was one of these.

Arturo had presented in analysis three years earlier, following a panic attack. An athlete and a big man of more than 220 pounds and about 6 feet tall, he had practiced various extreme sports to an agonizing level – exposing himself, he told me 'to significant risks, but always without feeling any fear.' Since I had asked him for an example of this, he evoked an episode that was a complete syllabus, if read between the lines as pertaining to a view of the two of us, beyond the deeper, atemporal, and absolute levels of his oneiric reality.

In a cross-country motorcycle race, he had found himself competing on a mountain track located in the center of an enormous hollowed-out area of ground, a kind of crater, with spectators watching from up above, all around the rim, while the motorcycles roared along their infernal track in a highly exciting spectacle. Unfortunately, he had taken a bad fall in that makeshift arena, seriously injuring one of his legs, and he could not get up. An ambulance quickly departed from above, the medical caregivers came out at great speed (to clear the race course as well), and they had carefully laid him on a wheeled stretcher that they immediately loaded into the rear door of the ambulance. They then departed very quickly, with sirens turned on, heading for the high rim of the track, following a direct path up the steep slope.

Unfortunately, in their hurry, they had forgotten to carefully close and lock the rear door of the ambulance. Halfway up the steep ascent, it had come open, and to the astonishment and shouts of hundreds of spectators, the wheeled stretcher with the patient on board had rolled out the back, beginning a breakneck descent – with Arturo waving his arms, terrified, while the ambulance and its occupants, unaware of this, proceeded toward the summit.

Essentially, Arturo retraveled the entire steep hill back again on that medical projectile, only to be traumatically thrown off it at the same point from which he had been picked up. The roar of the crowd (presumably terrified and excited at the same time, due to the unusual spectacle) had at last alerted the ambulance crew at the top, and with dismay the paramedics had done an about-face to return and recover the hapless victim.

'Doctor, I let them come close, pretending to be stunned; then, when the first two bent over to pick me up, I grabbed both of them by their necks and knocked their heads together! After that, no one wanted to come get me,' Arturo told me triumphantly.

In identifying with him, I had been dismayed during the first part of his subjective account, and then I had instinctively dissociated myself from his traumatized subjectivity in order to acquire, in a more distanced and protected way, the point of view of the spectators, making an enormous effort not to laugh. I felt at that point a long shudder down my back, and, with a sort of involuntary intuition, I experienced a confused fear that I would meet the same end as the two paramedics.

In the end, that surreal story – with its extremely rapid sequence, full of sudden and unexpected events worthy of a silent film – conveyed, in a syncopated way, the numerous implications of the situation, hidden among the pockets of its factual concreteness.

Arturo was consciously presenting to me traumas experienced in the recent past (those obvious ones of the manifest account), and unconsciously the dark internal traumas of the remote past (presumably, a disabling 'break'/castration, in a painful condition of impotence and *Hilflosigkeit*). But he was also communicating the potential traumas of a near and frightening future: the idea of being aided analytically by me in an inappropriate and hurried way (like the paramedics who arrived so quickly had done), with insufficient holding and containment (like the doors of the vehicle that could not contain, that came open and let him fall out the back), and even more with the shame of being exposed (wounded and 'stretched out' in a regressive state, in a ruthless psychoanalytic arena, to the mockery of a persecuting, jeering 'public' spectators/analyst, ready to amuse themselves/himself at the patient's disgrace).

What I could not yet know during that period, but could only vaguely intuit, were the levels of the remote past and feared future that were being reproposed transferentially, in an atemporal circularity, in the representation of that scene that was so exciting. In Arturo's subjective experience, the colossal counterphobic challenging of the fear of insufficiency and helplessness came to rest ignominiously in the demand for an analytic/maternal-care type of 'first aid,' of which he had a desperate need, but of whose inadequacy he was transferentially certain, and thus he was *a priori* rendered furious.

Fear in childhood and adolescence

'You must not be afraid!' we have been told since we were children; and at times it was true, because there was actually no big thing to be afraid of. At other times it was a trick, because indeed there *was* something to fear! And it was the adults who expressed impossible expectations with regard to a courage that – to say it in Manzoni's terms – one cannot give to oneself.[3]

Children, as has been noted, have many fears – some natural, some pathological. Simona Argentieri and Patrizia Carrano wrote *The Bogey Man: A Little Catalogue of Childhood Fears* (1994), for which they interviewed parents and children, and they drew out an interesting fact: while the children referred to their fears with great sincerity, the parents tended to deny the children's fears, perhaps to reassure themselves. 'It seems,' wrote Argentieri in a subsequent 2002 article,

> that there has been a reversal of the ancient illusion, according to which at one time it was the children who believed that parents weren't afraid of anything! In the past, in fact, fears and bugbears were confidently used by 'grown-ups' to keep children good, with a sort of pedagogic sadism; while today a child who expresses his fear arouses alarm, in a hodgepodge of guilt and inadequacy.[4]

---

3 *Translator's note*: This is an allusion to the words of Italy's most famous novelist, Alessandro Manzoni, whose cowardly character Don Abbondio in *I Promessi Sposi* [The betrothed] notes that: '*Il coraggio uno non se lo può dare*' – one cannot give oneself courage. That is, a person cannot decide on his own to feel an emotion, such as courage; either he has that emotion or he does not.

4 Translation by Gina Atkinson.

In short, it is difficult to accept that our little ones must have the experience of fear; even though it is commonly seen that one of the pleasures of grown-ups – a bit of a sadistic one, in fact – is that of saying and doing something that can induce fear, in order to then reassure the real child and the child who exists in the adult about the comforting intervention of a grown-up who can always pull the chestnuts out of the fire.

An extreme example of protection of the child from fear is provided by Roberto Benigni in the 2000 film *La vita è bella* [Life is beautiful], through the acrobatic maintenance of an illusion and a misunderstanding of reality, here used to a good end.

Despite the entire collection of neurotic and psychotic defenses that psychoanalysis has patiently identified and described since the time of Freud, children remain the most direct experts and communicators on the subject of fear: they feel it, they say it, they are not very ashamed of it, and they tell about it more accurately than do adolescents or adults.

In adolescence, the complex drive-related and narcissistic transformations completely change the picture: of fundamental importance are the devices of splitting, dissociation, and denial, which make strange and paradoxical solutions temporarily possible. The excess of internal stimulation that the organism is not capable of mastering, modulating, or circumscribing often pushes adolescents to seek counterphobic solutions or representations in external reality (Golinelli, 2000), and it is the dream that often takes them by surprise.

Alessio, aged 16 – turbulent and conflictual – years, tells me of a partial nightmare, which impressed him and scared him a lot for the better part of its contents:

With his parents, he is following a path on the valley floor of a beautiful mountain area, in a calm and sunny atmosphere, when suddenly, far away, a threatening rumble becomes noticeable, at first in the background and then increasingly closer. Raising his eyes, he notices that from the snow-clad peaks that surround the valley, due to a sudden melting of glaciers, an enormous mass of water and mud is rushing down, which in a few minutes will reach him and his parents and will be able to bury them.

Terrified, he instinctively begins to run toward higher ground with all his might, climbing up the mountainous hillside to gain ground as quickly as possible, and – by a hair's breadth – he makes it. The enormous mass of water came very close to where he was, but he got himself away from it, panting and trembling with fear.

But suddenly a thought flashes across his mind: what about his parents?!? He whirls around and sees them – they are saved.

It is only the representation of a conflictual desire, but behind him, I, too, breathe a sigh of relief.

I do not interpret to him that puberty has loosened and put back into circulation – in a very brief time period, almost suddenly – quantities of various kinds of drive materials that latency had frozen up there on the spotless peaks of a milky-white color, and that rescuing himself and his love objects during this phase of psychoemotional development is a difficult task, one that often involves serious losses as well as precarious and tormented adjustments.

Instead, I comment that in life, too, as in the dream, one can do all possible to rescue what is salvageable without becoming paralyzed by fear in situations that can seem insurmountable to us. There will be time to give more names to things later on, and for now it is enough for me that Alessio enjoys a respite in which to catch his breath, following his race to save himself.

Fear and glamour

I am in a psychotherapy session, vis-à-vis, with a woman who is still emotional at the memory of a meeting the evening before, after a book presentation in a sort of citywide literary salon. 'And then, look, doctor, believe me – he is not like he seems on television. . . . He is nice . . . Just imagine that, when the buffet was served, he gave me a place ahead of him in line, smiling. . . . In fact, for me he is a true gentleman!'

This woman, rather excited, is evoking before me the impact of a few seconds (sufficient to establish that he is a gentleman) with the honorable Mr. X, a fearsome and feared personality of the local political and social news, a regular when it comes to insults and brawls on television, with men and women. I notice that her excitement is not limited to the dimension of elation, typical of closer contact with a famous person; there is a further level of enthusiasm, of being emotionally touched, that evokes for me an atmosphere of a more pronounced internal split.

This patient has come to me not long before, and she seems far from having sincere contact with herself. My idea is that she is in the process of achieving the task of growing closer to the analysis, taking a very broad curve.

She has a problem of profound devaluation of the self, noticeable precisely in her hypocritical idealizations of objects (actually persecutory and feared) to which she entrusts the assignment of representing a way of being *'comme il faut,'* in which she can co-participate through very rough and approximate identifications. I don't have doubts about the fact that I, too, like the honorable Mr. X, am at present an idealized persecutor, and I await the appropriate moment for exploring this area, counting on the possibility of a slow process of drawing closer and of improvement of the object relationship. Since at this point my task is first of all that of listening and of fostering her gradual adaptation to a working situation, I abstain, of course, from premature comments, and I limit myself to some internal reflections.

In general, people love being treated with humanity and kindness, and this is obvious. Less obvious is the fact that most of them, as a rule, recognize and repay this attitude in kind. Narcissistic personalities, in fact, consider it a sort of expected, natural right, something that is their due; entrenched in its benefits without any particular gratitude, they accept this right, and that's the end of it – this is normal for them.

Sadistic personalities, whose libido follows a different course (and, in their way, a more 'object-related' one) from that of the 'pure' narcissist, in contrast capture in others' kindness a potential sign of weakness, a tasty morsel, and they often try to profit from it, crushing the interlocutor in various ways.

Now, one thing that never ceases to strike me is the way that people can be literally conquered, entranced, moved, when a notoriously violent and overpowering personality produces – in a once-in-a-lifetime occurrence! – an act of kindness, or demonstrates for an instant a really humane aspect. This is what happened, for example, to the woman just described, in her encounter with Mr. X. The situation of having been able to almost enjoy, for an instant, the benevolence of a wicked person, in fact, has a seductive effect a thousand times greater than that produced by contact with a normal person who habitually behaves correctly.

In a way, on a moral level, this paradoxical phenomenon has some commonalities with the magical resonance of the return of the prodigal son, in the parable from the gospel, in relation to the zero attribution to the other sons who remained at home to work. Thus, it seems to disproportionately reward, in an undeserved fashion, those who give little of themselves and who do so rarely, and, even more so, those who, from a demonstrated position of power, are wont to mistreat others.

Usually, the reasons for all this are not at all conscious and stem on the one hand from fear and on the other from narcissistic defenses put into play in order not to have to recognize the bitterness – first of all, in relation to the self – of having had to be afraid, in fact, of the interlocutor. In effect, it is extremely anxiety-provoking to have to tolerate the idea or the vision of a person's dehumanized aspects, and one cannot wait to be able to negate them: 'It isn't true; I was mistaken; reality cannot be so terrible, ugly, and cruel.'

In addition, it is profoundly humiliating to have to recognize having felt a sense of undefended impotence (and, all in all, a fear of helplessness, *Hilflosigkeit*) in relation to the wicked person 'on duty' at the moment. The narcissistic aesthetic of our times, which valorizes indomitable women and decisive men, dictates that he who feels afraid would have to feel shame at having allowed this experience to dwell in the self.

It is better, then, to twist the argument, to fall back on the conventional ambiguity provided by a cheap psychology that reassures us with the platitude that aggressive and overbearing people are like that 'as a defense,' and actually, underneath, they are timid, afraid, and in need of comprehension themselves, etc. (I remember many journalistic readings, in this regard, about timid, inhibited persons who were actually clamorous 'externalizers,' all presented as individuals oppressed by fear – in contrast to land-registry clerks, notoriously bold and reckless.)

All well and good, but it must be clarified once and for all that this vision of things neglects a fundamental detail – that is, the *Fixierung*, the fixation on pleasure (Freud, 1905) – which often intervenes as a characterizing factor, with all the equipment of secondary gains that derive from this way of behaving.

It is well understood that there are few doubts about the pathogenetic course we can reconstruct, from its source: the overbearing person, in the initial phases of the foundation of his character, has truly made active recourse to the use of aggression because he was himself passively wounded in the past and was dominated by his

195

unbearable distress. That is, he has turned passive into active, transforming himself from victim into persecutor (Ferenczi, 1932), and, having verified very early on that this device worked well, he has derived relief, benefit, and pleasure from it and has gradually structured himself in this way. The subsequent passage is in fact that of structural consolidation, through the splitting and systematic projection into the other of one's own vulnerable and frightened self, and through the development of a specific technical ability (which tends toward shrewdness, in perversion) in intimidating and subordinating the other.

These individuals, then, in order not to have to recognize defeat and/or re-experience fear, can arrive at thinking that the interlocutor 'might be right,' while the truth is that this person 'has obtained a right over him (the other)' – that is, he conditions him and blocks him internally.

And they, those who intimidate, how do they manage these painful and ambiguous relational patterns of intrigue? One can sketch out two characteristic profiles.

The first is constituted by those who, to say it once again with the merciless La Rochefoucauld, 'pass off their unrestrained brutality as frankness.' This is the category of *head-on intimidators*, who strike the interlocutor in a direct way with unexpected and violent attacks and then take him under their arm, solemnly explaining that they prefer 'to be sincere' and that, at any rate, they are 'made' like this – in that once things are said, they do not harbor any ill feelings (appearing so magnanimous, while in reality it is the other who would have cause to be furious!), and, overall, they have done it 'for the good of the other.'

The second example is that of *intimidation Mafia-style*, which can be put forward by subjects who have nothing to do with the Mafia; it is the style that is the same. It consists of *making things felt without saying anything*. During an apparently normal conversation, and in a way that is usually extremely difficult to specify, the recipient feels a shiver running down his spine and begins to feel mysteriously upset and worried.

It is strange, because his interlocutor smiled and was so nice . . . but something must have been transmitted to him, because afterward he began to feel bad. But the most extraordinary thing is that, at a certain point, everything was resolved, when the other – the smiling one – explained to him with affection what he had to do: then the clouds were cleared away, and the sun and calm returned. Yes, certainly, there is a price to pay; but it's nice to feel you have a friend who has your interests at heart, who gives you the right directions, who advises you for the better.

This process occurs in a way that some authors (Kaës, 1993; Losso, 2003) have defined as *transpsychic:* the projective identification bypasses both the intersubjective area — the transitional space — and the ego apparatus of the targeted person, introducing into the other unelaborated contents, often really unelaborated projectiles.

In my opinion, the Mafia message penetrates the victim primarily through an *uncontrollable but controlling anal intrusion, invading and violating, denied in an intentionally confusing way by contradictory messages at other levels, conscious and precisely head-on.* Here it is clear that we are grappling with highly pathological secret passages, in an area of delinquency. The ego of the victim becomes confused, ensnared, and stunned; the persecution is introduced as a way of inducing fear and submission, but the real and final success is the *replacement of the self of the assaulted one with something else.*

This 'something else' is a *preformed, transgenerational nucleus,* a kind of fully equipped 'kit,' part of a genome, which — once it is installed — will be able to produce a definitively compliant victim, defeated and won over, or, alternatively, in the case of an energetic transformation from passive into active and of identification with the aggressor, a new Mafia member, in turn an exporter of violence.

Fear, therefore, seems to lose itself on the street, transformed into devotion or converted into delinquent activism. Little or nothing seems to remain, then, of the frightened child who is in each of us, or of the natural biological dignity of this necessary sentiment.

12

TRUST IN ONE'S SELF

Pseudomaturity and disarticulation between ego and self in panic attacks

A psychoanalytic contribution on the theme of panic attacks must take into account the fact that the dynamics of anxiety states do not have an absolute specificity, from a psychogenic viewpoint, nor do they seem to be reducible to a single explicative formula.

This is the fundamental thesis of this chapter, and if on the one hand this statement may appear obvious, it is also true that a consultation of the psychoanalytic literature on this topic suggests the idea that, even today, a certain difficulty persists in resigning oneself to the fact of not being able to turn to a single key idea in order to resolve the enigma of this disconcerting and fearsome pathology.

Actually, the causal factors can be multiple, more or less as is the case in medicine for febrile symptoms or for syndromes of collapse. It is just this varied and complex etiology that has in the past induced some researchers, such as Bria and Ciocca (1993), to prefer the phrase 'crises of panic' to that of 'disturbance of panic attacks'. Bria and Ciocca intended, that is, to emphasize the clinical–phenomenological individuality of the symptom of panic more than the pathogenetic one.

Once the field has been cleared of the pretext of a simple and unified psychodynamic key to panic attacks, it must be said that the contribution of psychoanalysts on this subject nevertheless appears to have been significant, bearing in mind that many patients have in effect achieved lasting benefits from their work on the couch. The analytic laboratory allows a sharper and deeper view of the internal processes involved in the pathology of panic, as well as in the processes of transformation and subsequent therapeutic reparation.

I believe I have communicated up to this point how my theoretical point of view is integrated with awareness (an integration of the 'and/and' type, rather than the 'or/or' one) and the way in which it is pragmatic (the use of theories as metaphors, as tools for work and for fruitful but not sacred investigation). For me, the substance of the whole of my theoretical point of view is made up primarily of the more or less harmonious quality of the game that every analyst plays with theoretical elements, interrelating them among themselves with his own clinical mediation and with his own preconscious evocation.

I maintain that today's analyst knows the most important theories well enough, to the point of being able to keep them conceptually separate from each other. He is an analyst who can essentially tolerate the complexity of his own theoretical field, not reducing theory to an erotized fetish with which to control reality, or to a superego–related object to which he must be faithful at any (clinical) price. Nonetheless, it seems important to me to grasp from theory the point of maximal opportunity of clinical utilization and to leave open potential spaces for further conceptual integrations, valuable for throwing light on other aspects of what one is going through in analysis (Bolognini, 2002a, 2004e).

In this chapter, I will try, then, at the cost of many omissions, to identify a red thread running through the labyrinth of psychoanalytic theorizations on the subject of panic. I will present a brief summary of two typical clinical histories and, finally, I will formulate some reflections on 'trust in one's self' – that is, on what I consider (to say it extremely briefly) the most mature and realistic compromise that an individual can achieve along his developmental journey, toward his own knowledge of and faith in himself and in his own psychic resources.

That compromise is truly realized after the individual has accepted the limits of his own capacities for self-control and self-regulation, after having increased his sensitivity to and tolerance for anxiety signals, and after he has acquired a feeling of trustworthiness in his own dialogue with the preconscious, as well as a sufficient degree of harmony and trust between the ego functions and the nature of the self.

Theoretical aspects

Freud's theories on panic anxiety can be schematically reviewed in two general formulations, separated from one another by about thirty years. In 1894 (in 'On the Grounds for Detaching a Particular Syndrome from Neurasthenia under the Description "Anxiety Neurosis"'), Freud hypothesizes that the libido that did not appropriately discharge itself comes to be displaced, and this might cause tension that would put pressure on the defenses. Thus, the displaced ego might generate – or be transformed into – anxiety.

Freud's second theory, more complex, was formulated in 1926, in *Inhibitions, Symptoms and Anxiety*. It concentrates on the ego and distinguishes two types of anxiety: *primary* or *automatic anxiety* [*Primäre Angst*], and *signal anxiety* [*Angstsignal*], both responses of the ego – in very different ways – to the increase of instinctual and emotional tension.

Primary anxiety has the birth experience as its prototype (even though Freud contests Rank's theories), coupled with the neonate's state of psychophysiological impotence, and derives from an excess of stimulation that the organism is unable to dominate, modulate, or circumscribe. In the infantile and adult experience that repeats such a protocondition, the ego's control of reality (internal and/or external) can no longer be maintained, resulting in a temporary destructuralization and functional disorganization of the subject.

Signal anxiety, less pervasive and destructive, fulfills a warning function with the aim of protecting the individual precisely from the overwhelming experience of primary anxiety. As powerful triggers of internal anxiety, Freud envisions three types of danger situations. The most archaic one is the vestiges of the loss of the love object (the mother), on whom the baby depends *in toto*. Subsequently, as a sense of the bodily self is progressively constructed, the potential bodily losses or wounds (castration) become important. And later, in latency, what succeeds this is the danger of the loss of love on the part of the internal parents (the superego).

If these fundamental Freudian formulations are the object of recurring and almost dutiful historical citation in written works on panic anxiety, less noted, by contrast, are the passages of *Group Psychology and the Analysis of the Ego*, in which – already in 1921 – we find allegorical group representations relative to the phenomenon of panic (for example, Freud speaks of the libidinally cohesive functioning of

HudsonBooksellers

NEW ORLEANS INT'L AIRPORT
PO BOX 20205
NEW ORLEANS, LA 70141
STORE: 00459 REG: 001 CASHIER: NICKOLAS
CUSTOMER RECEIPT COPY

HUNGER GAMES MTI
9780545425177 1 @ 12.99   12.99
SUBTOTAL   12.99
SALES TAX (10.7500%)   1.40
TOTAL   14.39
AMOUNT TENDERED
Amex   14.39
ACCT: ************5003
EXP: ******
APPROVAL: 504824

TOTAL PAYMENT   14.39
Transaction: 86811   3/28/2012 7:36 AM

Comments/Inquiries? (800)326-7711
or Email comments@hudsongroup.com
Thank You for shopping with us.

0868110045500103282012

HudsonBooksellers

NEW ORLEANS INT'L AIRPORT
PO BOX 20205
NEW ORLEANS, LA 70141
STORE: 00459 REG: 001 CASHIER: NICKOLAS
CUSTOMER RECEIPT COPY

HUNGER GAMES MTI
9780545425117 1 @ 12.99   12.99
SUBTOTAL   12.99
SALES TAX (10.75000%)   1.40
TOTAL   14.39
AMOUNT TENDERED

Amex   14.39
  ACCT: ***********5003
  EXP: ******
  APPROVAL: 504824

TOTAL PAYMENT   14.39
Transaction: 86811   3/28/2012 7:36 AM

     Comments\Inquiries? (800)326-7711
     or Email comments@hudsongroup.com
       Thank You for shopping with us.

0868110045900103282012

armies). These representations are extremely illuminating when they refer to the 'functional internal grouping' of the individual, understood in the metaphorical sense of the unity of internal parts and various ego functions within the individual.

> . . . that the essence of a group lies in the libidinal ties existing in it, is also to be found in the phenomenon of panic, which is best studied in military groups. A panic arises if a group of that kind becomes disintegrated. Its characteristics are that none of the orders given by superiors are any longer listened to, and that each individual is only solicitous on his own account, and without any consideration for the rest.
>
> (Freud, 1921, pp. 95–96)

As is evident, we are dealing here with a very effective allegorical representation of an individual intrapsychic phenomenon.

Freud concentrates in particular on cases in which the group comes to be seized by panic without the danger having surpassed the usual limits that are normally tolerable:

> It is not to be expected that the usage of the word 'panic' should be clearly and unambiguously determined. Sometimes it is used to describe any collective fear, sometimes even fear in an individual when it exceeds all bounds, and often the name seems to be reserved for cases in which the outbreak of fear is not warranted by the occasion. If we take the word 'panic' in the sense of collective fear, we can establish a far-reaching analogy. Fear in an individual is provoked either by the greatness of a danger or by the cessation of emotional ties (libidinal cathexes); the latter is the case of neurotic fear or anxiety.
>
> (Freud, 1921, p. 97)

The analogy is striking, in fact, if one imagines that in the interior of an individual who is close to a panic attack, the functional ties among parts of the self may already be inefficient, in a condition of only slight cohesion – exactly as in an army, as Freud says (or, I would add less dramatically, as in the internal workings of a sports team), in which interpersonal investments may have been withdrawn and one may have lost the integrated sense of functional unity.

These Freudian representations seem to precede by about fifty

201

years the concepts of 'cohesion' (which will be developed by Kohut and self psychology) and the individual's 'internal groupness.' In particular, in this group allegory, we can see represented – though in a generic, barely differentiated way – a relational network that is multiobjectual in the interior of the subject. The quantitative aspect of the ties (= the libidinal quantities in play) remains important, but the quality and structure of the internal relationships to the subject assume a specific importance.

To depart from the anonymity of an overly scholastic report, I will immediately say that, personally, I hold these progressive Freudian formulations to be indispensable and fundamentally useful. The contemporary analyst, attentive to object relations, to the state of the self, to attachment phenomena, and inclined to place the experience of panic in a perspective of theoretical complexity and multifactorial genesis, cannot neglect *a priori* the 'quantitative' aspect described by Freud in 1894. This description proposes the genesis of anxiety as tied to – in extreme synthesis, and in nontrivial correspondence with a somatic event – a sort of 'colic' deriving from libidinal obstruction.

Similarly, the Freudian analysis of 1926, relative to the traumatic vicissitudes of the ego, turns out to be at times illuminating in describing an 'electrical short-circuit' aspect in which, due to a sudden increase in tension and an intolerable excess of stimulation, as in traumas, the ego itself (not protected by a 'transformer' or an 'automatic circuit breaker,' in some way close to the 1920 Freudian concept of a 'protective barrier') is not capable of modulating or circumscribing excessive inputs, which end up overpowering it and deactivating it.

Ultimately, the aspect of 'fragmentation and destructuralization' described by Freud in 1921, when the internal structures lose their cohesive ties (primarily libidinal ones) as happens in large groups, is also, in my opinion, valuable as a metaphor for something else: the analyst's working ego, which must make appeal to other theoretical constructions, useful if different, in a natural and creative way, without feeling itself in overly rigid contradiction to them.

Edoardo Weiss (1966), too, was fundamentally concerned with the topic of anxiety, referring to phobias that could be divided into two categories: 'projection' phobias, in which an instinctual, internal, and unconscious danger is transformed into a perceptible, external, and conscious one in the form of a more controllable 'phobic object'; and other phobias, in which anxiety is connected with an undefined, internal sensation of psychophysiological malaise. The implied risk is that of a loss of the sense of self: the 'sensation of the bodily ego' (Weiss, 1966) is compromised.

From Federn, his analyst, Weiss borrowed the concept of *ego emotion,* and this formulation became the precursor of others; it is part of the inherited legacy of psychoanalysis, like the *sense of the self* and the *sense of identity,* which are organized from the starting point of bodily sensations – in particular, those of the skin and tactile sensations, the zone that truly borders the self (Greenacre, 1958; Winnicott, 1969; Anzieu, 1985; Gaddini, 1980, 1984).

Among authors who wanted to take a scientific approach to the abyss of the panic experience, one who is historically mentioned is Mahler (1968), who referred to *organismic panic.* She used this term to describe extremely intense forms of anxiety accompanied by the ego's tendency toward disorganization and regression.

In Mahler's view, which concentrated primarily on the processes of separation–individuation, the primitive panic stemming from separation could find a natural, specific defense in the establishment of a symbiotic organization, with little differentiation between representations of the self and those of the object, and with the child's attempts to induce the mother to behave like an extension of his own body. If such a physiological defense cannot be established in the correct ways and at the right times, the child may tend toward autistic withdrawal.

Possible early disorganizations of this symbiosis involve the risk, then, of subsequent panic experiences, with anxiety about disintegration and a loss of the sense of entity and identity. There may be a terror of being swallowed up or cancelled out by the symbiotic object, which has been rendered persecutory by the projection of destructive, nonneutralized aggression beyond the weak boundaries of the self.

I maintain that the experience of working with patients suffering from panic attacks often presents us with the urgent and explicit requirement, on the part of some of them, of a symbiotic use of the analytic relationship – and vice versa, on their part, of an intense, specific difficulty in temporarily accepting the same necessary symbiotic phase. The method and aims of these relational configurations (primarily resistant or usefully reintegrating of unsaturated needs) must be understood and evaluated case by case, and, I would say, time by time, such that the theoretical models of reference do not degenerate into 'model-isms.'

Subjective experience and the condition of the self

Whether of primarily internal origin (i.e., due to uncontainable conflicts) or of primarily external origin, originating in impact with events that overwhelm the physiological mental processes, or even if of mixed and complex origin, panic anxiety seems to involve some common features regarding the subjective experience and the complex conditions of the self.

The subjective experience is well described in Semi's (1989) observations:

> The traumatic event is usually perceived by the subject as a certain cause of death . . . the last signal that the ego emits before being overpowered. In other words, although the event evidently does not provoke death . . . the sensation of death signals the immediately following and transitory eclipse of the ego. For the ego . . . death is representable only as a real absence.
>
> (p. 65)[1]

Diamond (1985), referring to Kohut, Tolpin, Stolorow, and Lachmann (all of whom were proponents of self psychology), maintains that the common element in panic attacks, in hypochondria, and in agoraphobia (symptoms very often associated with mixed syndromes) may be the threat to the constancy and cohesiveness of the self, expressed by patients as a fear of no longer being themselves or of going to pieces: the state of fragility and of potential fragmentation of the self would thus constitute the real nucleus of the underlying pathology.

In spite of a defective mechanism of anxiety regulation, which has existed since infancy and from which vulnerability to self-fragmentation derives, the patient may have structured a reasonably cohesive self, thanks to compensatory defensive structures. But if these defenses are weakened, cohesion is lost and panic surges up as an experience of internal fragmentation.

Panic states have long-term consequences, setting in motion a regression to a precohesive state and evoking an acute need of objects – appropriated selves from that period of development that was prematurely disrupted. Transferential vicissitudes indicate that

---

1 Translation by Gina Atkinson.

the therapy comes to be experienced as a vital self–object for the maintenance of the integrity of the self. More recently, from the perspective of the mind–body relationship, De Masi (2004) has advanced a hypothesis that interests me: that the crisis of panic may have a specifically psychic origin, capable, however, of triggering a specific and automatic neurobiological response. He notes that one can identify two distinct moments of the attack: the first moment, in which anxiety is still psychically anticipated; and the second one, in which bodily participation is prevalent, and terror becomes uncontrolled psychic anxiety.

De Masi also reevaluates the first Freudian model of panic because, in his opinion, it contains an important intuition that a panic attack is not necessarily the result of the repression of emotional conflicts, but, rather, is based on primitive mechanisms, automatic and preverbal ones. Therefore, it would be – at least in many cases – a–conflictual.

Panic and oedipal conflict

Turning now, more specifically, to the sources of internal conflict that can propel the ego toward failure resulting in a panic attack, the findings of a longitudinal study – based on a total of 25 cases – are of particular interest. The study, from which various writings emerged, was carried out by a mixed group of researchers at Cornell University and Columbia University and was guided by Busch, Milrod, and Shapiro (see Busch, Cooper, Klerman, Shapiro, & Shear, 1991; Busch, Shear, Cooper, Shapiro, & Leon, 1995; Busch et al., 1999; Milrod et al., 1997). These researchers developed a general psychodynamic formulation for 'panic disorders,' which also includes a concept of neurophysiological 'diathesis': children at risk for panicked disorganization have a neurophysiological vulnerability that exposes them to an intense fear of the strange and the unknown, often connected to traumatic experiences.

These children experience basic sensations of inadequacy and anxious dependence on their caretakers; when parental sustenance is then inadequate, the child at risk of panic becomes angry with the parents and fears that his aggression could destroy them. This substantially conflictual, oedipal perspective was integrated in one of this group's contributions with observations of subsequent factors, this time of the oedipal type, that serve to aggravate the situation

(Busch et al., 1999). Competitive urges with the parent of the same sex, and fantasies or effective realizations of personal success, can cause panic attacks, with a regression to states of impotence and dependence. A vicious cycle is then triggered because this regressive condition can also be experienced as dangerous, inasmuch as it is associated with fearsome homosexual fantasms; this can then be followed by an aggressive oedipal reaction that makes the situation worse, and so on. A panic episode could then be the implosive result of these forces in conflict among themselves, made more acute by the perception of a relational regression that is poorly tolerated by the subject.

Beyond this specific psychopathogenetic profile, which seems to me highly probable in a number of cases (though not all), I also find very interesting some of the general observations on the subject of 'weakness of the ego and defenses' (Busch et al., 1999, p. 776). These studies go beyond the more specifically oedipal side of the problem: individuals vulnerable to panic live as though incapable of modulating or managing internal tensions and external stimuli; with terror, they keep themselves incapable of carrying out normal developmental tasks, especially if connected to separation and autonomy. In addition, they have difficulty recognizing emotions, including rage (Vanggaard, 1989), which are feared as uncontrollable and are therefore isolated and distanced.

The point is that this leads them to defensively screen, and thus to lose, the signal-anxiety function [*Angstsignal*], exposing them to a nonprogressive passage from insensitivity to a pervasive and overwhelming experience. A vicious cycle ensues: ego weakness – fear of autonomy – intolerance of dependence – imperceptibility of affects – deactivation of signal anxiety (Busch et al., 1995); in a structural and dynamic way, this leads to an increased vulnerability, sometimes associated with oedipal-level conflicts.

Such a condition brings patients to a characteristic defensive style: these patients who are predisposed to the risk of panic often repeatedly try to confirm to themselves their own strength, tenacity, and health. They use counterphobic defenses and cultivate unrealistic fantasies of total independence.

They are *afraid of being afraid*.

Arturo, a patient of this type whom I will describe in this chapter, was essentially organized in this way.

The psychotic aspects and defective results of regression stemming from panic

The self-experience of panic can constitute a trauma that is more or less mentalizable, with difficulty, and lends itself to a mode of functioning that is like that of the past. The panic experience can become a phobic object to be avoided in memory, or, vice versa, one to be compulsively sought out in equivalent forms (e.g., by periodically putting oneself in dangerous situations) in order to put the durability of the defenses to the test and, in some cases, to attempt an elaborative re-approach to the trauma as well.

Sullivan (1931), referring mainly to serious situations in psychiatry, outlined three possible results after significant and protracted episodes of psychotic panic: displacement onto persecutory guilt and paranoia; an enduring regressive state; and hebephrenia, which very rarely occurs when there is a regressive state with schizophrenic disintegration.

Pao (1979), Sullivan's student, addressed attempts at self-protection of the mind, describing a psychotic sequence in five phases:

1 An untenable conflict generates panic.
2 A paralysis of the ego's integrative functions is produced.
3 There is an attempt at reorganization of the ego.
4 Symptoms are formed in the service of avoiding direct contact with anxiety.
5 Pathological reorganization of the self takes place, with a relative loss of earlier levels of ego functioning, a consequent major functional deficit, and nonintegration of the premorbid personality.

As can be noted from this sequence, Pao initially makes reference to panic anxieties caused by internal processes, more than to panic of traumatic origin caused by external events.

In fact, panic can be caused by both internal and external situations; in addition, it can be caused by internal situations that are experienced as external ones, and by the internal vicissitudes of external situations: repression, denial, projection, and displacement are the more common defenses, as in phobias in general and in paranoia (Frances & Dunn, 1975).

Traumatic neuroses may reflect such difficulties of metabolization, and the durability of defenses set up against a panic situation can be of varying degrees. In this sense, we might recall Waelder's (1967) clinical observation of the fact that panic reactions accompanied by hyperactivity and by shouting are to be thought of as less harmful, and prognostically less severe, than those earmarked by stupor, which imply an apparent recourse to dissociation.

Sullivan (1931), in agreement, described a catatonic condition following protracted states of panic as the destructive result of an untenable condition. The self-destructive aspect was also pointed out by Greenson (1959), who extended it to the economic-libidinal area; for Greenson, panic is a state of psychic impotence, with a reduction of ego functioning and loss of investment of both the internal object and the external one, to the point that there is a possible regression to a state of lacking objects (perhaps stimulated by a primitive hostility that leads to temporary destruction or disinvestment of internal objects).

Regarding Waelder's observation of the benign prognosis of shouting (an observation of a very concrete element, but, in my opinion, not to be underestimated), Greenson (1961), with his usual richness, considers that the great emotions (panic, anger, pain, ecstasy, orgasm) are without words, but not without sounds; they have a common factor – that is, the sensation of the ego's being overpowered, either all to the good or all to the bad. According to Greenson, the involuntary shout certainly fulfills a discharge function, but at the same time it is a request for help. And at any rate, I would specify that it is also a relational act.

Continuing this line of thought, we come to Silber (1989), who, in his extremely interesting work, reports material about some panic attacks occurring in sessions to one of his patients. Silber fully supports a relational perspective in emphasizing the profound differences between his patient's panic attacks and those described in general in the psychiatric literature:

> Those [panic attacks] described in the literature might occur to people who have in some way given up in their efforts to establish contact with a psychological object and have taken their own body as the only remaining available object. The attacks could be their affective cry of despair as well as their acknowledged loss of hope of involvement with another person. In contrast, the patient I described always manifested her wish to be involved with another person and demonstrated her capacity to fulfill this wish.
>
> (p. 362)

Later in this chapter, in discussing my patient Elsa, I will return to Silber's contribution.

Again in the sphere of primitive and basic aspects of mental functioning, I will mention here those cases in which an insufficient transformative function of the mind, with respect to the gathering of unelaborated elements in its interior, produces a dimension of hallucinosis or of frank hallucination that can, in turn (see Ferro, 1996), generate unbearable anxieties for the ego apparatus, to the point of real panic. One finds oneself before a dis–metabolic disturbance of the mental apparatus: a 'poisonous/dis–metabolic' aspect, in the Bionian sense, that is produced when the psychic apparatus is struggling with experiences and mental contents that are quantitatively uncontainable with respect to the real structure, and/or qualitatively indigestible with respect to the transformative capacities of an insufficient alpha-function (Ferro, 1996).

I am aware of having condensed – with extreme synthesis – a very broad range of theoretical perspectives and clinical configurations, which the various schools of thought have gradually addressed, pointing them out with preferential emphases. And I can add that very often they have been of great help to me in orienting myself in moments of difficulty: there is some truth in all these contributions, and I think this may be an experience that many colleagues can recognize having shared.

In the coincidence of the complex conditions described by various authors, the ego of patients suffering from crises of panic fails, and subjective sentiments of psychic death and physical death intertwine and become confused with one another. A vital, basic experience becomes impossible – the experience, that is, that I will define in the final part of this chapter as *trust in one's self*.

First clinical case: Arturo

In the previous chapter, I have already described this patient with an impressive sports curriculum, which he referred to with pride and the evident regret of one who refers to past glories: he had already been a rugby player, a black belt in karate, a military parachutist, a deep–sea diver, a volleyball champion, and a 'rally' pilot. Since adolescence he had constructed a fearless personality, phallic and noisy, in continual challenges with others and with his own limits.

While Arturo listed his accomplishments during our first meeting, Balint and Balint's (1959) description of a philobat came to my mind, while I simultaneously experienced a sense of my total inadequacy in the comparison induced in me by the patient's exploits. I thought that this very pervasive countertransferential element might correspond in some measure to a deep experience of the patient's.

Then Arturo described a disabling lesion at the cruciate ligament of his knee, with the air of attributing to this event (which had occurred five years earlier) a sense of 'the beginning of all my problems.' But after a brief pause – in which I had the impression that he believed himself to be actively studying me, while in reality his psyche was involuntarily undergoing changes in a depressive direction – he admitted that, at about the age of 20, he had become subject to a series of severe panic attacks, which in short order restricted his lifestyle to a humiliating state of inactivity, agoraphobia, and extreme dependence on his parents.

During these periods of crisis, Arturo became fragmented as a result of very acute anxieties and sensations of mentally breaking into pieces, refinding cohesion (or, as he called it, 'rescue') only if he succeeded – wherever he found himself – in defecating.

The patient did not refer to delirious phenomena or misperceptions (nor did these appear later). But during his urgent searches for a place in which to defecate, he was quite capable of running over anyone or anything, sometimes becoming embroiled in bizarre situations that were painful or grotesque.

I will disclose, for example, that during a weekend break in the second year of analysis, he was seized by extreme anxiety while in front of the palace of the Fieristica Esposizione, to which he had come for business reasons; he was wearing a dark suit and tie. Not finding an available public restroom (the analyst's *gabinetto*[2]), Arturo elected to squat, in a contorted position, in the shrub of a traffic roundabout. And when, a few moments later, he was ordered by a pair of police officers to cease and to tidy himself, given that it was a public place, Arturo felt compelled to explain his disorder in all its drama, with the result that the officers resigned themselves to making a protective barrier around him!

---

2 *Translator's note*: In Italian, a *gabinetto* can be either a closet, a small room or study, or a bathroom. Here there is an equation of the patient's need for a bathroom and his need for the analyst in his office.

This protective function, in a metaphorical form, was one that I also fulfilled for Arturo in subsequent years, utilizing my ideals of 'psychoanalytic aesthetics,' until a sufficiently structured containing function could be instilled in the patient himself.

In Italian, we speak of *farsela addosso* – 'putting oneself over' or 'surmounting' – a fear or other difficulty. But in this case, this unpleasant and humiliating situation of failure, there also seemed to be an associated positive aspect of 'halting the fall': if, as a container, the patient could not manage to hold himself back, at least as contents he seemed to 'find the bottom' and to calm himself. The defecation – probably through an evacuative, 'magical' act that drove out the internal persecutory contents – seemed, that is, to allow him to achieve an organizing *ubi consistam*,[3] with the recovery of a minimal level of self-cohesion, at least at a corporeal/anal level; at that level, he 'was there.' Of course, that obligated him to undergo adventures and to take the daring actions required by his painful compulsion.

As a consequence of the derivative narcissistic injury of no longer being able to behave in life as he had before (i.e., as a sort of human fireball, actually the result of his counterphobic setup), Arturo had completely shut himself up. 'It is better to die than to feel myself and see myself reduced to these conditions!'

In the manner of a wounded philobat, Arturo asked of the analysis a complete *restitutio ad integrum* [restitution of integration]: 'In the past, when people got into a car with me, it was *they* who had to surmount their fear! I want to go back to my life like it was before!' He intimidated me with a threatening determination – communicating, at any rate, the prospect of a turbulent psychoanalytic voyage in which we would share in alternating systems of active and passive roles.

In the fourth month of analysis, a phase was reached that I consider classic in the treatment of patients exposed to the risk of panic attacks. At that time, the patient was coming to three sessions a week on the couch, waiting for a fourth session that would become available presently. The middle session of the week began as follows: 'Doctor, I am much better, and my parents are also very happy at my progress toward cure!' Arturo is then silent and seems to be awaiting my supporting confirmation, which doesn't arrive. 'I haven't had any more of those tremendous panic attacks. [He tries to communicate

---

3 This is a Latin metaphor that literally means 'Where can I solidly place myself' and metaphorically means to find a secure coping method.

the feeling of a problem that has been overcome.] . . . I am happy, too, because I've adapted well to the Xanax dose . . . it's much better like this!'

I think that the patient has merely established a more flexible symbiosis with me, and he associates me in some way with a deep fantasy of magical-omnipotent control of the object, as happens with a pharmacist. I answer him: 'Well, this is a favorable foundation on which to be able to work here in analysis!'

I perceive a slight movement of delusion and disappointment on Arturo's part; with my measured consideration, I was not fully sharing his enthusiasm. I did not think that he was already 'cured'; on the contrary, I invited him to continue the analytic task.

Arturo makes some other remark characterized by a sense of security, and I note his tone: he speaks like a sort of self-made man, mature and experienced. I think of an elderly uncle, an Alpine soldier, or a seasoned old sea captain: figures of 50- to 60-year-old men who have seen it all and who 'look far away.'

With part of myself, I feel inadequate and clumsy. Being in my forties at the time, I am about fifteen years older than Arturo, who is speaking to me concretely, at an age twenty years less than his internal idealized object, 'from the height of which' – in a system of identification similar to that of a young boy who, in Japanese animated cartoons in the 1980s, entered into the maxi-robot and 'became' Goldrake – he deludes himself about grandiosely taking part in a conversation. Yet again, the problem seems to be that of one who is not of the same level as someone else.

In the subsequent session (the last of the week), the patient was terrorized, and the 'soldier/sea captain' had fled from the scene. Arturo was in the phase – a dreadfully genuine one – of needing the bathroom, and I had to work in depth to contain his anxiety and his tendency toward acting out.

Earlier I spoke of a certain typical aspect of this phase at the beginning of analysis with this type of pathology: the initial fusional effect brings relief and well-being, but modest discontinuities in the setting (the weekend separation) or the dialogue (a lack of confirmation by the analyst, for example) are sufficient to throw a symptomatic amelioration into crisis when it is not supported, for the moment, by any effective structural change.

The state of projective identification with an incorporated or interiorized object, but one that is not introjected (Grinberg, 1976), is at the base of the false self, and the ego's occasional reinforcement through a certain degree of temporary fusion with the object-analyst cannot settle the matter. The problem pertains, then, to the internal formative levels of the self, its authenticity and effective consistency, as well as the ego's rapport with the self (Bollas, 1987): in the sense that if the ego does not know the self and does not have contact and familiarity with it (Bolognini, 1991, 2002a, 2004e), it sets up an 'investiture' of the false self in a deceptive way, based on identifications with objects that are internalized but not introjected, and a validating 'investment' over the false self is created, with naturally disastrous results.

The introjective difficulty and the tendency toward an incorporating '*escamotage*' [a primitive solution], so typical in these pathologies, were expressed in Arturo's case through his habitual clinging to drugs, which, however, never really reassured him. In fact, drugs (and in this respect also, Arturo was absolutely typical) demonstrated a 'psychological half-life' of some weeks.

Functioning as orally incorporated parents, fantasied guardian angels, bodyguards, or nursemaids, the effect of the pills faded with time, to the point of their being invalidated on each successive occasion of acute anxiety, losing their magically redeeming and protective halo. Arturo could not utilize them as a valid, even if partial, means of help – according to the primitive law of 'all or nothing,' the pills would have had to render him completely invulnerable, or, in the opposite situation, they would have been thrown out like a shield with holes in it.

Frustrated in the area of drugs (which were prescribed to him by one of my psychiatrist colleagues), Arturo began to question me about psychoanalytic technique, as though to snatch away from me the secrets of alchemy and to prescribe the most powerful potion. He feared, however, that I – like the magician Merlin – was jealous and did not want to give it to him. In short, his pervasive magical thinking made of him a hero who had been thrown from his horse – one who intended to return to the saddle as quickly as possible, with the help of the gods and of stolen sorcery.

I cite this metaphorical representational context – which continued to form in my mind, session after session, in response to the pressures and investigations that Arturo exerted on me – in order to give an idea of the highly primitive nature of the intrapsychic and interpersonal scene that the analysis gradually allowed to emerge. In particular,

Arturo's phallic idea proved to be grandiosely primitive; it constituted an ideal in itself and, at the same time, a fundamental, defensive skeleton for profound experiences of inconsistency and insufficiency.

He had, in fact, devised an original self-therapeutic system to keep his impending panic crises at bay. Terrified by the idea that, because of psychiatric factors, his license to carry weapons (his most precious possessions, presumed proof of his demonstrable and fearsome phallic completeness) might be withdrawn, he was obliged to go about with an enormous revolver hidden under his armpit – such that he could not have been 'permitted the luxury,' in a certain sense, of having a panic crisis; for if he did, the emergency-room staff would discover the revolver and he would be prohibited from possessing it (a fantasy stemming from losses and wounds to the bodily self; castration related in a broader way to his sense of identity).

This '*escamotage*' with which the ego-ideal recaptured the patient's impoverished ego, threatening castration to the illusory self-representation of an ideal self, functioned in effect for some time, but it began to assume an emotional weight that was gradually less bearable.

It is difficult to cite an analytic dialogue with Arturo that was not based on concrete facts; in practice, fearing castration of his phallic false self (a castration that did not depend as much on me as on his slow but inevitable increase in awareness), Arturo did everything to transfer into me his fear and all his deep, chronic state of inadequacy and helplessness, with the typical mechanism of the 'reversal' – that is, of an inversion of roles.

It was thus that he arrived at his session one day carrying an immense dark case, similar to those for transporting cellos. He leaned it against my desk and stared fixedly at me, sneering with a sadistic air: 'Now we'll see if a psychoanalyst has any balls!'

He opened the case, and inside it was a dismantled gun in various pieces. He proceeded to put it together with the speed born of knowledge and experience.

I was afraid, given that he seemed excited.

Then he picked up the gun and pointed it at me, asking what effect it had.

Analyst: I think you want me to feel the way one feels when threatened by danger . . .
Arturo (*excitedly*): Very effective, eh?

Analyst (*nervously*): However, if you want me to help you, it would
be better to put that thing away.

Arturo (*pointing the weapon at the analyst's eyes*): Oh, yeah? And what
does a psychoanalyst start to feel with a gun pointed at his head?

Here I would like to be able to recount that I made an elegant
interpretation, along the lines of 'You want me to understand that
you feel "under fire," or even that you "fear for the safety of your
head,"' or something of that type. Instead, I acted on impulse and said
something very different.

Analyst: And what do you want me to feel?? Of course I'm afraid!
Certainly, anyone would be afraid with a gun planted in their
face! Come on, put it away.

Arturo was quite struck by my words and immediately dismantled the
gun; he asked my pardon with an ashamed air, put the parts in the case,
and lay down on the couch.

After a certain silence, he told me that he was startled by the fact
that I was not ashamed of my fear and that, on the contrary, I had
presented it as a very natural thing that could be shared, an inevitable
consequence and even obvious. For him, it was not like that.

Can a hero, a Superman, a human missile, actually be afraid?

Panic is — as I learned from Arturo — for some patients a bill paid
all at one time by someone who does not want to pay small debts,
the small human fears of everyday life, those that make us feel poor
and defenseless, unarmed and inadequate, defective and deluded. In a
certain sense, such patients are *afraid of being afraid*. Giants with feet of
clay fear the collapse of their illusion, and from a certain point of view,
they are not completely wrong: the collapse of the illusion is always
just around the corner.

Several years more of analysis were needed before Arturo could
accept speaking with me of his weaknesses — his inadequate erections,
his relational difficulties, and his infantile fears. These emerged gradually, with difficulty and with anger — all the pain and desolation of an
infantile self wounded and mortified by a mother who was always
absent; she was spirited, feisty, and captivated by a thousand outside
interests. Those interests were of the phallic–professional–athletic
type, given that she was a hard woman and in perennial distrust of
men, whom she hated and explicitly scorned. Simultaneously, she

assumed an attitude of secret admiration, consistently putting aside her basic maternal functions.

Arturo's mother was a rock climber, hunter, noted fisherwoman, and champion of clay-pigeon shooting; she was an 'invincible' object, internalized by her son, but barely introjected. It was she who was the 'Alpine solider' and the 'tough old sea captain'! Arturo 'did' his mother, 'became' her, when he felt at risk of being afraid, insufficient, or inadequate. He could not be himself because he would have been ashamed at his truly human nature, and therefore he identified with his mother (identification with the 'aggressor'? With the 'abandoner'? With the 'humiliator'?), putting into place his false self.

Arturo's panic attacks diminished, little by little, in the course of seven years of analysis, in parallel with the humanization and acceptance of his self-image (ego-ideal) as less idealized and fictitious, gradually more painfully authentic and resized, but also progressively more reliable. 'Super-Arturo' (as after a while we called his antique, idealized self-image, in our familiar analytic lexicon) yielded his place to a modest, very human 'poor Arturo,' who, however, had his feet firmly planted on the ground, who accepted listening to fear – even through the alarm bells of an 'anxiety-signal' – and who could begin to trust in himself.

'All in all,' Arturo said to me toward the end of the analysis, 'My healthy part brought me to analysis. If I had gone forward on the same challenging road, I would have ended up against a tree at 300 kilometers an hour – or maybe in a madhouse.'

Second clinical case: Elsa

I will present some notes about this second patient primarily to illustrate differences with respect to the first one, but also to support my initial thesis regarding the panic crisis as a symptom of complex derivation, multifaceted and substantially nonspecific, whose treatment often requires a profound analytic revision of the individual's psychic organization.

Elsa, 24 years old, seemed to me the most seriously ill among all the agoraphobic persons I had seen – not only on the basis of her incapacity to be alone, whether at home or elsewhere, or the fact that she could not utilize public transport even if accompanied, but also because of her preoccupied disorganization of thought and her massive anxiety. She communicated the latter by speaking in an excited way, almost raving, always on the brink of acute breakdown and of a crisis of panic. From this last problem she had repeatedly suffered in a dramatic way.

Extremely thin at that time, almost bony, devoid of any intensity whatsoever in her gaze, Elsa gave the impression of not having any density but, rather, of being a mere bundle of anxious nerves, an aggregate of taut reflexes. I would have instinctively defined her as somewhat unattractive, without any precise aesthetic reason; it was not a matter of her features being rather unharmonious, given that hers were not at all so. Thinking about her again, I could reconstruct that on the occasion of our first meeting, it was really her expression – or, rather, her *in*expression – that was not pleasant and that tended to arouse sensations of impatience and detachment.

Even more strange, she aroused guilt feelings in the interlocutor when one saw that all her words were aimed at asking for help, which generated a curiously contradictory countertransferential effect. It was as though Elsa were asking for help, but instead induced a kind of rejection in the other person with her way of doing so; at the same time, she would attempt to cling inextricably to the other, with desperation.

She brought to my mind a story in *A Thousand and One Nights*, in which Sinbad the Sailor had to carry a wicked old man on his shoulders for a long time; this man had captured and enslaved Sinbad by inexorably squeezing his legs around Sinbad's neck – a very clear representation of a parasitic symbiosis, which Elsa repeatedly tended to reproduce toward a rejecting internal object. This situation of rejection was reproduced in the analysis precisely by her way of placing herself in respect to the other, through inductions in the unconscious game of transference–countertransference.

The basic symbiotic object for Elsa was her father, a self-centered and domineering man who was also her employer, truly 90% of her world. As a sort of 'spare tire,' she had acquired a young and uninfluential husband, whom she had married more than anything else to guarantee the constant presence of another emergency symbiotic object.

After three years of marriage, their sexual life was rather impoverished; the first thing that came to Elsa's mind in the way of sexual material was that, at whatever hour of the day or night, her father (who was equipped with a key to their apartment) could have entered,

catching them in the act; for the same reason, she had never mastur-
bated in her life.

From the beginning, these anamnestic elements pointed to an area
of hysterical organization, with an underlying oedipal situation of
enormous proportions placed there in the middle of this young
woman's developmental course, thereby obstructing the passage to
genitality and fostering violent crises of anxiety that were ascribable –
as in the first Freudian formulation of 1894 – to libidinal obstructions
not easily dischargeable because of excessive conflict.

Actually, these things revealed themselves to be much more complex over time, beginning with the fact that Elsa did not suffer only
from more or less unsuccessful repressions; she also completely lacked
any contact with vast areas of herself that she seemed to fear like the
plague. At that time she had a sparse and fragile consistency, and
she was not capable of having an experience or of learning from it.
She had habitually taken shelter in life behind the basic object, to
which she also delegated the functions of self-knowledge. In analysis,
if left alone (e.g., by a protracted silence on my part), she tended
toward panic.

Elsa's mother appeared in the analysis as a shadowy and lifeless
figure. She had been irredeemably marked by the tragedy of a second
daughter who was stillborn when Elsa was 4 years old; she had subsequently suffered from a long and serious depression. Elsa remembered having seen her in bed for months at a time, in a semi-dark
room, as though dead; her mother had remained a frightened woman,
devoid of liveliness, even though endowed with feminine graces and
refinement.

Resolute in this 'distanced' vision of her mother, Elsa was accustomed, materially and metaphorically, to seeing the world from
behind glass, impeded and at the same time protected from it. Since
she was little, she had seen other children run and play in the garden,
observing them from behind the glass window of the kitchen of the
upstairs condominium where she lived. Her parents, rendered hyper-
protective by the fear of losing their only remaining child, did not
allow her to go down and join them. But, ultimately, Elsa herself
would not have wanted to play with them; the other children 'certainly
wouldn't have welcomed me!' she thought, with a projection that for
a long time had served her unconscious desires to maintain a state of
uniqueness.

As a young adult, Elsa always preferred to place her father, and later her husband, between herself and others (furthermore, they were so predictable that they became transparent for her, just like the glass), to protect her. But protect her from what? From that which she would have been able to feel – from life experiences, in a certain sense.

In Elsa's sessions, if I was silent for a long period, she no longer felt accompanied or protected and became agitated, looking out the windows of my office. Dyspnea, tachycardia, and anxiety about death appeared. In fact, at such times, she risked having thoughts of her own – that is, of being born, of existing without the other, and of discovering herself to be separate.

The element of glass reemerged during panic attacks as well, together with the sensation of being sucked up and then scattered in the cosmos, outside the glass porthole of a spaceship, like the astronaut in *2001: A Space Odyssey*. For her, this meant a return to the nightmare of being separated from the figures that surrounded her like glass, rendering her deaf to others' invocations and impossible to contact.

From an apparently casual conversation with her mother, Elsa learned – in the sixth year of analysis – of having been placed between the glass walls of an incubator for almost a month following her premature birth. This condition of separation and early isolation, and of noncontact with her mother in a phase that would have required an integrating and sustaining containment of the intrauterine membranes, became in time an understandable model of Elsa's agitation and fragmentation on occasions not mediated by the presence of the equivalent of a primary object (the analyst in sessions, her father or her husband in daily life).

As was pointed out by Lewin in 1952, panic attacks of internal origin are not events detached from the past, but are often re-enactments of the unelaborated experience of panic states in early childhood, and, as Silber (1989) noted, they can at times be utilized in analysis to recuperate in some way (by memory or by reconstruction) important aspects of the repressed past, since they give a factual representation to affective contents of archaic experiences. This interpretive perspective permitted us, in the work of reconstructing the past as a link to understanding the present, to give a more profound meaning to Elsa's panic experiences and to improve her feeling of 'ego continuity' (Blos, 1968). Furthermore, and more than a historical fact in itself, the 'feeling of being behind glass' became useful in analysis as a shared metaphor – a product of reconstruction that was reinvoked on multiple occasions as a description of what was happening between the two of us.

Elsa's analysis lasted ten years, taking shape as a truly constructive operation of entire sectors of her personality, accomplishing the reintegration and completion of a self that in certain areas could have been defined as embryonic at the beginning. Orality was finally rehabilitated with moments of pleasure and with a certain humor, where once projected greed and aggression (e.g., her hostility toward other children) had burdened her world with external persecutors. The sadomasochistic anality aimed at parasitic control of the symbiotic object (as in the story of Sinbad the Sailor) was transformed into tenacity and professional precision. Hysterical phallicism gradually evolved into promising signs of pride and high-functioning assertiveness. The beginnings of a genitality, which had been unthinkable at the start of the analysis, made her a woman capable of giving and receiving pleasure. Elsa also began to love herself for her feminine image, including her very personal elegance, and to develop an intensely human gaze and an expression that was finally warmer and more communicative.

I wish to emphasize that there was no precise moment that marked the end of her panic crisis, nor were there specific technical interventions.

This was a long analysis, whose fundamental difficulties could be summarized as:

1   Accepting separation.
2   Accepting herself.

The creation of a sufficient working alliance was initially made more difficult by an implicit experience of 'high treason' toward the symbiotic-father object (and we are well aware that separation and guilt may be closely associated). Three years of analysis were needed before Elsa could permit herself a certain confidence with me in discussing material about family relationships, and the unveiling of certain highly significant behind-the-scenes events required much more time.

The development of Elsa's internal setup was made more difficult by her reluctance to abandon the conspicuous secondary gain to which she had by now become accustomed. Pitied, catered to, and relieved of any responsibilities, this patient was saved from all the situations that could have made her anxious, such as standing in lines, riding on public buses with strangers, the need to wait in stores, and so on. These situations had many times been the source of panic attacks that had led to a course in the hospital, anxiety about death, ECT, injected benzodiazepine, and so forth.

Together with the work of recognition and empathic comprehension of her weak and undeveloped parts, an attentive attitude of reconnaissance was necessary in the face of implied narcissistic pretensions with which the patient unconsciously self-legitimized her secret right to privilege, uniqueness, and treatment which caused her to regress. Over the course of the years, therefore, Elsa and I coined an entire intra-analytic jargon, with expressions like 'accepting being a whomever,' 'liberating the slaves' (first her family members and then me), 'liberating Sinbad the Sailor,' and 'wrapping it up' (i.e., the recognition that one must resign oneself to accepting certain things and then throw them away), and similar terms. Certainly, this could seem like a sort of moralistic pedagogy, but in our context, it was not. The patient really felt that 'we were working' because we struck — in a nonpersecutory way — 'confoundedly true notes.'

After ten years, her panic attacks were a painful memory, but one that no longer caused her fear. Other aspects of her life and of her relationships in general had perhaps become the source of conflicts, uncertainties, and new anxieties, within the framework of that 'common unhappiness' described by Freud (1895).

Comparison of the two cases

What were the evident differences between Arturo and Elsa? And what were the similarities? And why — their differences notwithstanding — had these two patients been affected by the same panic symptomatology, instead of developing symptoms and defenses of a different nature? I will try to answer these questions a little at a time.

The most evident *differences* pertained to their premorbid dispositions. Before the panic episodes, Arturo had been a philobat, whereas Elsa was a textbook ocnophile[4] — the first a participant in extreme sports; the second, claustrophilic and cowardly. Arturo cultivated a

---

4 The *ocnophile*, at the opposite end of the spectrum from the *philobat* (see fn. 2 in the previous chapter), tends to cling to the stable and the secure (Balint & Balint, 1959).

grandiose phallic ideal; Elsa, an ideal of conformity to the desires of the paternal superego, in order to guarantee her symbiosis.

If not contained by parental equivalents or protoparental ones such as doctors, Arturo's 'panicked collapse' hit bottom and thereby arrested itself – though with a traumatic impact of its own – in the anal *ubi consistam* (solid ground), inglorious and unacceptable, but evidently consolidated in some manner in early childhood. Elsa's 'panicked collapse' was never spontaneously arrested; a parental equivalent with a magical or containing function was necessary, and her rescuing *ubi consistam* was, in the end, of the adhesive type.

Regarding the fifth phase of the defensive sequence described by Pao (1979) – that relative to the pathological reorganization of the self with defective results – one can see that in Arturo, this process had established a false-self system, based on the grandiose phallic model and secured through systematic recourse to projective identification with the phallic, nonintrojected mother. Unable to fully acquire the qualities of this object, then, Arturo 'became it.' Elsa, on the other hand, did not 'become' her father or her depressed mother. (Elsa was not depressed; she tended toward 'non-being' more than anything else.) More than having a false self, she was characterized by an insufficient self; discouraged by the impossibility of comparison with a powerful father and a stereotypically feminine mother, she cultivated a basic fantasy of being the eternally needy and dependent young girl – while Arturo's basic fantasy was that of a hero.

Arturo, however, was more than a little bit oedipal in his heroism: he did not confront any 'third,' but, rather, he was a St. George who had not yet begun to consider the dragon, being instead taken in by the desire for a great sword that might redeem him from the shame of an infantile 'little dagger.' From an oedipal point of view, perhaps Elsa was slightly more developed. The hypothesis of Busch et al. (1999) regarding success anxiety during the oedipal phase, with subsequent ruinous regression in the face of conflict, could be a little more pertinent to her, all things considered, even if it was clear that this father was also a male 'mamma,' and that the oedipal function and the basic symbiotic function were inextricably intertwined.

I believe a conflictual oedipal component was also much in evidence in Arturo, who by virtue of his physical endowment and military training would have been well able to outdistance both me and his father (in addition to outdistancing himself in challenging real limits) – even though the component of competition between two

222

people, and envy, appeared more important than any triadic issues or jealousy.

From a countertransferential point of view, in the first part of the analysis, Arturo had induced experiences of inadequacy and fear in the analyst; Elsa, sensations of parasitic clinging and of annoyance. The analyst was restricted to experiencing within himself a part of Arturo's self that had been rejected by Arturo's ego–ideal; with Elsa, a part of the omnipotent parental object that she had looked for and 'claimed.'

The *similarities* between these two patients, on the other hand, were: the common 'landing place' of the panic experience and the defensive agoraphobic modality, in line with the theorizations cited by Weiss (1966); the weakness of the ego, in aspects well described by Busch et al. (1999); the fragile cohesion of the self, as referred to by Diamond (1985); and, more generally, the inadequacy of the containing functions of the mind, which necessitated external support on the spur of the moment, as well as, in perspective, a structural evolution (Bion, 1959, 1962, 1963).

On the basis of these clinical observations and others that I cannot report here due to space constraints, I propose the following *typical psychodynamic pictures, which form the setting for panic attacks of internal origin:*

- The threat of the collapse of scaffolding of a false self.
- The risk of dissolution, proximate or in actuality, of a visible or invisible symbiosis (Bleger, 1967; Mahler, 1968).
- The approach of the subjective experience to a traumatic-conflictual area, repressed and feared, as in phobias.

In all these cases, a rupture in the defensive system will be signaled both dramatically and unconsciously, a tenacious and primitive alarm in the way and of the time period in which it had its genesis.

Trust in one's self

The patient who, after having experienced helplessness and a feeling of the collapse of the ego in a crisis of panic, enters into therapeutic treatment is the carrier of an implicit thought that I would formulate as follows: 'I don't trust myself any more.'

The patient has good reasons to think this way, and, in a certain number of cases, we would not render him a good service by denying or minimizing his difficulties and sound reasoning. Ultimately, the fact that he is conscious of these is in itself a good sign. We have seen that for some this first depressive step may already be difficult and that, basically, it may be more gratifying, from a narcissistic point of view, to cultivate the illusion of a self who is 'strong and secure,' with stubborn aspirations toward a restored, integrated state of pre-crisis or pre-thought (or anti-thought).

After a considerable period of treatment, many patients could describe the phase in process by saying, 'I still don't trust myself.' Elsa experienced this situation for years in analysis. The feeling that 'it might be working,' and that something substantial had begun to consolidate within Elsa's self, gave her the strength to patiently complete her individual formative journey.

Toward the end of treatment, the patient must feel within himself the birth of the thought: 'I can begin to trust myself.' The proof of this is the patient's perspective that he can function by himself, without the analyst, with a disposition that is both wishful and resigned, tinged with the correct degree of worried preoccupation that appropriately accompanies the gradual experience of separateness and that, conversely, is characteristically absent in reactions of pseudo-independence of a narcissistic–manic–oppositional kind.

'Trusting the self' can be, for many, the developmental task of a lifetime. One could state that, in large measure, it consists of beginning to recognize (and then gradually knowing in greater depth) the real self – of establishing contact and gaining familiarity with it, and of fostering its harmony with the functional systems of one's own ego, which have in large measure taken on defensive aims (Bolognini, 1997b, 2002a, 2004e).

An experience that is both commonplace and emblematic can effectively illustrate what I am describing: that of 'playing dead' in water, which I cited in chapter 2. This is a bodily equivalent of the experience of letting one's self go mentally as well (e.g., with evenly suspended attention), while trusting in the body's ability to float. This indeed can prove to be a pleasure in containing the ego's initial alarmed reaction in the face of what is unusual and the loss of motor control based on muscular tension.

The harmonious state of an ego that has become gradually more trusting, relaxed, and competent, and of a self that can be 'left to live,' is one of the most fortuitous results of a sufficiently successful analytic treatment. This capacity to fluctuate with pleasure in the preconscious area of mental life, emerging and reemerging without excessive fear from either the primary or the secondary process, is a significant goal for patients who have suffered from panic attacks – people who, to continue the analogy, have run the risk of mentally drowning in a sea of anxiety. Seen in this light, the phenomenon of panic attacks takes on a complex meaning that goes well beyond that – though real and factually determined in itself – of the dynamic of neurotransmitters.

Very often, panic presents to us as a persecutory event, unexpected and lacking in meaning, on the part of pseudo-mature people who have lost (or have never achieved) internal contact with important parts of the self. Such a psychic organization demands functional performances of the ego that are untenable, given the defensive charge it is placed under, and given the missing integration with the self.

The investigation of authenticity suffered, of feared separation, and of sufficient harmony between the elements of one's own internal world becomes, yet again, the true developmental task of the individual. To that, psychoanalysis can make a determinative and lasting contribution, without deductions, miracles, or shortcuts, with patience and a methodical approach.

References

Accerboni, A. M. (1990). Il segno di un'amicizia [The sign of friendship]. In *Topsy: Le ragioni di un amore* [Topsy: the reasons for love], ed. M. Bonaparte. Turin: Bollati Boringhieri.

Adler, A. (1911). Beitrag zur Lehre von Widerstand. *Zentralblatt für Psychoanalyse*, 1: 215.

Ambrosiano, L. (2005). The analyst: His professional novel. *International Journal of Psychoanalysis*, 86: 1611–1626.

Andrade de Azevedo, A. M. (1994). Validation of the psychoanalytic clinical process: The role of dreams. *International Journal of Psychoanalysis*, 75: 1181–1192.

Anzieu, D. (1985). *The Skin Ego*. New Haven, CT: Yale University Press.

Argentieri, S. (2002). Elogio della paura [Eulogy to fear]. *Psiche*, 8(1): 193–200.

Argentieri, S., & Carrano, P. (1994). *L'Uomo nero. Piccolo catalogo delle paure infantili* [The black man: a little catalogue of childhood fears]. Milan: Mondadori.

Aron, L. (1996). *A Meeting of Minds: Mutuality in Psychoanalysis*. Hillsdale, NJ: Analytic Press.

Atwood, G., & Stolorow, R. (1984). *Structures of Subjectivity*. Hillsdale, NJ: Analytic Press.

Balint, M., & Balint, E. (1959). *Thrills and Regressions*. London: Hogarth Press.

Baranger, M., & Baranger, W. (1961–62). La situación analítica como campo dinámico. *Revista Uruguaya de Psicoanálisis*, 4(1): 3–54. [The analytic situation as a dynamic field. *International Journal of Psychoanalysis*, 89 (No. 4, 2008): 795–826.]

Barlow, D. H. (2002). *Anxiety and Its Disorders: The Nature and Treatment of Anxiety and Panic*. New York: Guilford Press.

Beres, D., & Arlow, J. A. (1974). Fantasy and identification in empathy. *Psychoanalytic Quarterly*, 43: 26–50.

Berti Ceroni, G. (2002). *Fattori terapeutici specifici comuni e fattori terapeutici propri della psicoanalisi* [Ordinary specific therapeutic factors and real therapeutic factors in psychoanalysis]. Paper presented at the 12th National Congress of the Società Psicoanalitica, Trieste, Italy.

Bezoari, M., & Ferro, A. (1992). L'oscillazione significati/affetti nella copia analitica al lavoro [Characters in sessions as functional aggregates in the analytic field]. *Rivista Psicoanalitica*, 38: 381–406.

Bion, W. R. (1959). Attacks on linking. In *Second Thoughts*. London: Heinemann, 1967.

Bion, W. R. (1962). *Learning from Experience*. London: Heinemann.

Bion, W. R. (1963). *Elements of Psycho-Analysis*. London: Heinemann.

Bion, W. R. (1967). *Second Thoughts*. London: Heinemann.

Bion, W. R. (1970). *Attention and Interpretation*. London: Tavistock.

Birksted-Breen, D., Flanders, S., & Gibeault, A. (Eds.) (2010). *Reading French Psychoanalysis*. New Library of Psychoanalysis. Hove, UK: Routledge.

Blanton, S. (1957). *Diary of My Analysis with Sigmund Freud*. New York: Hawthorn.

Bleger, J. (1967). *Symbiosis and Ambiguity: The Psychoanalysis of Very Early Development*. London: Free Association Books, 1990.

Blos, P. (1968). Character formation in adolescence. *Psychoanalytic Study of the Child*, 23: 245–263.

Bollas, C. (1987). *The Shadow of the Object: Psychoanalysis of the Unthought Known*. New York: Columbia University Press.

Bolognini, S. (1984). *Empatia* [Empathy]. Paper presented at the Veneto Center for Psychoanalysis, 10 April.

Bolognini, S. (1991). Gli affetti dell'analista. Analisi con l'Io e analisi col Sé [The analyst's affects: analysis with the ego and analysis with the self]. *Rivista di Psicoanalisi*, 37: 339–371.

Bolognini, S. (1994). Transference: Erotised, erotic, loving, affectionate. *International Journal of Psychoanalysis*, 75: 73–86.

Bolognini, S. (1997a). Empathy and empathism. *International Journal of Psychoanalysis*, 78: 279–295.

Bolognini, S. (1997b). Empatia e patologie gravi [Empathy and serious pathologies]. In *Quale psicoanalisi per le psicosi?* [Which psychoanalysis for the psychoses?], ed. A. Correale & L. Rinaldi. Milan: Cortina.

Bolognini, S. (1997c). Empatia e differenza [Empathy and difference]. In *Differenza, indifferenza, differimento* [Difference, indifference, deferment], ed. G. Sacerdoti & A. Racalbuto. Milan: Dunod.

Bolognini, S. (1997d). The 'kind-hearted' versus the 'good' analyst: Empathy and hatred in countertransference. In *Squiggle and Spaces*, ed. G. Bertolini, A. Giannakoulas, M. Hernandez, & T. Molino. London: Rebus Press.

Bolognini, S. (1998). Compartir y malentender. *Revista de Psicoanálisis*, 55: 7–20.

Bolognini, S. (2000). Lavoro del sogno, lavoro con il sogno [Dream work, work with the dream]. In *Il sogno cento anni dopo* [The dream one hundred years later], ed. S. Bolognini. Turin: Bollati Boringhieri.

Bolognini, S. (2001). Empathy and the unconscious. *Psychoanalytic Quarterly*, 70: 447–473.

Bolognini, S. (2002a). *L'empatia psicoanalitica* [Psychoanalytic empathy]. Turin: Bollati Boringhieri.

Bolognini, S. (2002b). The analyst at work: Two sessions with Alba. *International Journal of Psychoanalysis*, 83: 753–766.

Bolognini, S. (2003a). Vrais et faux loups. L'alternance du refoulement et du clivage dans les tableaux cliniques complexes. *Revue Française de Psychanalyse*, 67: 1285–1304.

Bolognini, S. (2003b). Parler mots, parler choses. *Libres Cahiers pour la Psychanalyse*, 7: 15–20.

Bolognini, S. (2004a). Intrapsychic–interpsychic. *International Journal of Psychoanalysis*, 85: 337–357.

Bolognini, S. (2004b). La complexité de l'empathie psychanalytique. Une exploration théorique et clinique. *Revue Française de Psychanalyse*, 68: 877–896.

Bolognini, S. (2004c). Misunderstandings on empathy. *Bulletin of the British Psychoanalytical Society*, February.

Bolognini, S. (2004d). Fidarsi di sé. Pseudomaturità e disarticolazione Io–Sé negli attacchi di panico [Trusting one's self: pseudomaturity and disarticulation between ego and self in panic attacks]. *Psicoterapia psicoanalitica*, 11: 47–68.

Bolognini, S. (2004e). *Psychoanalytic Empathy*, trans. M. Garfield. London: Free Association Books.

Bolognini, S. (2005a). *La famiglia interna dell'analista* [The analyst's internal family]. Paper presented at an INT seminar of the SPI, Milan, 18 June.

Bolognini, S. (2005b). *Il coraggio di avere paura* [The courage to be afraid]. Paper presented at a Congress at the Psychoanalytic Center of Rome, 'The Emotions of Living,' 26 February.

Bonaminio, V. (1996). Esiste ancora uno spazio per l'individualità del paziente? [Does a space for the patient's individuality still exist?]. *Rivista di Psicoanalisi*, 42: 97–110.

Bonaminio, V. (2003). La persona dell'analista. Interpretare, non–interpretare e controtransfert [The person of the analyst: interpreting, not interpreting, and countertransference]. In *Forme dell'interpretare. Nuove prospettive nella teoria e nella clinica psicoanalitica* [Forms of interpreting: new perspectives in theory and psychoanalytic clinical practice], ed. P. Fabozzi. Milan: Angeli, pp. 25–52.

Bonino, S., Lo Coco, A., & Tani, F. (1998). *Empatia. I processi di condivisione delle emozioni* [Empathy: the processes of sharing emotions]. Florence: Giunti.

Botella, C., & Botella, S. (2001). *The Work of Psychic Figurability*, trans. A. Weller. Hove, UK: Brunner-Routledge, 2004.

Bria, P., & Ciocca, A. (1993). *La psicoterapia breve nel trattamento delle crisi di panico*

[Brief psychotherapy in the treatment of panic crises]. Rome: Edizioni Universitarie.

Busch, F. N., Cooper, A. M., Klerman, G. L., Shapiro, T., & Shear, M. K. (1991). Neurophysiological, cognitive-behavioral and psychoanalytic approaches to panic disorders. *Psychoanalytic Inquiry*, 11: 316–332.

Busch, F. N., Milrod, B. L., Rudden, M., Shapiro, T., Singer, M., Aronson, A., et al. (1999). Oedipal dynamics in panic disorder. *Journal of the American Psychoanalytic Association*, 47: 773–790.

Busch, F. N., Shear, M. K., Cooper, A. M., Shapiro, T., & Leon, A. (1995). An empirical study of defense mechanisms in panic disorders. *Journal of Nervous & Mental Disease*, 183: 299–303.

Camon, F. (1981). *The Sickness Called Man*, trans. J. Shepley. Chicago, IL: Northwestern University Press, 1993.

Campbell, R. J. (1940). *Campbell's Psychiatric Dictionary*. New York: Oxford University Press, 2009.

Chianese, D. (1987). La relazione analitica come struttura [The analytic relationship as a structure]. In *Soggetto, relazione, trasformazione* [Subject, relationship, transformation], ed. C. Traversa. Rome: Borla.

Chianese, D. (1997). *Constructions and the Analytic Field: History, Scenes, and Destiny*. Hove, UK: Routledge, 2007.

Chianese, D. (2006). *Un lungo sogno* [A long dream]. Milan: Angeli.

De Masi, F. (2004). The psychodynamic of panic attacks: A useful integration of psychoanalysis and neuroscience. *International Journal of Psychoanalysis*, 85: 311–336.

De Moncheaux, C. (1978). Dreaming and the organizing function of the ego. *International Journal of Psychoanalysis*, 59: 443–453.

De Toffoli, C. (2000). L'analista e i suoi pazienti. Un campo psichico transpersonale [The analyst and his patients: a transpersonal psychic field]. *Rivista di Psicoanalisi*, 46: 269–283.

Diamond, D. B. (1985). Panic attacks, hypochondriasis, and agoraphobia: A self-psychology formulation. *American Journal of Psychotherapy*, 39: 114–125.

Di Benedetto, A. (1998). Sperimentare un pensiero che verrà [Experiencing a coming thought]. *Rivista di Psicoanalisi*, 44: 5–22.

Di Benedetto, A. (2002). *Prima della parola* [Before the word]. Milan: Angeli.

Eiguer, A. (1993). Un des traits specifiques du dialogue analytique. L'imprevisibilité. *Psychanalyse en Europe*, 42: 20–29.

Eisold, R. (1994). The intolerance of diversity in psychoanalytic institutes. *International Journal of Psychoanalysis*, 75: 785–800.

Etchegoyen, R. H. (1991). *The Fundamentals of Psychoanalytic Technique*. London: Karnac.

Faimberg, H. (1998). Transgenerationnel–intergenerationnel. In *Dictionnaire international de la psychanalyse*, ed. A. De Mijolla. Paris: Calmann-Lévy.

Faimberg, H. (2005). *The Telescoping of Generations: Listening to Narcissistic Links between Generations*. London: Routledge.

Faimberg, H., & Corel, A. (1990). Repetition and surprise: A clinical approach to the necessity of construction and its validation. *International Journal of Psychoanalysis*, 71: 411–420.

Fairbairn, W. R. D. (1944). Endopsychic structure considered in terms of object-relationships. *International Journal of Psychoanalysis*, 25: 70–92.

Falzeder, E. (1998). Family tree matters. *Journal of Analytical Psychology*, 43: 127–154.

Ferenczi, S. (1932). Confusion of tongues between adults and the child. In *Final Contributions to the Problems and Methods of Psychoanalysis*. London: Hogarth Press, 1955.

Ferro, A. (1996). Carla's panic attacks: Insight and transformation. *International Journal of Psychoanalysis*, 77: 997–1011.

Ferro, A. (1998). Il sogno della veglia. Teoria e clinica [The waking dream: theory and practice]. *Rivista di Psicoanalisi*, 44: 117–128.

Ferro, A. (2002). *In the Analyst's Consulting Room*, trans. P. Slotkin. Hove, UK: Brunner-Routledge.

Ferro, A. (2010). *Avoiding Emotions, Living Emotions*. London: Routledge.

Fiorentini, G., Frangini, G., Molone, P., Mori Ubaldini, M., Robutti, A., & Savoia, V. (2001). L'inconscio nelle prospettive relazionali [The unconscious in relational perspectives]. *Rivista di Psicoanalisi*, 47: 51–78.

Fonda, P. (2000). La fusionalità e i rapporti oggettuali [Fusionality and object relations]. *Rivista di Psicoanalisi*, 3: 429–449.

Foresti, G., & Rossi Monti, M. (2006). *Teorie sul transfert and transfert sulle teorie* [Theories on transference and transference onto theories]. Paper presented at the 13th National Congress of the Italian Psychoanalytic Society, Siena, 29 September.

Fosshage, J. (1997). The organizing functions of dream mentation. *Contemporary Psychoanalysis*, 33: 434–458.

Frances, A., & Dunn, P. (1975). The attachment–autonomy conflict in agoraphobia. *International Journal of Psychoanalysis*, 56: 435–439.

Freud, A. (1936). *The Ego and the Mechanisms of Defence*. London: Hogarth Press/ Institute of Psychoanalysis.

Freud, E. L. (1960). *Letters of Sigmund Freud*, trans. T. Stern & J. Stern. New York: Basic Books.

Freud, S. (1894). On the grounds for detaching a particular syndrome from neurasthenia under the description 'anxiety neurosis.' *S.E.*, 3.

Freud, S. (1895). The psychotherapy of hysteria. In *Studies on Hysteria*. *S.E.*, 2.

Freud, S. (1900). *The Interpretation of Dreams*. *S. E.*, 4/5.

Freud, S. (1901). *On Dreams*. *S. E.*, 5.

Freud, S. (1905 [1901]). Fragment of an analysis of a case of hysteria. *S. E.*, 7.

Freud, S. (1905). *Three Essays on the Theory of Sexuality. S. E.*, 7.

Freud, S. (1914). Remembering, repeating and working-through. *S. E.*, 12.

Freud, S. (1915a). Papers on metapsychology. *S. E.*, 14.

Freud, S. (1915b). The unconscious. *S. E.*, 14.

Freud, S. (1920). *Beyond the Pleasure Principle. S. E.*, 18.

Freud, S. (1921). *Group Psychology and the Analysis of the Ego. S. E.*, 18.

Freud, S. (1923). Remarks on the theory and practice of dream-interpretation. *S. E.*, 19.

Freud, S. (1925). Negation. *S. E.*, 19.

Freud, S. (1926). *Inhibitions, Symptoms and Anxiety. S. E.*, 20.

Friedman, L. (1996). Overview: Knowledge and authority in the psychoanalytic relationship. *Psychoanalytic Quarterly*, 65: 254–265.

Gabbard, G. O. (1997). A reconsideration of objectivity in the analyst. *International Journal of Psychoanalysis*, 78: 15–26.

Gabbard, G. O., & Westen, D. (2003). Rethinking therapeutic action. *International Journal of Psychoanalysis*, 84: 823–841.

Gaddini, E. (1980). Note sul problema mente-corpo [Notes on the mind–body problem]. In *Scritti*. Milan: Cortina, 1989.

Gaddini, E. (1984). L'attività presimbolica della mente infantile [Presymbolic activity in the child's mind]. In *Scritti*. Milan: Cortina, 1989.

Gamwell, L. (1989). The origins of Freud's antiquities collection. In *Sigmund Freud and Art: His Personal Collection of Antiquities*, ed. L. Gamwell & R. Wells. New York: Harry Abrams.

Garma, A. (1966). *Psicoanalisi dei sogni* [The psychoanalysis of dreams]. Turin: Boringhieri, 1971.

Giaconia, G., Pellizzari, G., & Rossi, P. (1997). *Nuovi fondamenti per la tecnica psicoanalitica* [New foundations for psychoanalytic technique]. Rome: Borla.

Giannakoulas, A. (2000). Holding dello spazio affettivo. Considerazione sulla tecnica e sull'esperienza analitica nella regressione alla dipendenza [Holding of the affective space: some considerations on the analytic technique and experience of regression to dependence]. In *Il Sé tra clinica e teoria* [The self in between clinical practice and theory], ed. A. Giannakoulas, M. Armellini, P. Fabozzi, & C. Lucantoni. Rome: Borla.

Girolami, M. (1967). *Il mio cane non conosce Cartesio* [My dog does not know Descartes]. Rome: Corso & Co.

Goldberg, A. (1994). Farewell to the objective analyst. *International Journal of Psychoanalysis*, 75: 21–30.

Golinelli, P. (2000). Paura. Perturbante e angoscia primaria [Fear: disturbing and primary anxiety]. *Psiche*, 8(1): 87–95.

Graves, R. (1955). *The Greek Myths: Complete Edition*. London: Penguin Books, 1992.

Green, A. (1993). *Le travail du negatif*. Paris: Editions de Minuit. [*The Work of the Negative*, trans. A. Weller. London: Free Association Books, 1999.]

Green, A. (1998). The primordial mind and the work of the negative. *International Journal of Psychoanalysis*, 79: 649–666.

Green, A. (2000). The intrapsychic and intersubjective in psychoanalysis. *Psychoanalytic Quarterly*, 69: 1–39.

Green, A. (2005). The illusion of common ground and mythical pluralism. *International Journal of Psychoanalysis*, 86: 627–632.

Greenacre, P. (1958). Early physical determinants in the development of the sense of identity. *Journal of the American Psychoanalytic Association*, 6: 612–627.

Greenberg, J. (2001). The analyst's participation: a new look. *Journal of the American Psychoanalytic Association*, 49: 359–381.

Greenberg, R., & Perlman, C. (1993). An integrated approach to dream theory: Contributions from sleep research and clinical practice. In *The Functions of Dreaming*, ed. A. Moffitt. Albany, NY: State University Press of New York, pp. 363–380.

Greenson, R. R. (1959). Phobia, anxiety, and depression. *Journal of the American Psychoanalytic Association*, 7: 663–674.

Greenson, R. R. (1960). Empathy and its vicissitudes. In *Explorations in Psychoanalysis*. New York: International Universities Press, 1978.

Greenson, R. R. (1961). On the silence and sounds of the analytic hour. *Journal of the American Psychoanalytic Association*, 9: 79–84.

Greenson, R. R., & Wexler, M. (1969). The non-transference relationship in the psychoanalytic situation. *International Journal of Psychoanalysis*, 50: 27–39.

Grinberg, L. (1967). Función del soñar y clasificación clinica de los sueños en el proceso analitico. *Revista de Psicoanálisis*, 24: 749–789.

Grinberg, L. (1976). *Teoria dell'identificazione* [The theory of identification]. Turin: Loescher, 1982.

Grispini, A. (2000). *Intrapsichico ed interpersonale nella prospettiva clinica* [The intrapsychic and interpersonal in the clinical perspective]. Paper presented at the Incontro Intercentri Congress, 'Analytic Spaces: Invariation and Transformations in Psychoanalysis,' Rome, March.

Grotstein, J. (1981). *Splitting and Projective Identification*. New York: Jason Aronson.

Grotstein, J. (2005). Projective identification: An extension of the concept of projective identification. *International Journal of Psychoanalysis*, 86: 1051–1069.

Haber, M., & Godfrind-Haber, J. (2002). *L'expérience agie partagée*. Paper presented at the 62nd Congress of French-Language Psychoanalysts, Brussels, May.

Herrigel, E., & Suzuki, D. (1953). *Zen in the Art of Archery*. New York: Vintage Books, 1989.

Herzog, J. (2000). Blood and love. *International Journal of Psychoanalysis*, 81: 263–272.

Hirsch, I. (1996). Observing participation, mutual enactment, and the new classical models. *Contemporary Psychoanalysis*, 32: 359–383.

Jacobs, T. J. (1986). On countertransference enactment. *Journal of the American Psychoanalytic Association*, 34: 289–307.

Jacobs, T.J. (1991). *The Use of the Self.* New York: International Universities Press.

Jones, E. (1961). *The Life and Work of Sigmund Freud*, ed. & abridged in one volume by L. Trilling & S. Marcus. New York: Basic Books.

Kaës, R. (1993). *Le groupe et le sujet du groupe.* Paris: Dunod.

Kaës, R., Faimberg, H., Enriquez, M., & Baranes, J.J. (1993). *Transmission de la vie psychique entre générations.* Paris: Dunod.

Kernberg, O. F. (2006). The pressing need to increase research in and on psychoanalysis. *International Journal of Psychoanalysis*, 87: 919–926.

Kestenberg, J. (1956). On the development of maternal feelings in early childhood: Observations and reflections. *Psychoanalytic Study of the Child*, 11: 257–291.

Klauber, J. (1981). *Difficulties in the Analytic Encounter.* New York: Jason Aronson.

Klein, M. (1955). On identification. In *New Directions in Psycho-Analysis*, ed. P. Heimann, M. Klein, & R. Money-Kyrle. London: Tavistock.

Kohut, H. (1971). *Analysis of the Self: A Systematic Approach to the Psychoanalytic Treatment of Narcissistic Personality Disorders.* Chicago, IL: University of Chicago Press.

Kohut, H. (1977). *The Restoration of the Self.* Chicago, IL: University of Chicago Press.

Kohut, H. (1984). *How Does Analysis Cure?* Chicago, IL: University of Chicago Press.

Kramer, M. (1993). The selective mood regulatory function of dreaming: An update and revision. In *The Functions of Dreaming*, ed. A. Moffitt. Albany, NY: State University Press of New York.

Laplanche, J., & Pontalis, J.-B. (1973). *The Language of Psychoanalysis*, trans. D. Nicholson-Smith. London: Hogarth Press/Institute of Psychoanalysis.

Le Guen, C. (2001). Quelque chose manque . . . de la repression aux répresentations motrices. *Revue Française de Psychanalyse*, 1: 37–50.

Lewin, B. D. (1952). Phobic symptoms and dream interpretation. *Psychoanalytic Quarterly*, 21: 295–322.

Lopez, D. (1983). *La psicoanalisi della persona* [Psychoanalysis of the person]. Turin: Boringhieri.

Lopez, D. (2004). Alcune osservazioni critiche sul lavoro di Gabbard e Westen, 'Ripensare l'azione terapeutica [Some critical observations on Gabbard and Westen's paper, 'Rethinking Therapeutic Action']. *Gli Argonauti*, 26: 291–308.

Losso, R. (2000). *Psicoanalisi della famiglia. Percorsi teorico-clinici* [Family psychoanalysis: theoretical–clinical journeys]. Milan: Angeli.

Losso, R. (2003). *The Intrapsychic, Interpersonal and Transpsychic in the Psychoanalysis of the Couple.* Paper presented at the Psychoanalytic Center of Florence, 30 January.

Maeder, A. (1912). Über die Funktion des Träumes. *Jahrbuch für Psychoanalytische und Psychopathologische Forschungen*, 4: 692.

Mahler, M. (1968). *On Human Symbiosis and the Vicissitudes of Individuation*. New York: International Universities Press.

Mantovani, M. (1989). Menzogna [Lie]. In *Trattato enciclopedico di psicologia dell'età evolutiva, vol. 2, parte 2* [Encyclopedic treatise on the psychology of the developmental age, Vol. 2, Part 2], ed. M. Batacchi. Padua, Italy: Piccin, pp. 847–859.

Marías, J. (1994). *Tomorrow in the Battle Think on Me*, trans. M. J. Costa. New York: New Directions, 2001.

Matte Blanco, I. (1981). *The Unconscious as Infinite Sets: An Essay in Bi-Logic*. London: Karnac, 1998.

Meissner, W. W. (2004). Sdraiarsi o non sdraiarsi (lettino o non lettino). Questo è il problema [To lie down or not to lie down (couch or no couch): this is the problem]. *Gli argonauti*, 26(102): 213–260.

Meltzer, D. (1967). *The Psycho-Analytical Process*. London: Karnac, 2008.

Meltzer, D. (1975). *Explorations in Autism: A Psychoanalytic Study*. London: Karnac, 2008.

Meltzer, D. (1978). Routine and inspired interpretations: Their relation to the weaning process in analysis. *Contemporary Psychoanalysis*, 14: 210–225.

Meltzer, D. (1992). *The Claustrum*. Strath Tay: Clunie Press.

Micati, L. (1993). Quanta realtà può essere tollerata? [Which reality can be tolerated?]. *Rivista di Psicoanalisi*, 39: 153–163.

Milrod, B. L., Busch, F. N., Cooper, A. M., & Shapiro, T. (1997). *Manual of Panic-Focused Psychodynamic Psychotherapy*. Washington, DC: American Psychiatric Press.

Minazio, M. (2002). *Introduction*. Paper presented at the 62nd Congress of French-Language Psychoanalysts, Brussels, May.

Mitchell, S. A. (1997). *Influence and Autonomy in Psychoanalysis*. Hillsdale, NJ: Analytic Press.

Moccia, G. (2002). Soggettività e oggettività dell'analista. Su alcune modificazioni della tecnica nella psicoanalisi relazionale nord-americana [The analyst's subjectivity and objectivity: on some modifications of the technique of North American relational psychoanalysis]. *Rivista di Psicoanalisi*, 48: 675–690.

Modell, A. H. (1990). *Other Times, Other Realities: Toward a Theory of Psychoanalytic Treatment*. Cambridge, MA: Harvard University Press.

Moll, A. (1898). *Untersuchungen über die Libido sexualis, Vol. 1*. Berlin: Fischer's Medicin. Buchhandlung. H. Kornfeld.

Money-Kyrle, R. (1951). *Psychoanalysis and Politics*. New York: Norton.

Money-Kyrle, R. (1956). Normal countertransference and some of its deviations. In *The Collected Papers of Roger Money-Kyrle, 1927–1977*. Strath Tay, UK: Clunie Press, 1978.

Neri, C., Pallier, L., Petacchi, G., Soavi, G. C., & Tagliacozzo, R. (1990). *Fusionalità* [Fusionality]. Rome: Borla.

Nissim Momigliano, L. (1984). Due persone che parlano in una stanza (una ricerca sul dialogo analitico) [Two people who talk in a room (an investigation of the analytic dialogue)]. *Rivista di Psicoanalisi*, 30: 1–17.

Ogden, T. (1994a). The analytic third: Working with intersubjective clinical facts. *International Journal of Psychoanalysis*, 75: 3–20.

Ogden, T. (1994b). The concept of interpretive action. *Psychoanalytic Quarterly*, 2: 219–245.

Ogden, T. (2003). On not being able to dream. *International Journal of Psychoanalysis*, 84: 17–30.

Ogden, T. (2005). *This Art of Psychoanalysis: Dreaming Undreamt Dreams and Interrupted Cries*. New York: Routledge.

Olden, C. (1958). Notes on the development of empathy. *Psychoanalytic Study of the Child*, 13: 505–518.

Pao, P. N. (1979). *Schizophrenic Disorders*. New York: International Universities Press.

Papadopoulos, R. K. (2002). Terrorismo e panico [Terrorism and panic]. *Rivista di Psicoanalisi*, 65: 165–182. [Annual volume, *Il terrore nell'anima* (Terror in the soul)]

Parsons, M. (1992). The refining of theory in clinical practice. *International Journal of Psychoanalysis*, 73: 103–115.

Pasquali, G. (2001). L'empatia e la clinica [Empathy and clinical practice]. *Rivista di Psicoanalisi*, 2: 253–264.

Perron, R. (2006). How to do research? Reply to Otto Kernberg. *International Journal of Psychoanalysis*, 87: 927–932.

Perron-Borrelli, M. (1985). Le fantasme. Une représentation d'action. *Revue Française de Psychanalyse*, 3: 903–913.

Perron-Borrelli, M. (2001). *Les fantasmes*. Paris: Presses Universitaires de France.

Ponsi, M. (1999). La partecipazione dell'analista. Un tema emergente nella psicoanalisi nordamericana [The analyst's participation: an emerging theme in North American psychoanalysis]. *Rivista di Psicoanalisi*, 45: 153–167.

Ponsi, M., & Filippini, S. (1996). Sull'uso del concetto di interazione [On the use of the concept of interaction]. *Rivista di Psicoanalisi*, 42: 567–594.

Quinodoz, D. (1994). *Le vertige, entre angoisse et plaisir*. Paris: Presses Universitaires de France.

Rabih, M. (1981). La pseudoalianza terapéutica. Algunas de ses manifestaciones clinicas. *Psicoanalisis*, 3: 169–191.

Racalbuto, A. (1994). *Tra il dire e il fare. L'esperienza dell'inconscio e del non verbale in psicoanalisi* [In between talking and doing: the experience of the unconscious and the nonverbal in psychoanalysis]. Milan: Cortina.

Racamier, P. C. (1992). *Il genio delle origini* [The genius of origins]. Milan: Cortina, 1993.

Rangell, L. (1982). Transference to theory. *Annual of Psychoanalysis*, 10: 29–56.

Reeder, J. (2002). *Hate and Love in Psychoanalytic Institutes*. New York: Other Press, 2004.

Renik, O. (1995). The ideal of the anonymous analyst and the problem of self-disclosure. *Psychoanalytic Quarterly*, 64: 466–495.

Renik, O. (1999). *Extreme Self-Disclosure*. Paper presented at a Meeting of the International Psychoanalytical Association, Santiago, Chile.

Riolo, F. (1997). Il modello di campo in psicoanalisi [The model of the field in psychoanalysis]. In *Emozione e interpretazione. Psicoanalisi del campo emotivo* [Emotion and interpretation: psychoanalysis of the emotional field], ed. E. Gaburri. Turin: Bollati Boringhieri.

Rocchi, C. (1997). *Intrapsichico, interpersonale, relazionale* [Intrapsychic, interpersonal, relational]. Paper presented at the Psychoanalytic Center of Rome, 18 December.

Rosenfeld, H. (1969). *The Importance of Projective Identification in the Ego Structure and the Object Relations of the Psychotic States*. Paper presented at the International Colloquium on Psychoses, Montreal, November.

Rosenfeld, H. (1987). *Impasse and Interpretation*. London: Tavistock.

Sandler, J., Kennedy, H., & Tyson, R. L. (1980). *Technique of Child Psychoanalysis: Discussions with Anna Freud*. Cambridge, MA: Harvard University Press.

Sassanelli, G. (2007). *Itinerari e figure della passione. Dall'A(more) alla V(endetta)* [Itineraries and figures of passion: from love to revenge]. Turin: Antigone.

Scanziani, P. (1978). Mistero dell'uomo e del cane [The mystery of man and dog]. In *Enciclopedia del cane* [Encyclopedia of the dog], ed. P. Scanziani. Novara, Italy: Istituto Geografico.

Schacht, L. (2001). The capacity to be surprised. *Richard & Piggle*, 9: 117–130.

Schafer, R. (1959). Generative empathy in the treatment situation. *Psychoanalytic Quarterly*, 28: 242–273.

Schafer, R. (1983). *The Analytic Attitude*. London: Karnac.

Schafer, R. (1972). Internalization: Process or fantasy? *Psychoanaytic Study of the Child*, 27: 411–436.

Searles, H. F. (1986). *Countertransference and Related Subjects: Selected Papers*. New York: International Universities Press, 1988.

Sechaud, E. (2000). Panel discussion: 'Self-Disclosure by the Analyst.' *International Journal of Psychoanalysis*, 81: 164–165.

Sechaud, E. (2003). *Introduction*. Paper presented at the 2nd Annual FEP Conference, Sorrento, April.

Segal, H. (1957). Notes on symbol formation. *International Journal of Psychoanalysis*, 38: 391–397.

Segal, H. (1991). *Dream, Phantasy and Art*. London: Routledge.

Segal, H. (1994). Phantasy and reality. In *The Contemporary Kleinians of London*, ed. R. Schafer. New York: International Universities Press, 1997.

Semi, A. A. (1989). Psiconevrosi e trauma [Psychoneurosis and trauma]. In *Trattato di psicoanalisi* [Treatise on psychoanalysis]. Milan: Cortina.

Semi, A. A. (1998). Il transfer nell'ottica freudiana. Una nota [Transference in the Freudian perspective: a note]. *Rivista di Psicoanalisi*, 44: 319–328.

Silber, A. (1989). Panic attacks facilitating recall and mastery: Implications for psychoanalytic technique. *Journal of the American Psychoanalytic Association*, 37: 337–364.

Smith, H. F. (1995). Analytic listening and the experience of surprise. *International Journal of Psychoanalysis*, 76: 67–88.

Smith, H. F. (1999). Subjectivity and objectivity in analytic listening. *Journal of the American Psychoanalytic Association*, 47: 465–483.

Smith, H. F. (2003). Hearing voices: The fate of the analyst's identifications. *Journal of the American Psychoanalytic Association*, 49: 781–812.

Soavi, G. C. (1989). The myth of the 'eternal return' and its importance in the structuring of the self. *Rivista di Psicoanalisi*, 35: 786–804.

Spurling, L. (2003). On psychoanalytic figures as transference objects. *International Journal of Psychoanalysis*, 84: 31–44.

Squitieri, G. (2002). Tra trasformazione e rappresentazione. Note sul 62° Congress of French-Language Psychoanalysts [Between transformation and representation: notes on the 62nd Congress of French-Language Psychoanalysts]. *Rivista di Psicoanalisi*, 48: 799–812.

Steiner, J. (1993). *Psychic Retreats: Pathological Organizations in Psychotic, Neurotic, and Borderline Patients*. London: Routledge.

Stolorow, R. D., & Atwood, G. E. (1992). *Contexts of Being: The Intersubjective Foundations of Psychological Life*. Hillsdale, NJ: Analytic Press.

Sullivan, H. S. (1931). The relation of onset to outcome in schizophrenia. In *Schizophrenia as a Human Process*. New York: Norton, 1962.

Teicholz, J. G. (1990). *Kohut, Loewald, and the Postmoderns: A Comparative Study of Self and Relationship*. Hillsdale, NJ: Analytic Press.

Thanopulos, S. (2003). L'interpretazione tra fantasma e interfantasmatizzazione nello spazio analitico [Interpretation between phantasm and 'interphantasimization' in the analytic space]. In *Forme dell'interpretare. Nuove prospettive nella teoria e nella clinica psicoanalitica* [Forms of interpreting: new perspectives in theory and psychoanalytic clinical practice], ed. P. Fabozzi. Milan: Angeli, pp. 125–164.

Vanggaard, T. (1989). *Panic: The Course of Psychoanalysis*. New York: Norton.

Vergine, A. (1981). Relazione analitica, codice, processo di significazione [Analytic relations, code, and process of meaning]. In *La relazione analitica* [The analytic relationship]. Rome: Borla.

Vergine, A. (1992). La relazione analitica e il caso clinico [The analytic relationship and the clinical case]. *Koinos*, 1: 19–36.

Waelder, R. (1967). Inhibitions, symptoms, and anxiety: Forty years later. *Psychoanalytic Quarterly*, 36: 1–36.

Wallerstein, R. S. (2005). Will psychoanalytic pluralism be an enduring state in our discipline? *International Journal of Psychoanalysis*, 86: 623–626.

Weiss, E. (1966). La formulazione psicodinamica dell'agorafobia [The psycho-dynamic formulation of agoraphobia]. *Rivista di Psicoanalisi*, 12: 240.

Widlöcher, D. (2001). The treatment of affects: an interdisciplinary issue. *Psychoanalytic Quarterly*, 70: 243–264.

Widlöcher, D. (2003). La personne du psychanalyste et les processus d'empathie et de co-pensées. *FEP Bulletin*, 57: 89–95.

Widlöcher, D. (2004). *Transference of Thoughts*. Paper presented at the Congress, 'Psychoanalysis and the Contemporary World,' Belgrade, 11 September.

Winnicott, D. W. (1949). Hate in the countertransference. *International Journal of Psychoanalysis*, 30: 69–74.

Winnicott, D. W. (1954). Methodological and clinical aspects of regression within the psycho-analytical set-up. In *Through Paediatrics to Psycho-Analysis*. New York: Basic Books, 1975.

Winnicott, D. W. (1958). *Through Paediatrics to Psycho-Analysis*. New York: Basic Books, 1975.

Winnicott, D. W. (1969). On the basis for self in body. In *Psychoanalytic Explorations*, ed. C. Winnicott, R. Shepherd, & M. Davis. Cambridge, MA: Harvard University Press, 1989, pp. 261–283.

Winnicott, D. W. (1971). *Playing and Reality*. London: Tavistock.

Winnicott, D. W. (1989). *Psychoanalytic Explorations*, ed. C. Winnicott, R. Shepherd, & M. Davis. Cambridge, MA: Cambridge University Press.

Index

Accerboni, Anna Maria 98, 99

acting out 44, 71, 78, 212; and action, distinction between 93

action(s): interpretive 93; speaking 93

aesthetic analytic technique 40

aggressor, identification with 92, 165, 216

agoraphobia 112, 204, 210, 216, 223

alcoholic drinks, as 'maniacal milk' 114

Alexander the Great 96

alpha-elements 47

alpha-function 209

ambivalence, tolerating 28

analysis: cooperative experience in, therapeutic nature of 31; fruitfulness of surprise in 120; 'negative' in 36; one-person 32; swimming metaphor of 38–43; termination of 57

analyst (*passim*): aptitude of for suspension of judgment 132; attention to self-cohesion of patient 35; awareness of dynamics of analysis of 81; capacity of to assess patient's progress 41; characterological exhibitionisms or perversions of 33; creative, caricature of 93; interior world of, group inhabiting 14; narcissism of 143; as object of desire, and patient's dream of kissing analyst (clinical example, Gianna) 112–113; –patient subjectivity 42; as post-

oedipal parent 17; psychic mucous membranes of 114; sadism of 175; self-disclosure of 33, 34; shared experience of, while listening 134; sharing of, vs. empathy 135; training of 136; working ego of 14, 17, 40, 117, 202; working self of 7, 14, 17, 82, 93 [plurality and complexity in 7–25]

analytic container, transformative function of, through reverie 162

analytic couple, unconscious fantasy of 68

analytic dialogue, experienced interpsychically from within 75

analytic experience, with serious pathologies, survival, containment, and con-viction in 161–176; clinical examples [Alfredo 163–165; Mario 170]

analytic function, introjected 57

analytic regression 30, 185

analytic relationship: asymmetry of 31; as complex system 72; symbiotic use of 203; truth in 50

analytic setting, asymmetrical 90

analytic space 37, 70, 169

analytic technique, aesthetic 40

'analytic third' 42

anxiety: internal, triggers of 200; neurotic 201; panic 200, 204; primary 180, 200 [or automatic 200];

239